I0795887

IMAGES
of America

THE MOOSEHEAD LAKE REGION
1900–1950

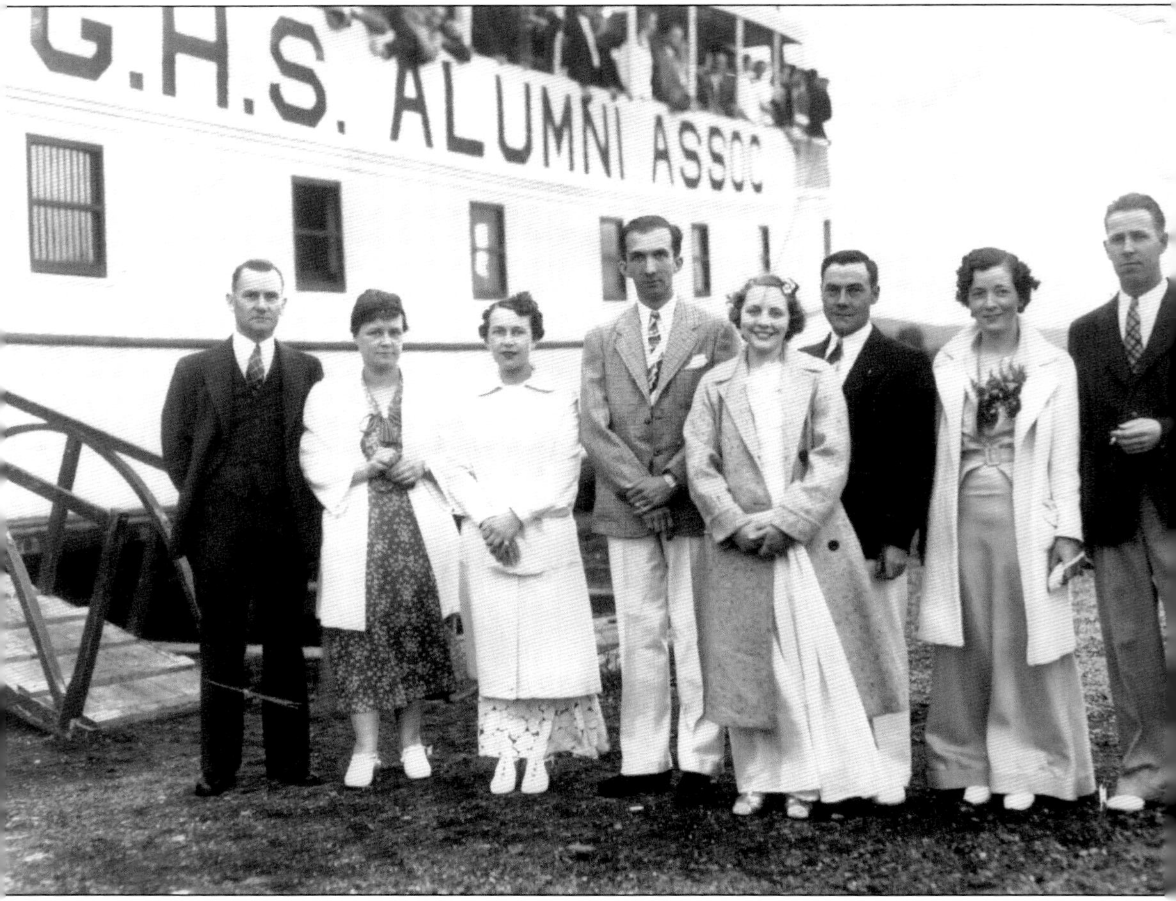

Pictured here are Greenville High School Alumni Association officers ready to travel to Kineo for an annual banquet. Shown from left to right are the following: Guy Hanson, Deltha Hanson, Erma Budden, Tom Young, Emile Hanson, Nick Hanson, Ruby Brett, and Rodney Brett.

IMAGES
of America

THE MOOSEHEAD LAKE REGION
1900–1950

Everett L. Parker

ARCADIA
PUBLISHING

ISBN 978-0-7385-3570-8

Published by Arcadia Publishing
Charleston, South Carolina

Printed in the United States of America

Library of Congress Catalog Card Number: 2004101333

For all general information contact Arcadia Publishing at:
Telephone 843-853-2070
Fax 843-853-0044
E-mail sales@arcadiapublishing.com
For customer service and orders:
Toll-Free 1-888-313-2665

Visit us on the Internet at www.arcadiapublishing.com

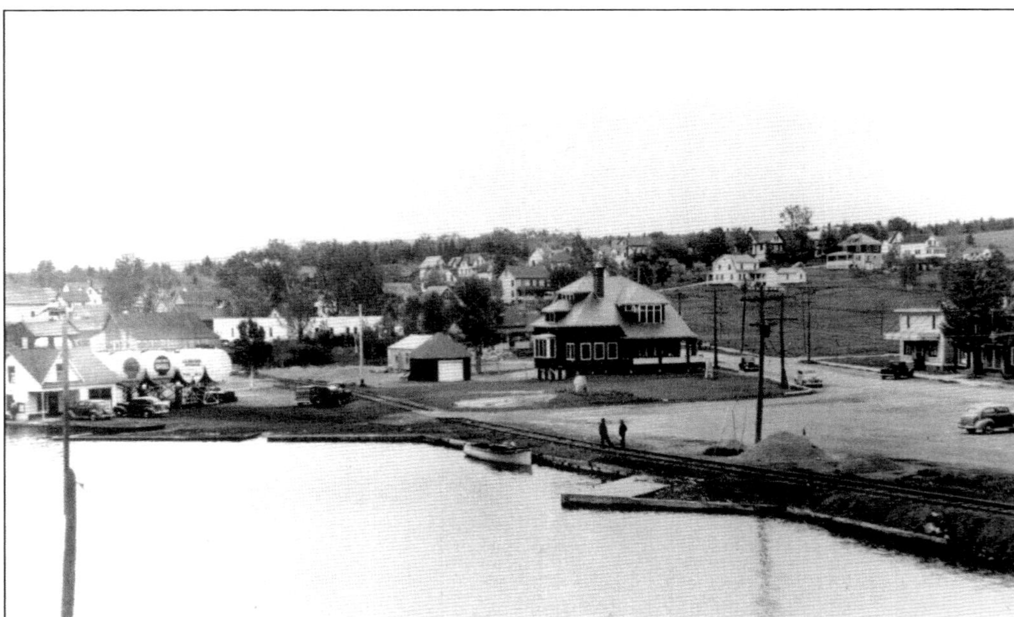

The east shore of Moosehead Lake at Greenville is shown here in the 1940s. The Lake House is at the right center and Knowlton's Bakery is at the far right (white building with overhang). The railroad tracks in the foreground went to the Atlas Plywood Mill.

Contents

ACKNOWLEDGMENTS

This book of photographs would not have been possible without use of the extensive photograph collection at the Moosehead Historical Museum in Greenville. There are thousands of photographs in this collection, from very early tintypes and ambrotypes to modern-day color photographs. Much of the collection has been broken down into name files, part of the thousands of people, places, and things vertical files at the museum. These collections have been gathered over the decades from the donations of many people.

Thus, special thanks are due to the generosity of many people who have donated collections of photographs and other ephemera and artifacts to the Moosehead Historical Museum since its beginnings in 1962. Among those—too many of whom are now deceased—are the following: Glenola Harrington, Glenys Pero, Randall and Margaret Whitten, Henrietta Bigney, Lawrence and Acelia Hall, Francis Crowley, Tony and Pinkie Bartley, Floyd and Colleen Ashe, Frances Bigney, Darell "Bee" Sawtelle, Clarence and Bea Laskey, Marion Phillips, Rodney and Ruby Brett, Lee R. Jacobson, Michael York, Madalene Burnham, Patricia Stankus, Harold and Alice Walden, Julia and Phil Sheridan, Dave Muzzy, Karlene G. Mahoney, Peter Templeton, Agnes Richardson Gott, Charlotte Dickinson, Wayne and Ellen Poole, Elizabeth Beverage, Melanie Breton, Ivon "Dodie" and Gail Turmel, Sandra Ryder, Elliott Levy, Marjorie McBurnie, Allyn Ward, the Keirstead and Jardine Collection, the Monson Historical Society, and the Moosehead Marine Museum.

Additional thanks are due to Frances Bigney, my assistant at the museum, who spends much of her office time scanning our photograph collection to preserve it for the future. It should be noted that the information in the captions is the best knowledge available. There likely will be errors, and they, along with amplifications, should be brought to the attention of the author in the interest of historical correctness.

INTRODUCTION

The Moosehead region has a long and colorful history. Many visitors speak of the pristine wilderness, suggesting perhaps that the area is just now being discovered. Nothing could be further from the truth. In fact, it could accurately be said that Native Americans were the first summer people in the Moosehead area, coming to Mount Kineo at least 11,000 years ago. Mount Kineo has been a tourist attraction for thousands of years, from the earliest Paleo-Indian period to the modern era when a large hotel dominated the peninsula. Euro-Americans first arrived in the region during the 1700s, but they were early explorers just passing through, often following Indian trails from the Penobscot River and through to Canada. It was not until the 1820s that permanent settlement began, particularly in the Greenville area. Within decades, settlements sprang up throughout the area, some continuing to this day and others disappearing with the sands of time.

From the earliest days, timber was the calling card that brought people to the Moosehead area. Great expanses of trees that resembled a vast ocean as far as the eye could see were a magnet to those who saw fortunes to be made. Lumbering became a way of life in what was to become known as the North Woods, and it was the stuff legends were made off, such as Paul Bunyan and his blue ox, Babe, and many others.

Several authors have written about the Moosehead region in these early days, but this is the first time that a careful examination has been made of the era from 1900 to 1950. The fact that this is a look at a half-century through the camera lens makes it even more exciting. The era featured here saw two world wars, the Great Depression, and periods of unparalleled growth. It was also a time when great changes were made in the Moosehead region. In the early days of the century, many visitors traveled by train to spend the summer at places such as the Mount Kineo House. But as the automobile came into greater use, trains were used less, and eventually passenger service all but ended. The second half of the era from 1900 to 1950 also saw the demise of the gigantic Mount Kineo House and the expansion of sporting camp operations throughout the region. People indeed continued traveling to the region, perhaps fewer during World War II, but rather than staying for months they stayed for a week or two.

How all of this evolved during the decades is described in the chapters that follow. While we have attempted to present each chapter in a chronological fashion beginning with photographs from the earliest days, not all will be shown that way. There are more than 200 photographs in the pages that follow, chosen from hundreds more to offer a cross section of the Moosehead region from 1900 to 1950.

One

Greenville

Greenville is the largest town in the Moosehead region and was a service center for the logging industry, and now tourism. Settlement began in the early 1820s, and the town was incorporated in 1836. In the early days, life was very difficult in this frontier settlement. Deborah Walden, the first Caucasian woman in the region, often jokingly said she was the "handsomest woman in town." (Of course, she was the only woman.) Stories have been passed down about Mrs. Walden, undoubtedly a woman of uncommon determination and inner strength, lying awake in bed at night listening to wolves howling, and about her dealings with local Native Americans. In the late 1800s, train service arrived in the form of the Bangor & Piscataquis (later Bangor & Aroostook) and Canadian Pacific Railroads, and by the beginning of the 1900s, several large structures had been built in town, including the Shaw Block in the village center. Greenville was by then a bustling town with a number of mills and other industries, and a larger population than today. Between 1902 and 1906, electric lights became available in town, followed by the telephone. The modern age was rapidly coming to Greenville.

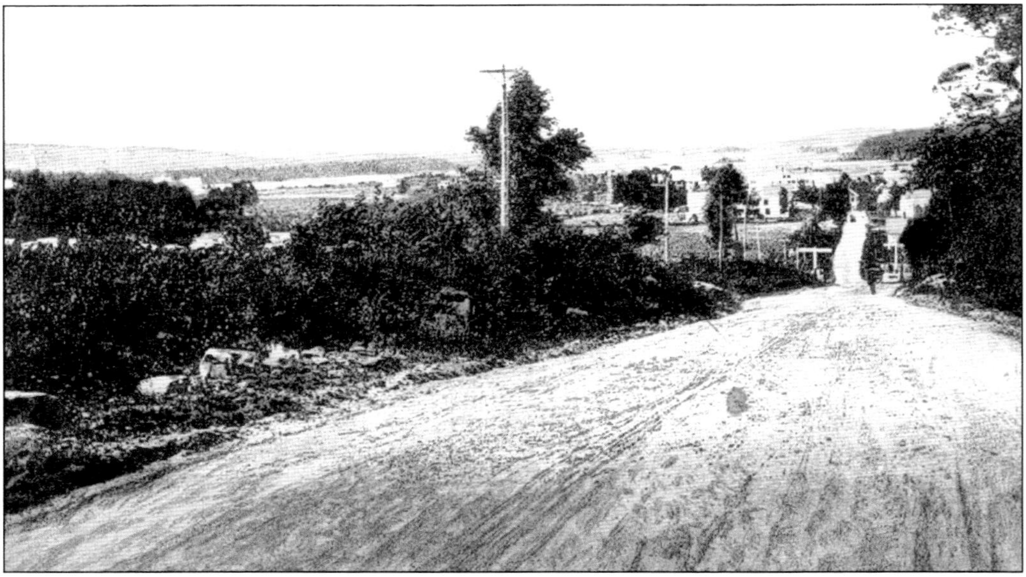

In the early 1900s, the road from Monson and Shirley over Indian Hill into Greenville was gravel. Notice the wagon tracks in the roadway showing this route was heavily traveled by horse-and-buggies. Greenville village is seen in the background.

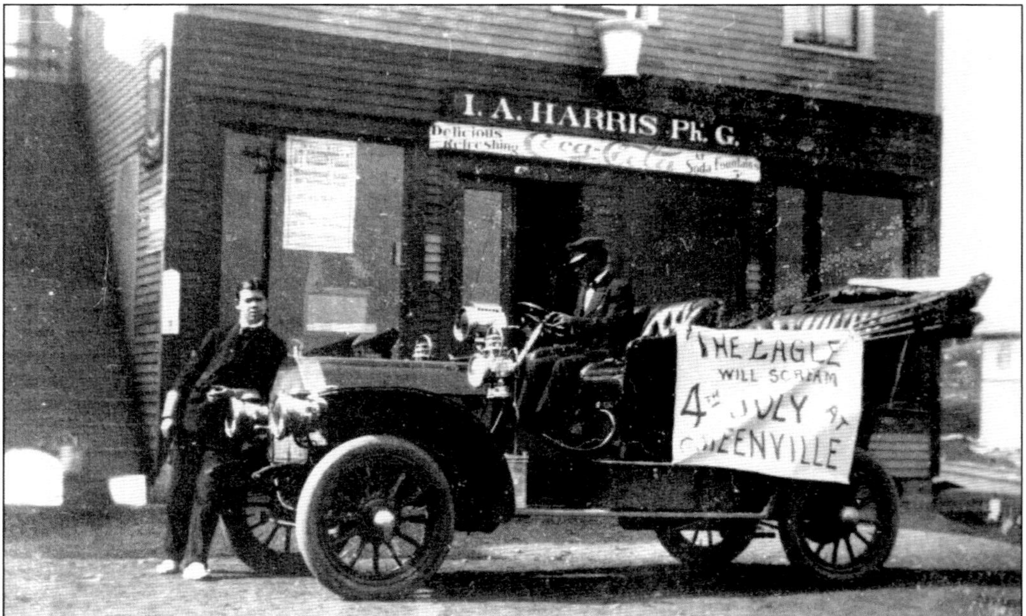

Henry Perley was at the wheel of a Grout automobile when this 1909 photograph was taken in front of the I. A. Harris Drug Store in Greenville village. Donald Davis is leaning against the car at the left. A sign on the side of the car notes, "The eagle will scream 4th July at Greenville," apparently referring to a Fourth of July parade that year.

The Greenville High School basketball team is shown here in 1907–1908. Even at this early date, Greenville had an active sports program in the school.

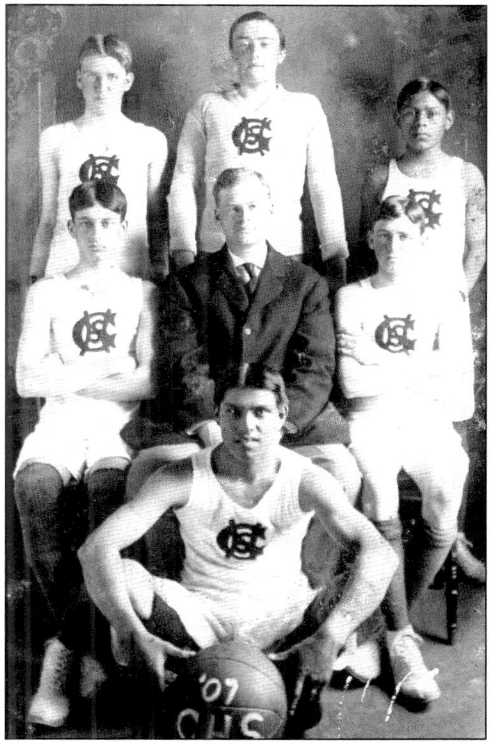

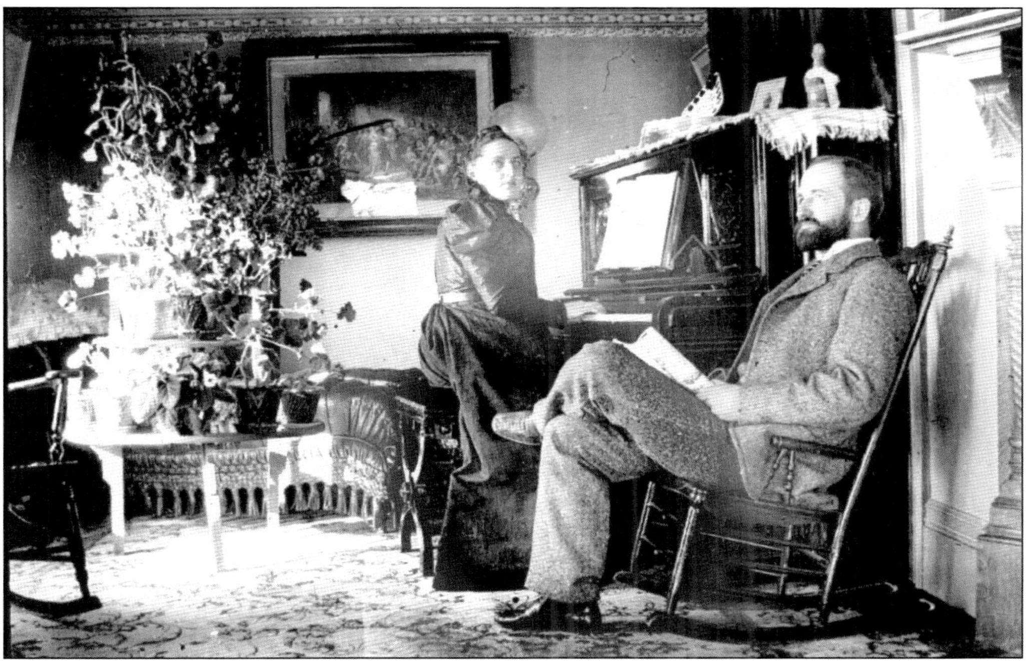

Most early photographs taken in the Moosehead region show outdoor scenes, but this rare view shows Harry Arthur Sanders Sr. and his wife, Octavia (Dean) Sanders, inside the parlor of their home in Greenville *c.* 1900. He was the son of D. T. Sanders, founder of Sanders Store.

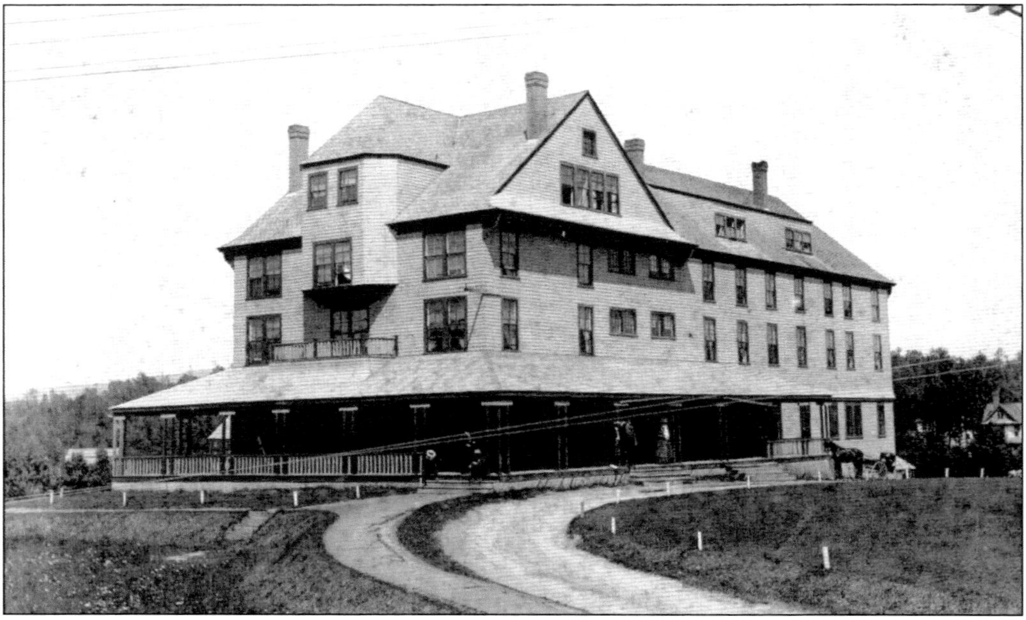

There were several impressive hotels in Greenville during the early 1900s. This is the Moosehead Inn, which was constructed in the 1880s and burned on March 5, 1912.

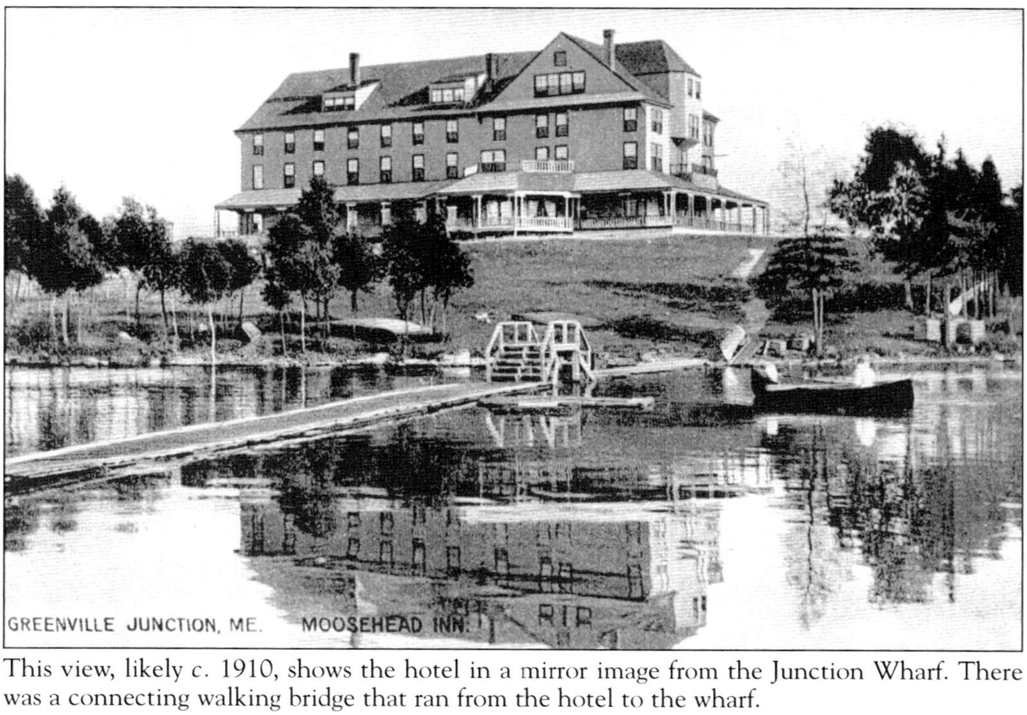

This view, likely *c.* 1910, shows the hotel in a mirror image from the Junction Wharf. There was a connecting walking bridge that ran from the hotel to the wharf.

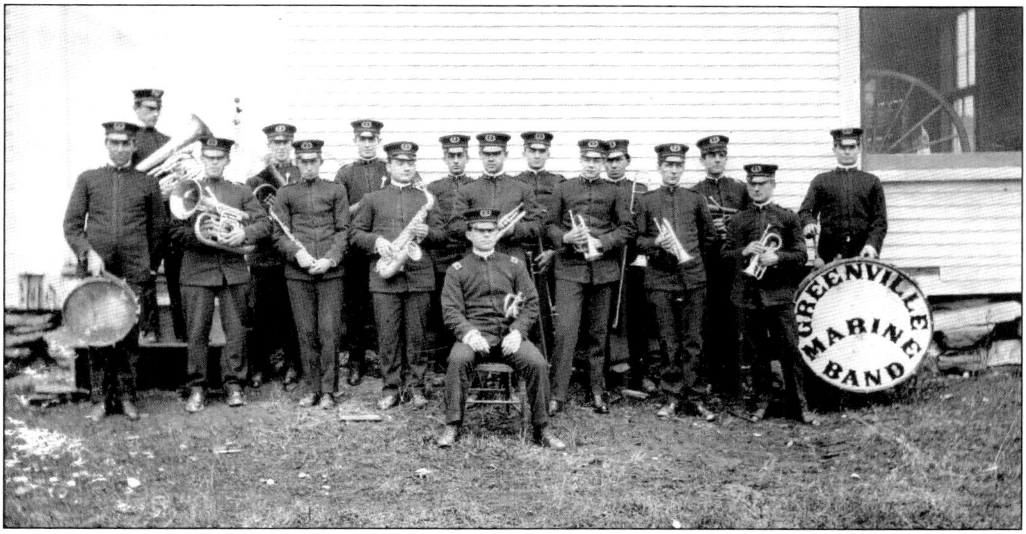

The Greenville Marine Band is shown here in 1906. Seated in front is band leader Ross St. Germain. Shown from left to right are the following: (first row) Thomas E. Wood, Fred E. Drake, Earl C. Buck, Edward Raymond, Donald H. Davis, Clifford Sawyer, Clair H. Savage, and Ralph B. Carleton; (second row) Edmund P. Bursley, Harry Mitchell, Malcolm B. Folsom, Harry E. Ray, Harley P. Budden, Henry Perley, Dick A. Young, and Ed Moore. Harold Walden is not shown.

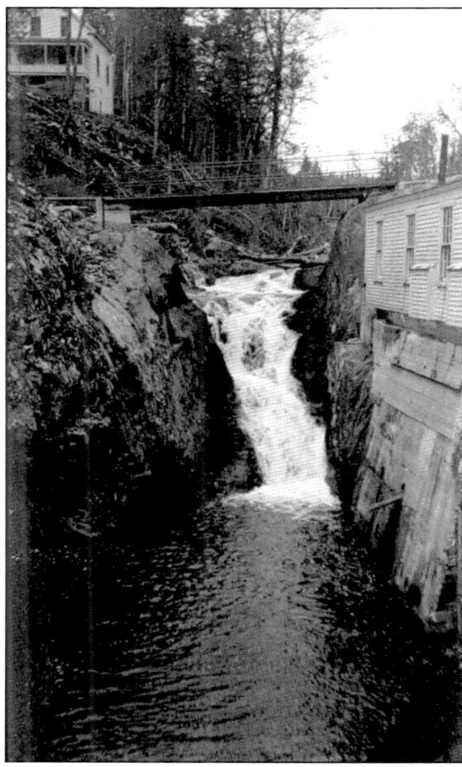

The Wilson Pond power station, east of Greenville, was one of the first places electrical power was generated in the Moosehead region. This *c.* 1910 photograph shows Wilson's Falls and the power generating plant on the right.

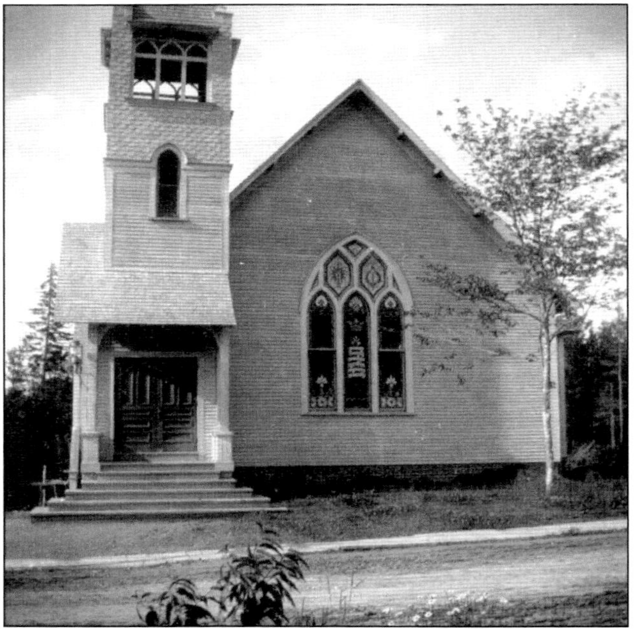

Methodism began in Greenville shortly after the first settlers arrived in the early 1820s. Methodist circuit riders preached in Greenville only occasionally. The first church was dedicated in 1869 and included Baptists, Methodists, Presbyterians, and Quakers. In 1900, the Methodist church (now United Methodist) in Greenville Junction was constructed. This view shows the church shortly after construction was completed, and at the time, West Street (now Pritham Avenue) was only a narrow gravel road.

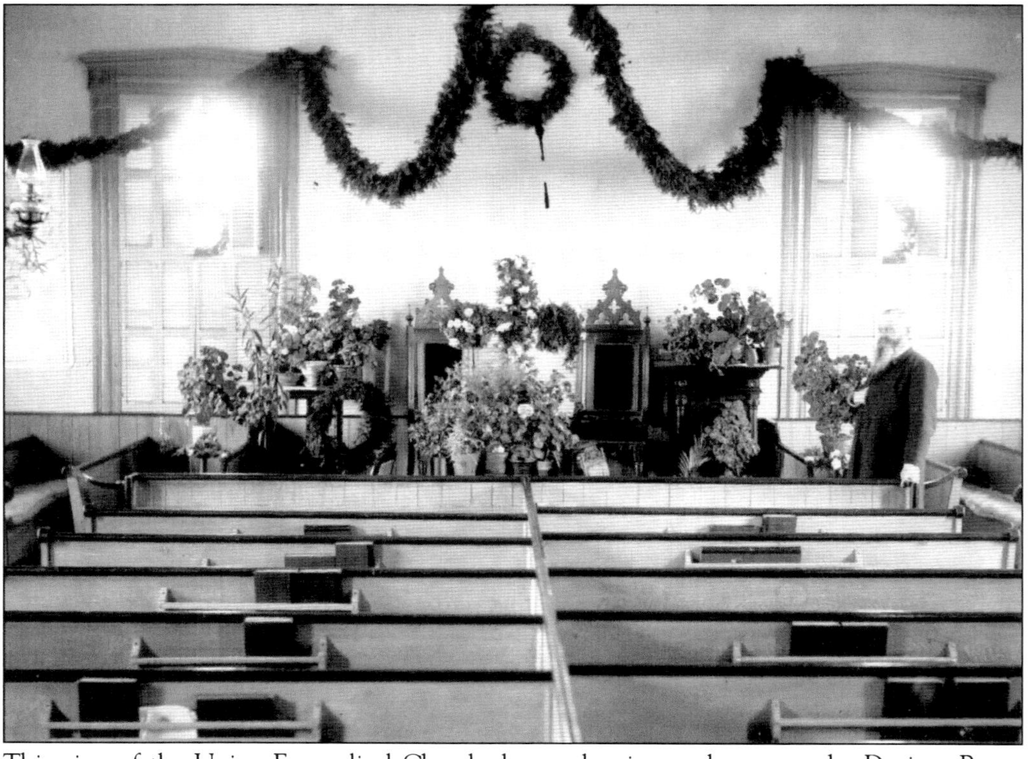

This view of the Union Evangelical Church shows what is now known as the Davison Room decorated for Christmas c. 1900. The Reverend Charles Davison, one of the church's early pastors, is shown at the right. This room was the original church, which was dedicated in 1869. In later years, the building was increased in size and is now several times larger than the original structure.

Greenville village had many sleepy residential streets during the second decade of the 20th century. This view shows Pleasant Street from near the top of Pleasant Street Hill, looking to the west, with Squaw Mountain in the distance. The roadway was still gravel during this time.

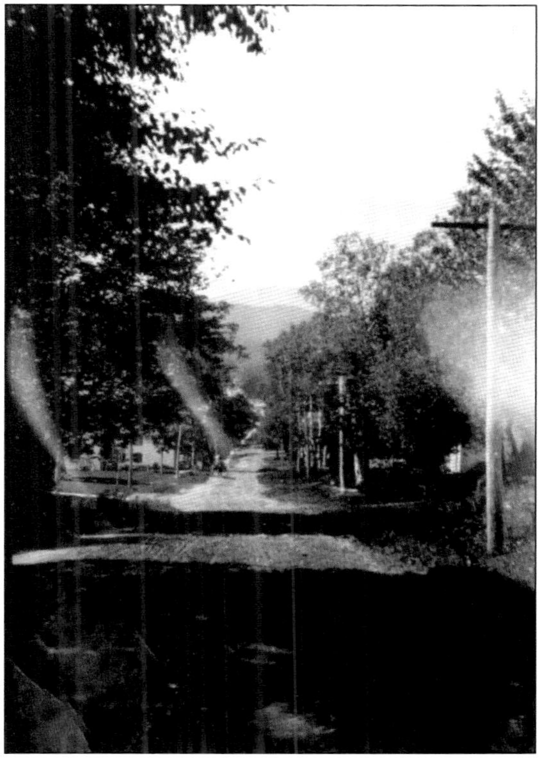

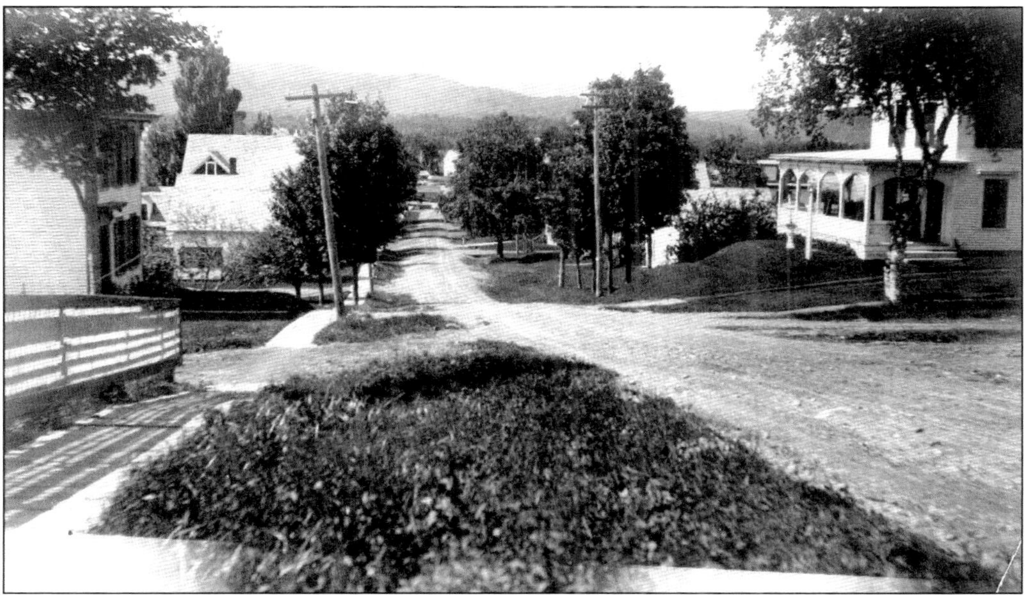

This view is similar to the one above but was taken farther down Pleasant Street Hill. Shown is the intersection of Pleasant and Shaw Streets. It looks much the same today, except the roads are paved and there is a lot more traffic.

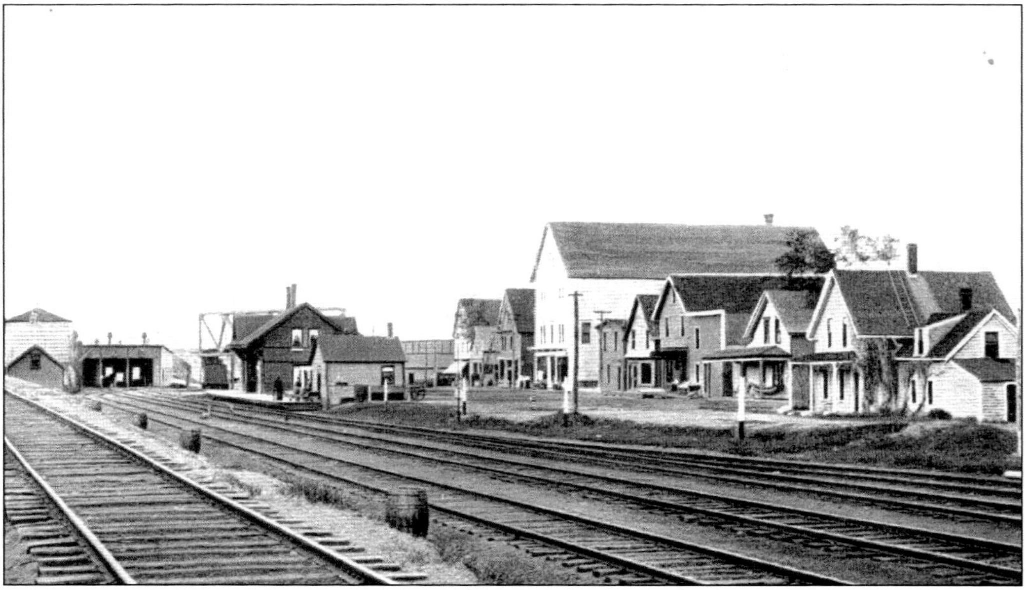

This view shows the Depot Street area of Greenville Junction during the early 1900s. Here, the Canadian Pacific Railroad and Bangor & Aroostook Railroad met, bringing many visitors to the Moosehead Lake region. From the Junction Wharf, people could travel by steamer to the Mount Kineo House and other areas. The three-story building in the center was the A. A. Crafts Store and is today known as the Depot.

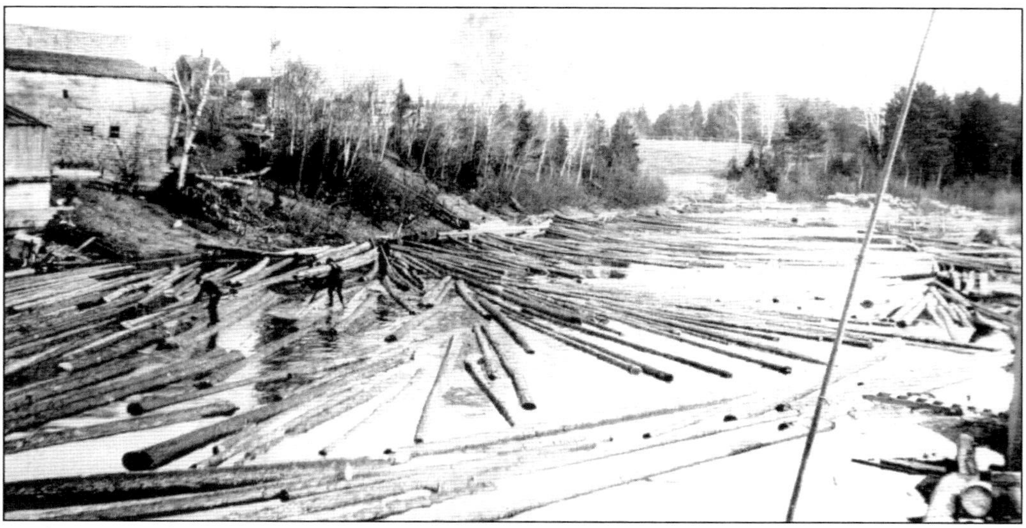

In the very early 1900s, long logs were floated down Wiggins Stream in Greenville Junction to Moosehead Lake and on to sawmills. This photograph was likely taken from the rear of the A. A. Crafts Store.

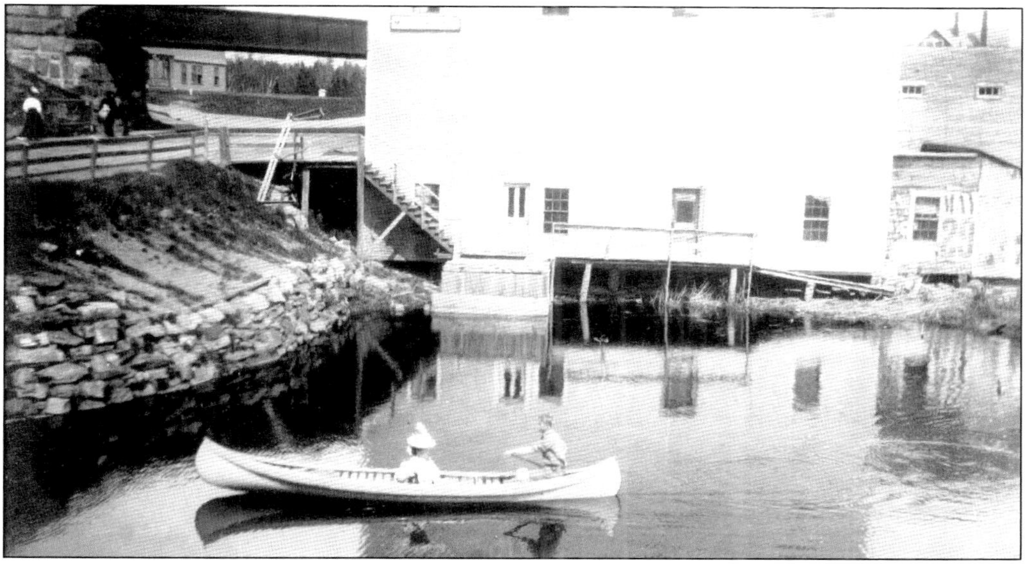

This view of Greenville Junction shows a calm stretch of water in Wiggins Stream with canoeists enjoying a fine day on the water near the outlet to Moosehead Lake. West Street (now Pritham Avenue) is seen to the left; the Canadian Pacific Railroad overpass and the Moosehead Inn are in the upper left corner. The photograph was taken in 1907. The large white building in the center and the Moosehead Inn are no longer standing, but otherwise the scene remains much the same today.

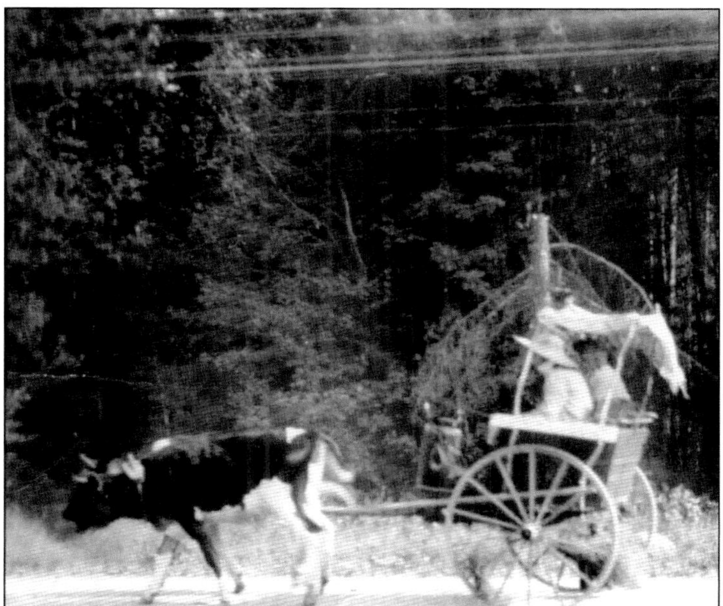

Parades have always been an important part of summer activities in the Moosehead region. This is a scene from the July 4, 1913, parade. John and Stan Walden are enjoying a ride in a small wagon, one of the floats depicting early life in the area.

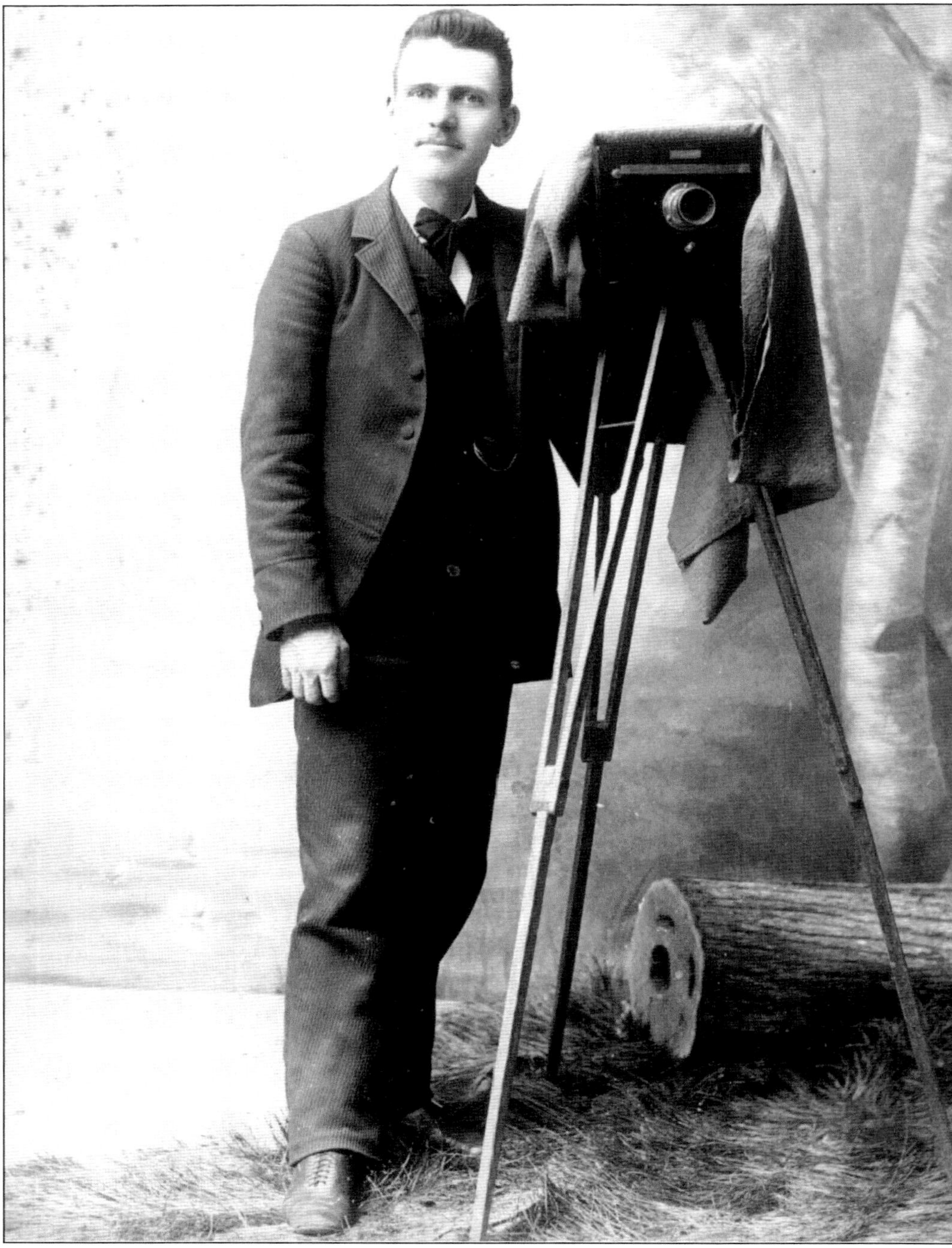

David O. Curtis was a well-known Greenville photographer in the early 1900s. He is responsible for many of the photographs that exist today of the region in the early twentieth century. He was born in Greenville on April 17, 1879, the son of Abel J. and Susan (Varney) Curtis. He was the grandson of Deborah Walden, the first white woman in Greenville, and the great-great-grandson of Nathaniel Haskell, one of the town's original settlers. He died on February 23, 1962, and is buried in the Greenville Cemetery.

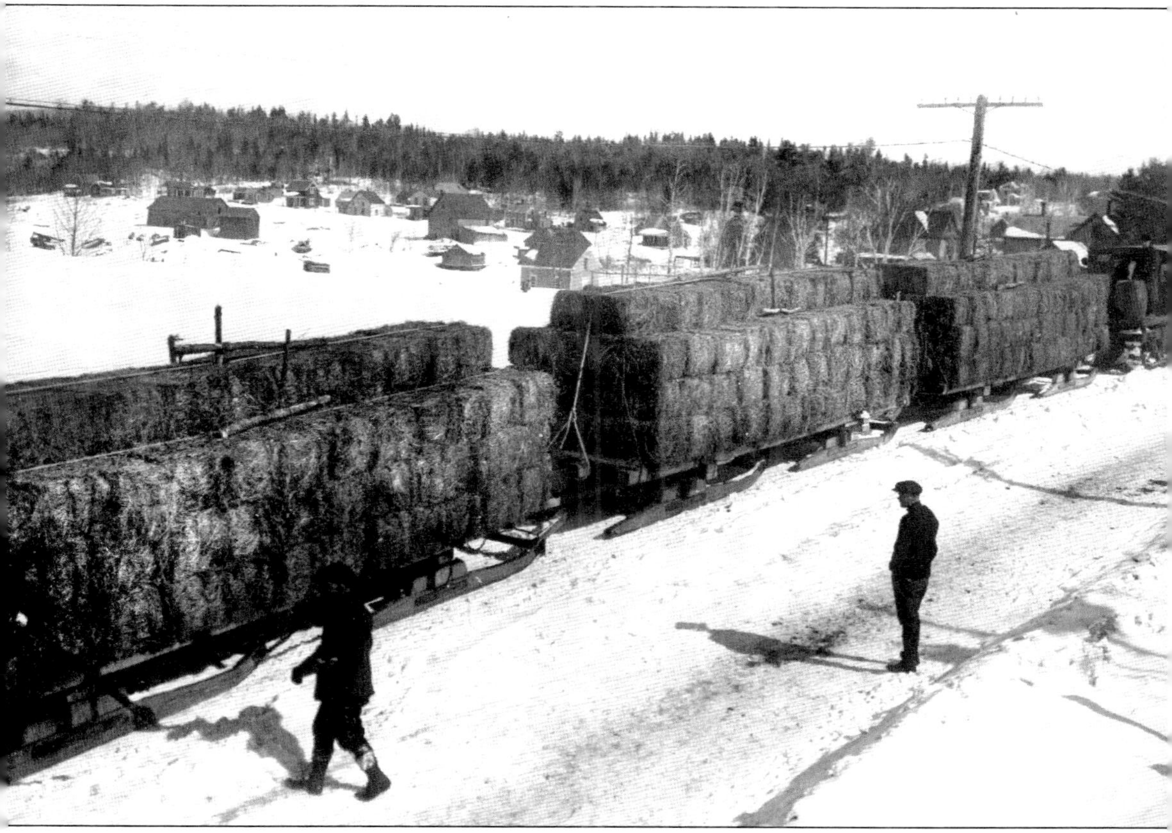

Lombard Steam Log Haulers were used throughout the North Woods in the early days of the 1900s. This view shows a hauler (far right) with three sleds loaded with hay bales. The photograph was taken by Greenville photographer Clarence W. Meade c. 1910. The location was near the Canadian Pacific Railroad depot, and the view looks south toward the Junction Wharf area.

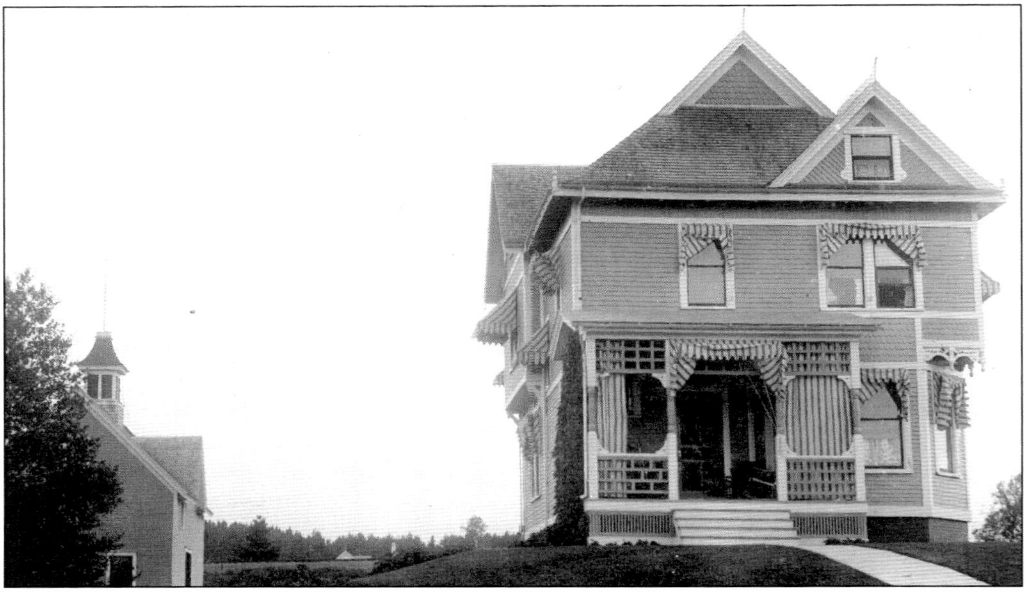

With its distinctive architecture, this house, built by John Eveleth in the late 1800s for his daughter Rebecca Eveleth and her husband, Arthur A. Crafts, was a landmark in Greenville Junction. The house was later enlarged and is today known at the Eveleth-Crafts-Sheridan Historical House, home of the Moosehead Historical Museum. This photograph was likely taken *c.* 1900. The carriage house is shown at the far left.

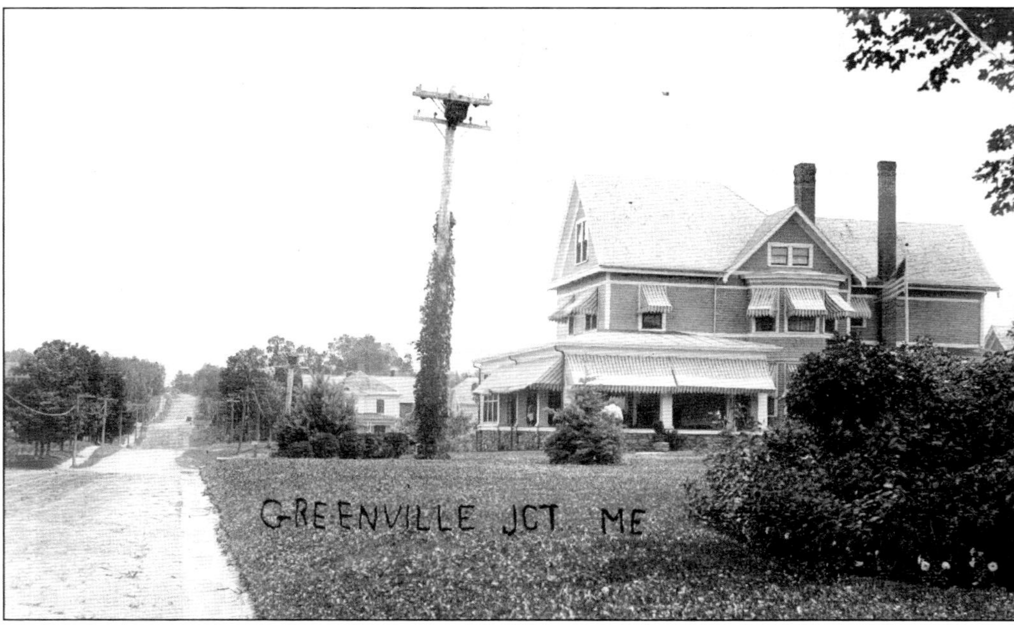

The Eveleth-Crafts-Sheridan Historical House was later owned by Rebecca and Arthur Crafts's daughter, Julia Crafts Sheridan and her husband, Phil Sheridan. This view shows the enlarged house following the expansion of 1913. The house remains much the same today.

Julia Crafts (right) pumps water from a hand pump on the south side of the Victorian mansion she occupied with her parents in this c. 1915 photograph. The woman on the left is unidentified. Julia Crafts later married Phil Sheridan and owned the Squaw Mountain Inn in Greenville Junction. She was an early member of the Moosehead Historical Society, joining in the early 1960s. She and her husband left major endowments for the society and museum.

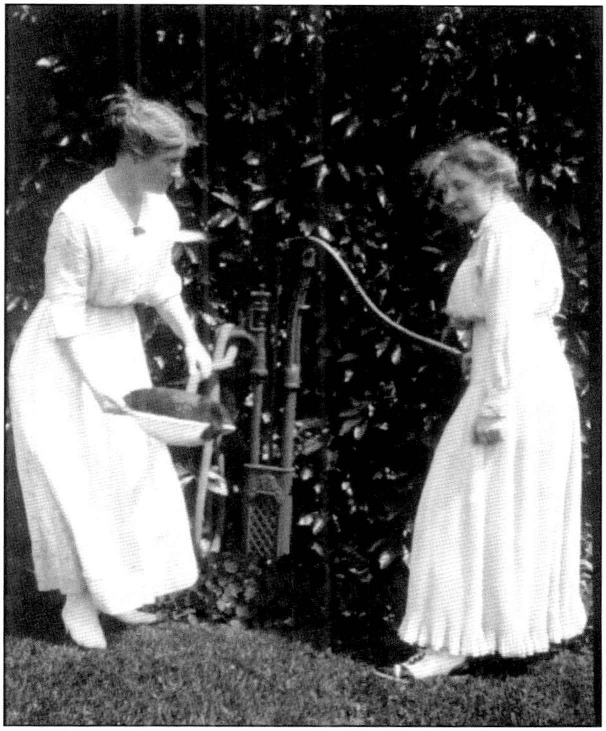

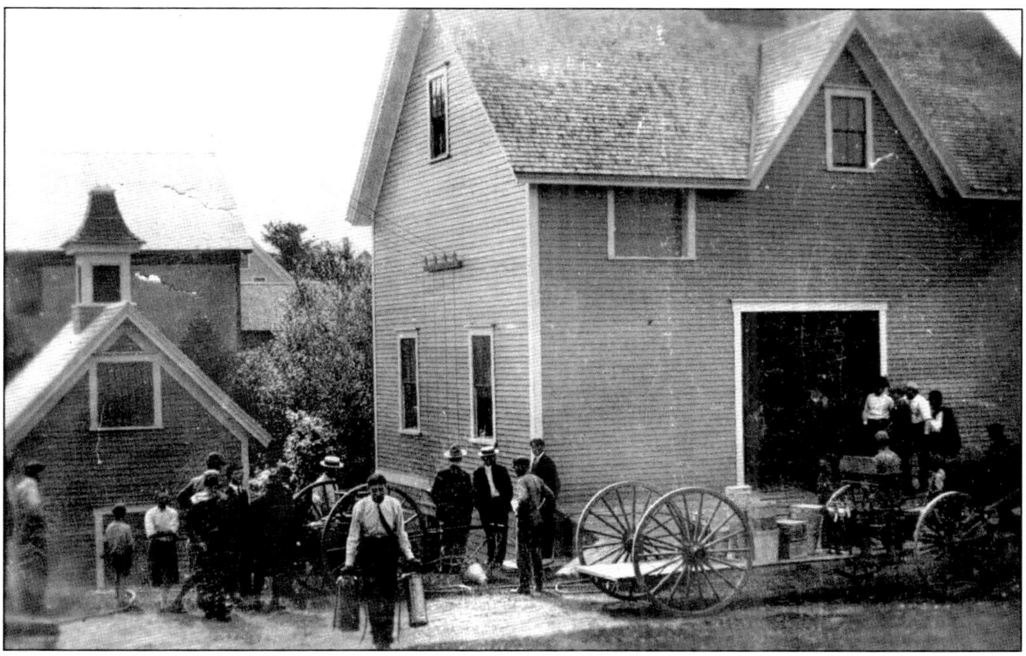

There was a lot of activity around the Crafts's estate when this early 1920s photograph was taken. It shows the carriage house on the right, and an icehouse and large barn to the left. The icehouse and barn are long gone, but the carriage house now houses the Lumberman's Museum and office space for the Moosehead Historical Museum.

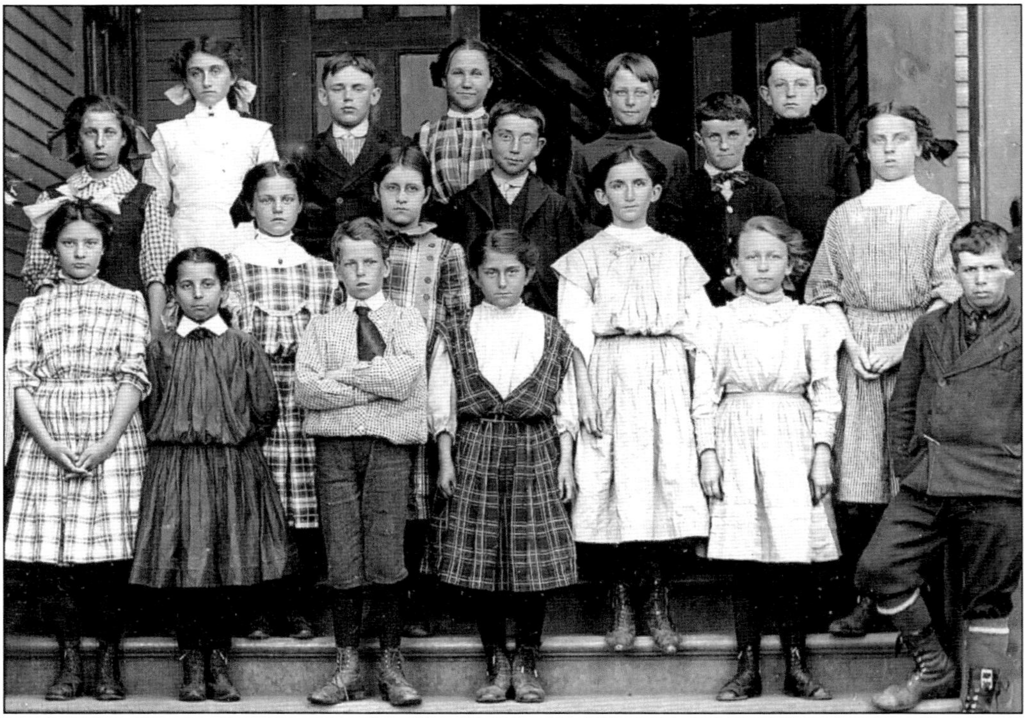

Miss Tardy taught the fifth grade when this photograph was taken in May 1910. Unfortunately, due to the passage of time, no one is identified.

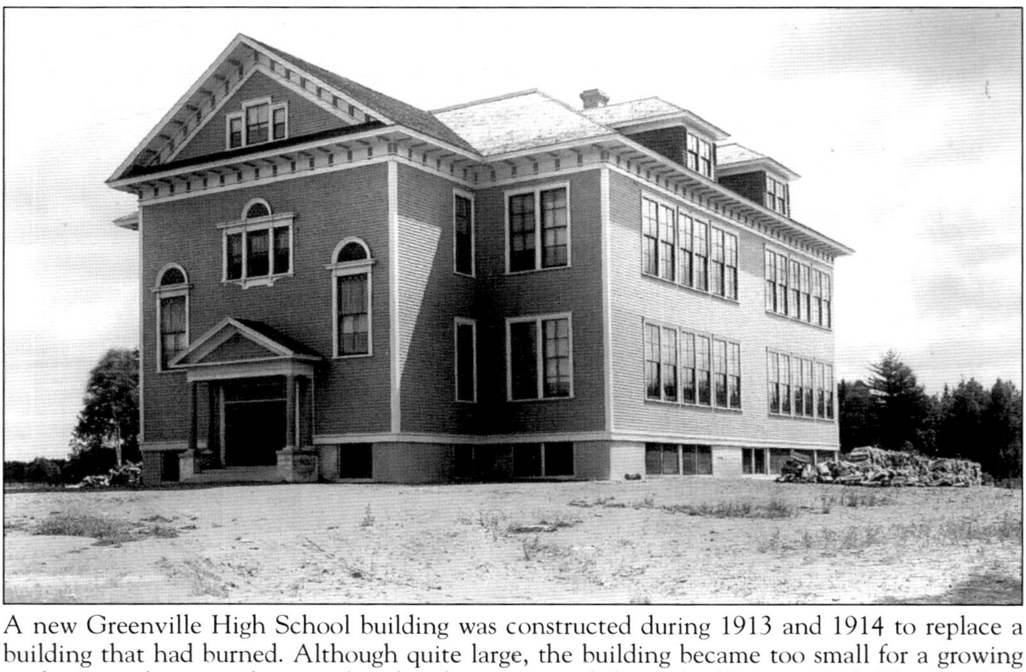

A new Greenville High School building was constructed during 1913 and 1914 to replace a building that had burned. Although quite large, the building became too small for a growing student population and was replaced with a new, much larger building in 1935. This building was located on the current school campus near the basketball court.

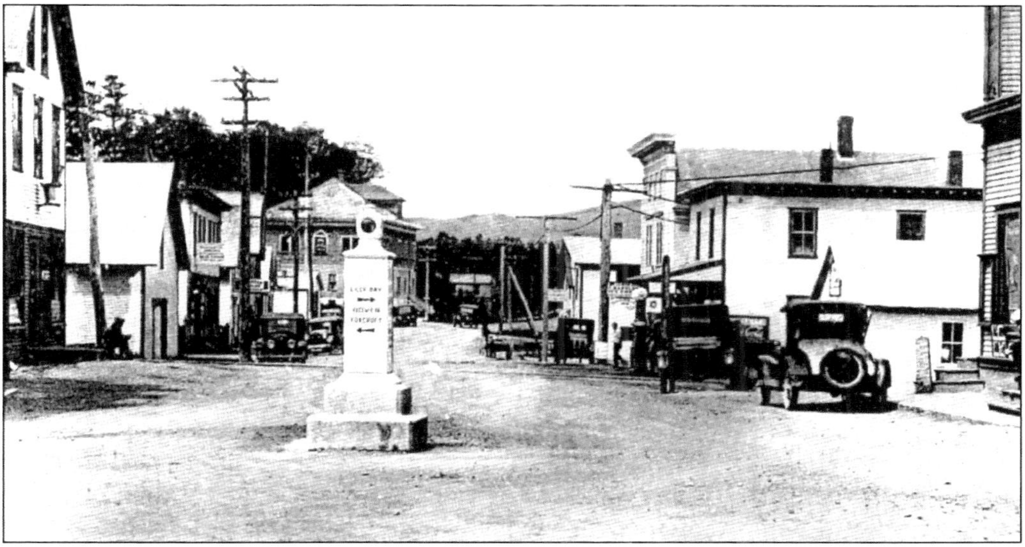

During the 1920s, a "silent policeman" made of concrete was located in the intersection of Main and West Streets, providing directions to Dover-Foxcroft, Lily Bay, and Rockwood. The monument was removed in later years when trucks had difficulty maneuvering around it.

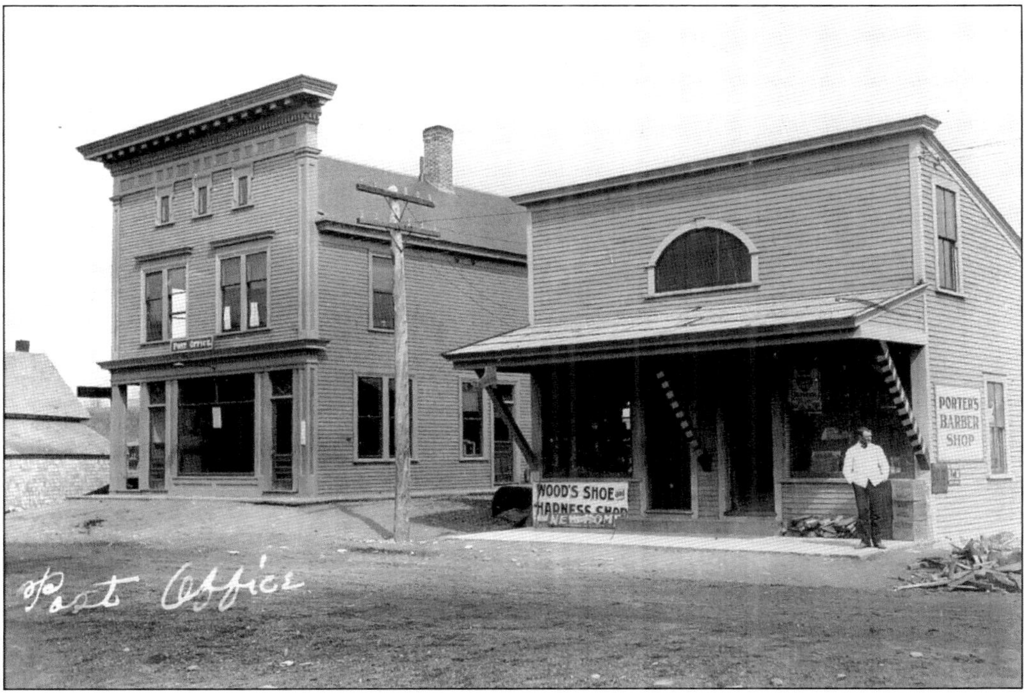

The Greenville Post Office was located in the building to the left in this c. 1920 photograph. It was later a bank and burned in the late 1980s. The building on the right contained Porter's Barber Shop and Wood's Shoe and Harness Shop. These buildings were located on West Street (now Pritham Avenue) in Greenville village.

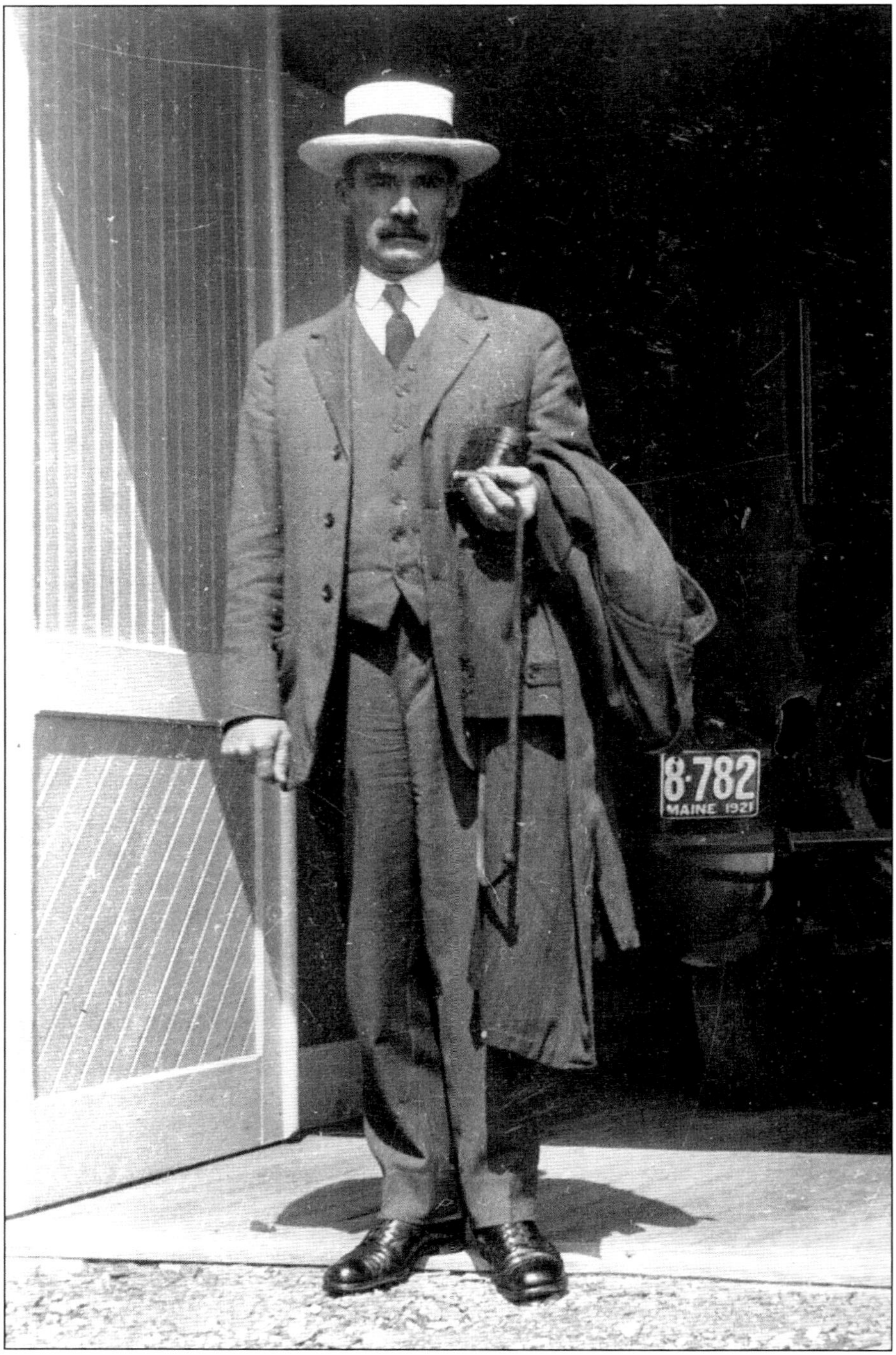

Louis Oakes was a well-known local surveyor who had an interest in forestry. He was also an entrepreneur who built the new Greenville Consolidated School building and donated it to the town in 1935. Oakes purchased the Mount Kineo House resort in 1938, and it was operated by the Oakes family into the 1960s. This photograph shows Oakes in the garage at the old stable in 1920.

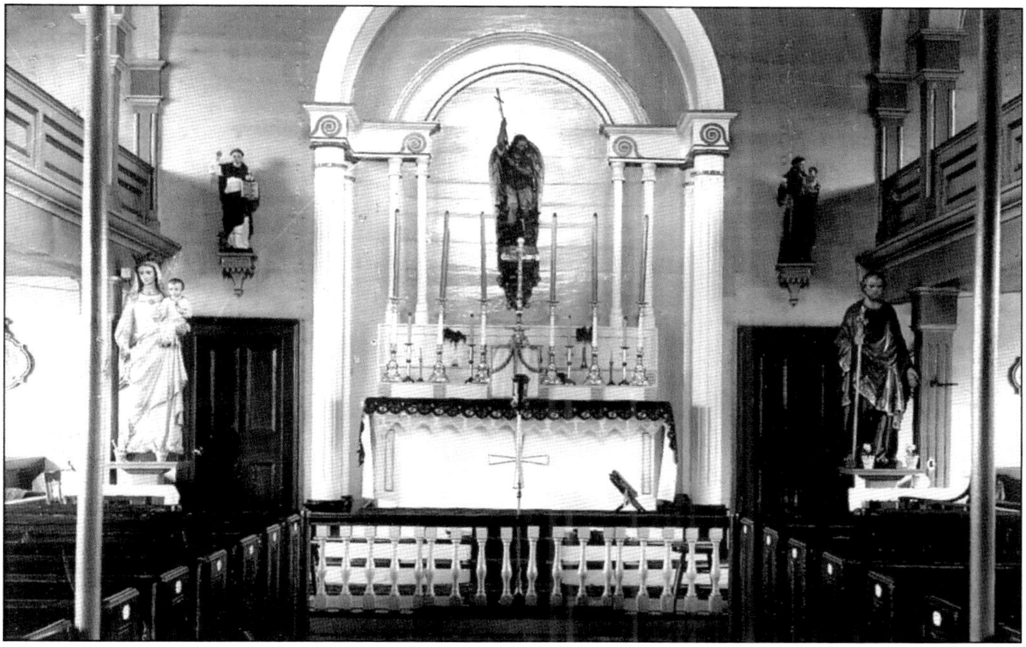

This is a *c.* 1920s interior view of the old Holy Family Catholic Church, located on Washington Street. The church was later expanded to a new site on West Street, across from the Greenville Consolidated School building, where it remains today.

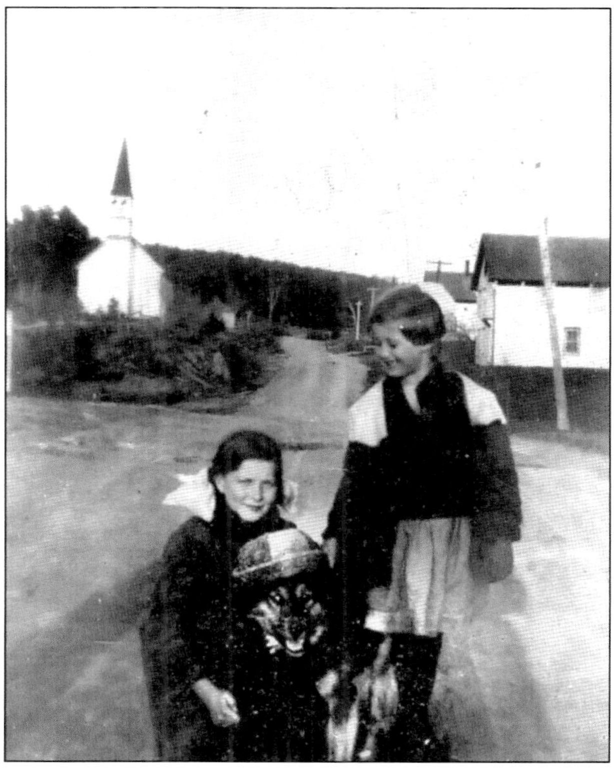

Priscilla Ells Ward and her sister Winifred Ells Rogers pose with the family dog on Washington Street. The old Catholic church is at the left in the background in this *c.* 1920s photograph.

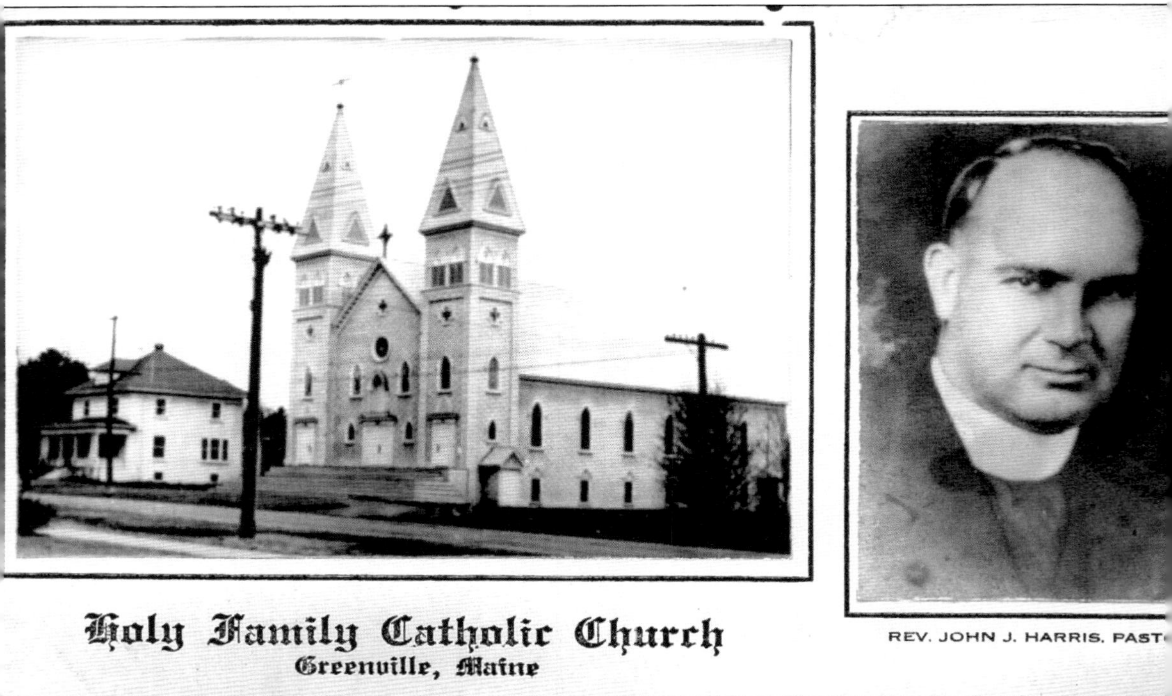

The new Holy Family Catholic Church is located on Pritham Avenue, across from the Greenville school buildings. This image shows the church and rectory, along with an inset of Rev. John H. Harris.

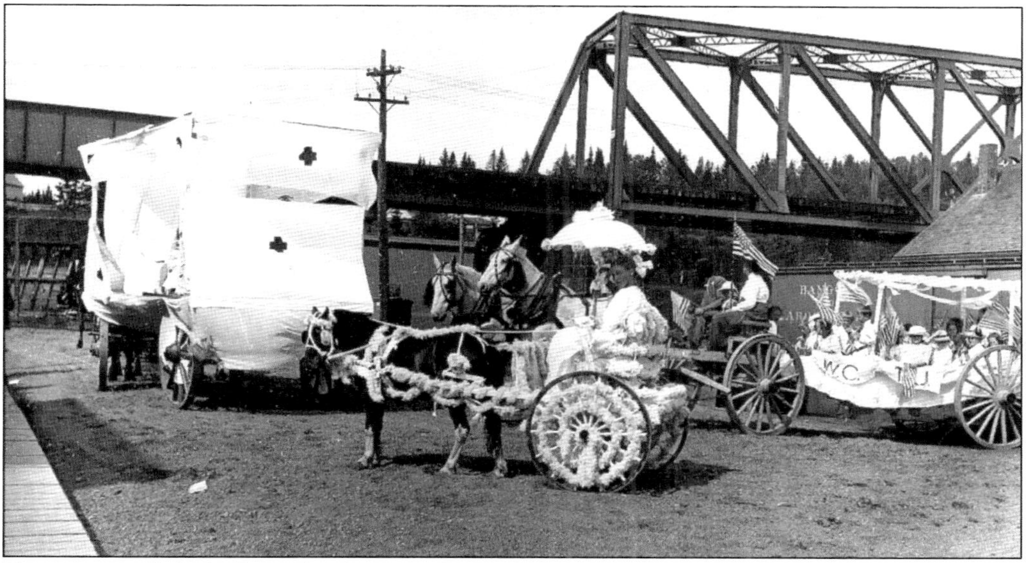

Floats were all decked out for the Fourth of July parade in Greenville Junction in this 1920s photograph. The float at the far left is believed to have been from the American Red Cross, and the float at the far right was prepared by the Women's Christian Temperance Union. The photograph was taken on the Junction Wharf. Note the Canadian Pacific Railroad trestle to the right and a boxcar of the Bangor & Aroostook Railroad partially hidden also on the right.

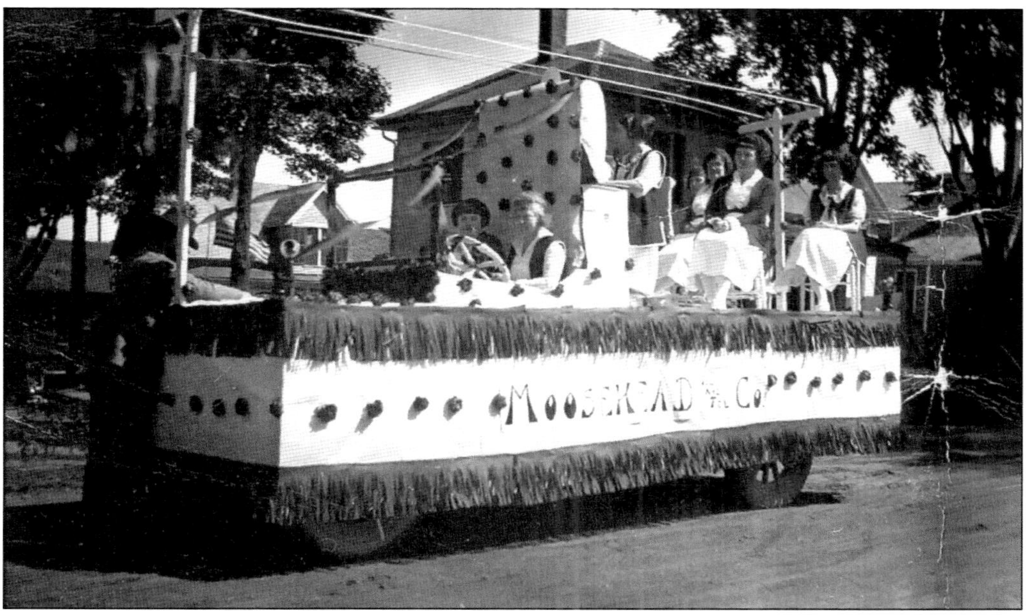

Several early telephone operators of the Moosehead Telephone & Telegraph Company are riding on this float in a Fourth of July parade c. 1920s.

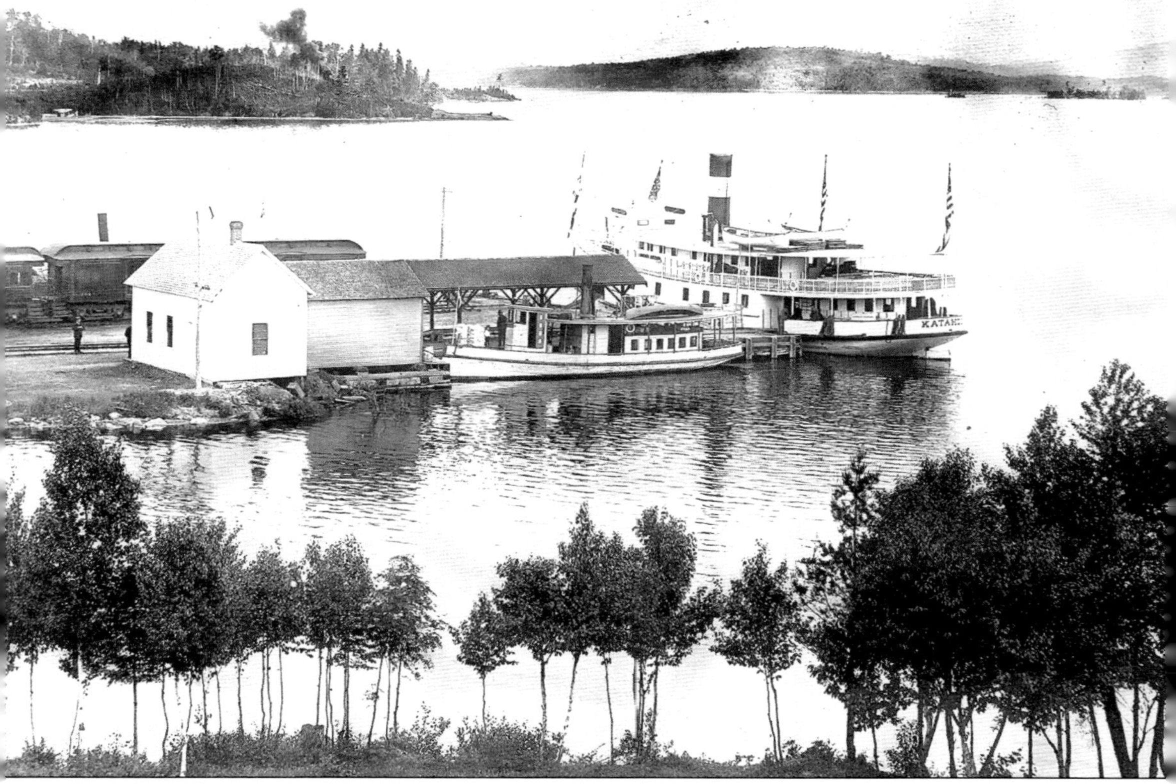

The Coburn Steamboat Company operated a ticket office at the end of the Junction Wharf, as seen in this 1920s photograph. The Bangor & Aroostook Railroad had a spur line that stopped at the end of the wharf. Two steamers are docked, likely preparing to transport passengers from the Bangor & Aroostook passenger cars up Moosehead Lake to Mount Kineo House and other destinations. The steamer to the far right is the *Katahdin* and the other is unidentified.

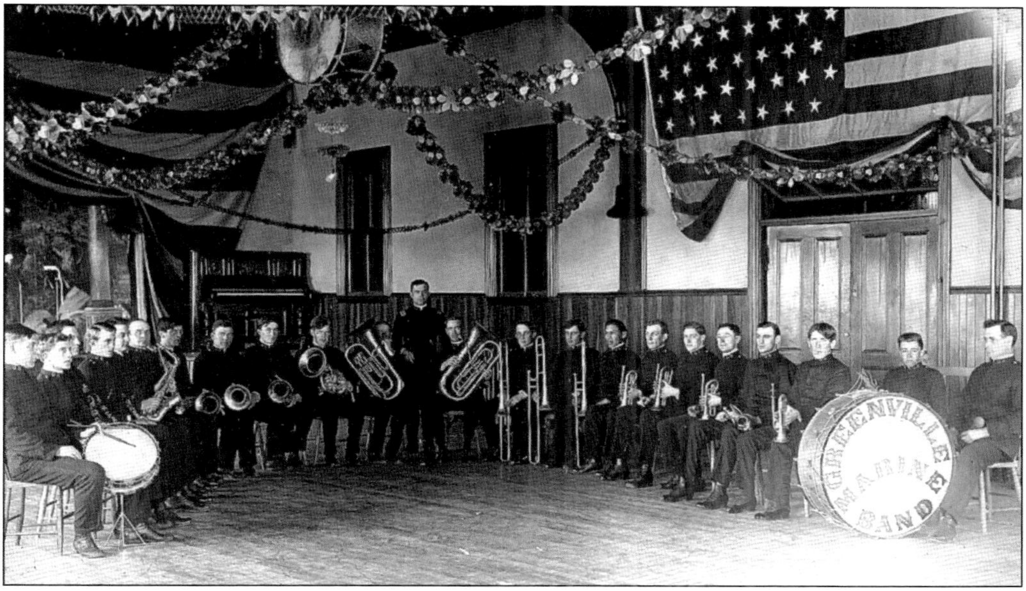

The Greenville Marine Band is shown here during the 1920s. Band members from left to right are as follows: Tom Wood, Phil Young, Harold Walden, Earl Buck, Eddy Raymond, John Gerrish, Dick Young, Jack Galusha, Fred Tweedie, Fred Drake, Harry Mitchell, Ross St. Germain (band leader), Malcolm Folsom, Harvey Budden, Harry Roy, Henry Perley, Clair Savage, Cliff Sawyer, Ralph Carleton, Dean Noyes, Roy Smith, Carroll Buck, and Ed Moore. The photograph was taken inside the Shaw Block in Greenville, where the band often performed.

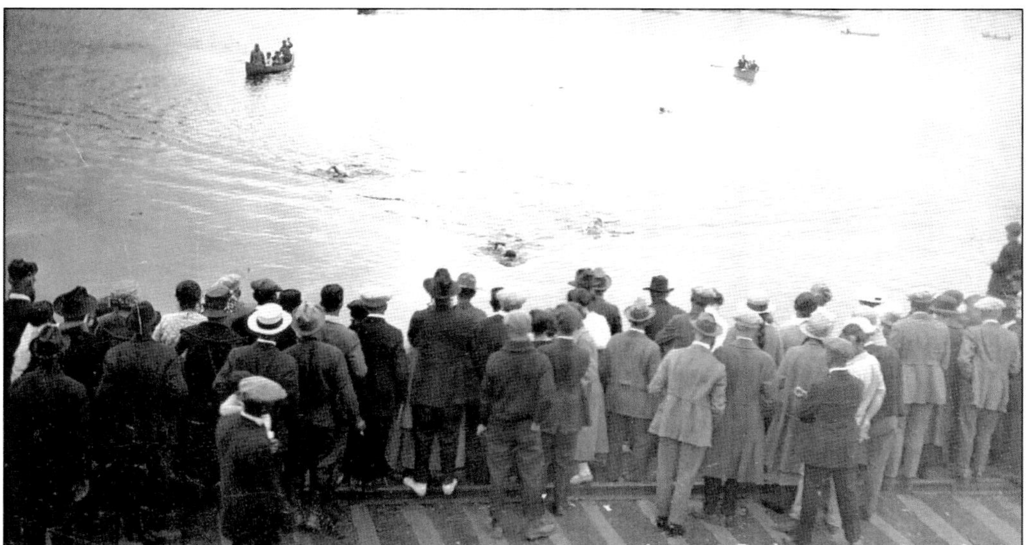

A swimming race in the East Cove of Moosehead Lake drew many viewers on July 4, 1923. It was one of several events that occurred during the annual Fourth of July activities.

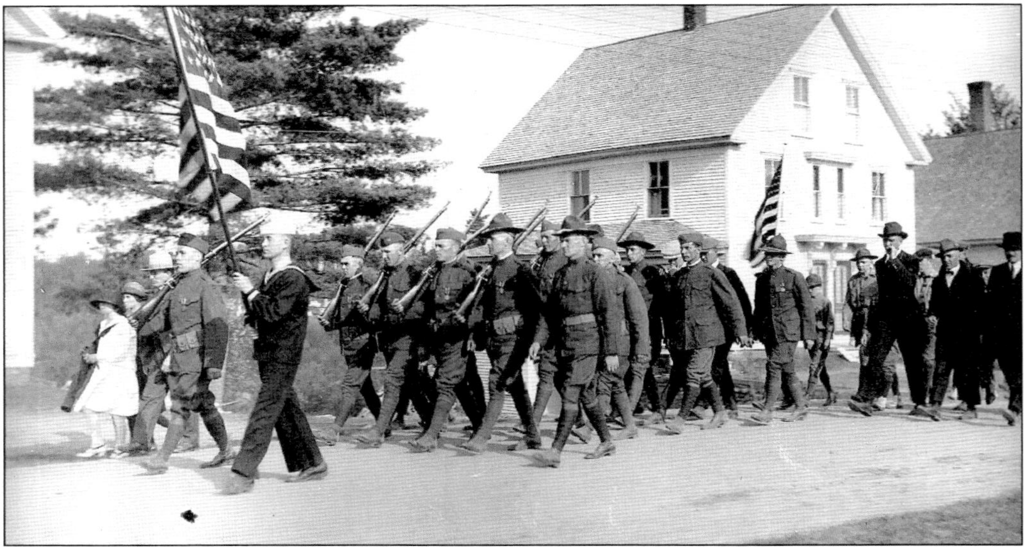

Memorial Day is another popular time for parades in the Moosehead region, and it is a time when veterans of all eras are given the opportunity to be recognized for their dedication. This photograph shows a 1920s parade that included men in uniform and older veterans in suits.

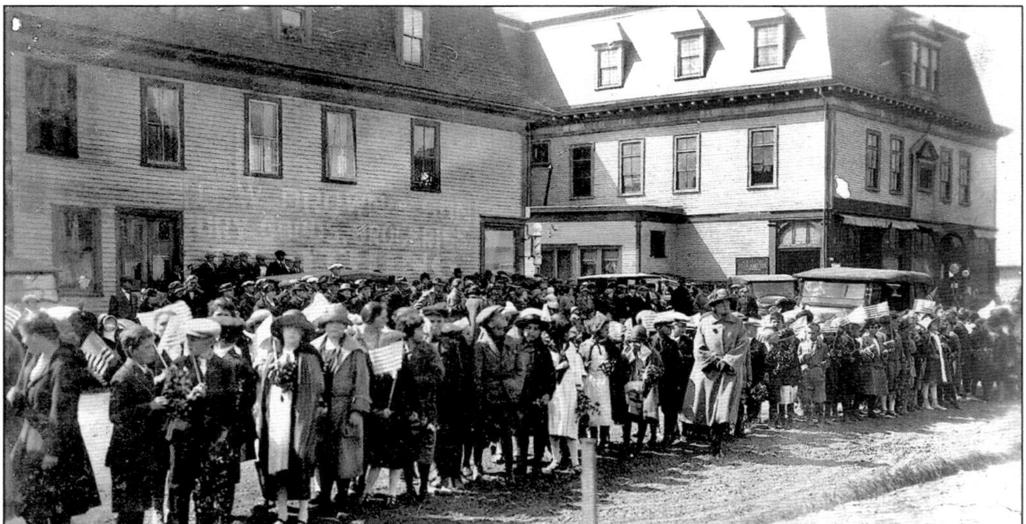

Hundreds of spectators gather at the intersection of Main and West Streets to view a Memorial Day parade in this 1920s photograph. The Shaw Block is to the right, and the building on the left was later partially burned and rebuilt as a two-story building that now houses the Corner Shop.

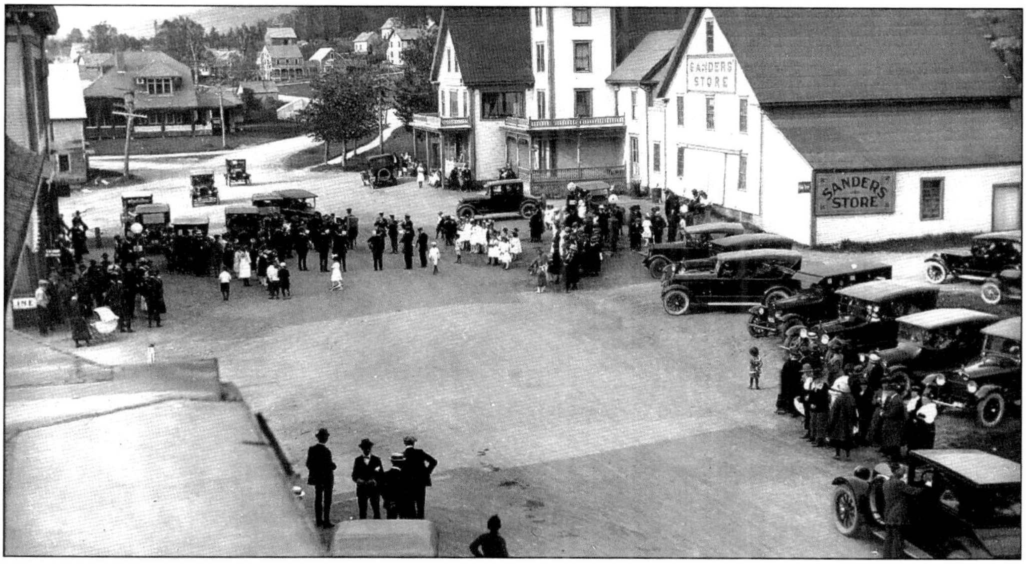

This 1920s photograph shows a view of the intersection of Main and West Streets in Greenville village shortly before a Memorial Day parade got under way. The Greenville Marine Band is shown in the top center preparing to provide music for the parade. There is an excellent view of Sanders Store to the right and the Lake House is in the upper left corner.

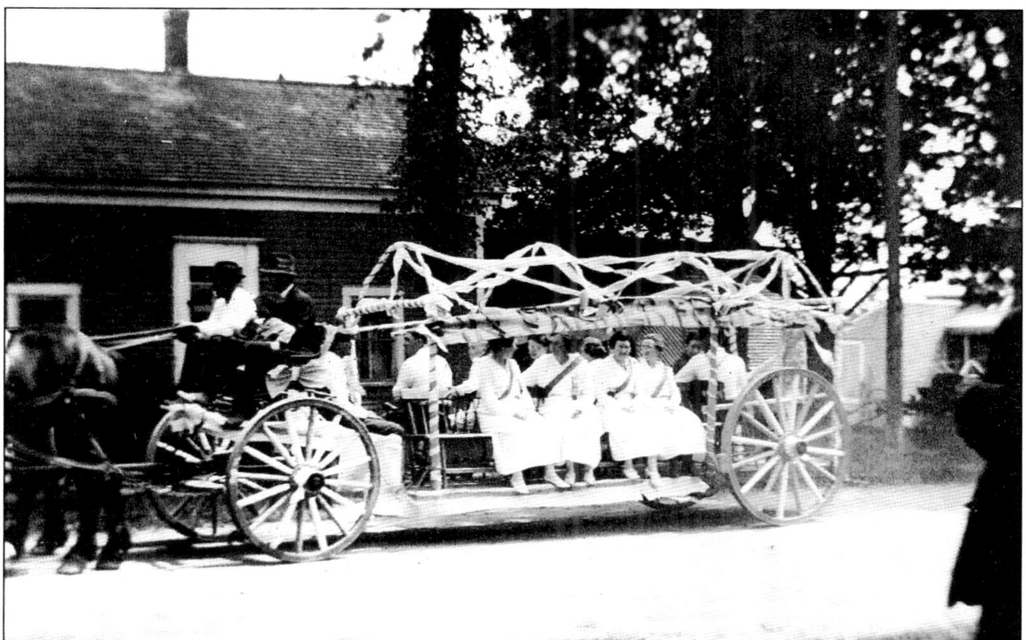

Here is another Fourth of July parade float with ladies in white dresses and sashes, perhaps representing a social organization. The photograph is from the early 1920s.

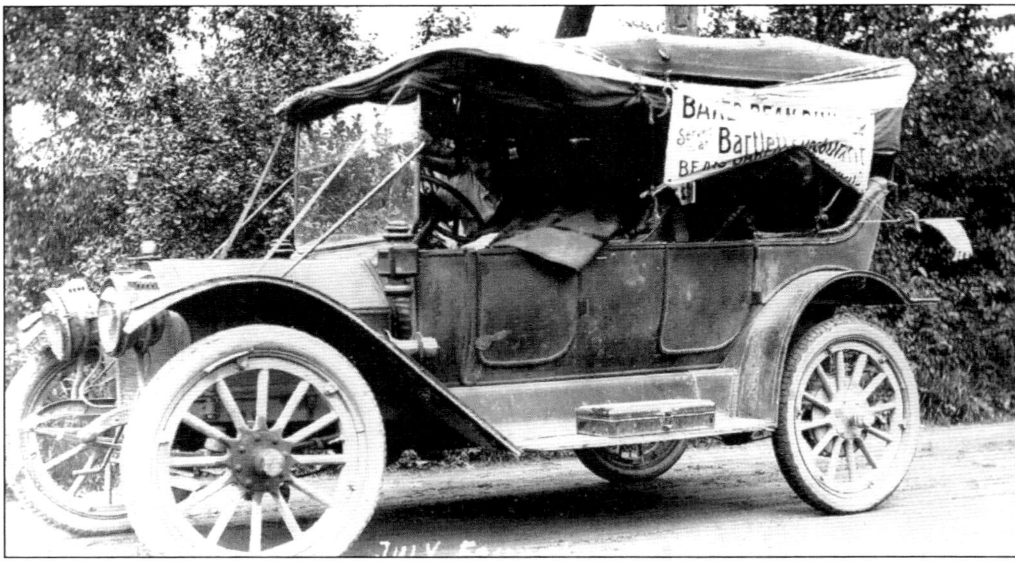

Many businesses participated in Fourth of July parades during the 1920s, and it is a trend that continues to this day. This 1920s photograph shows a car with a banner advertising a baked bean supper at Bartlett's Restaurant in Greenville village.

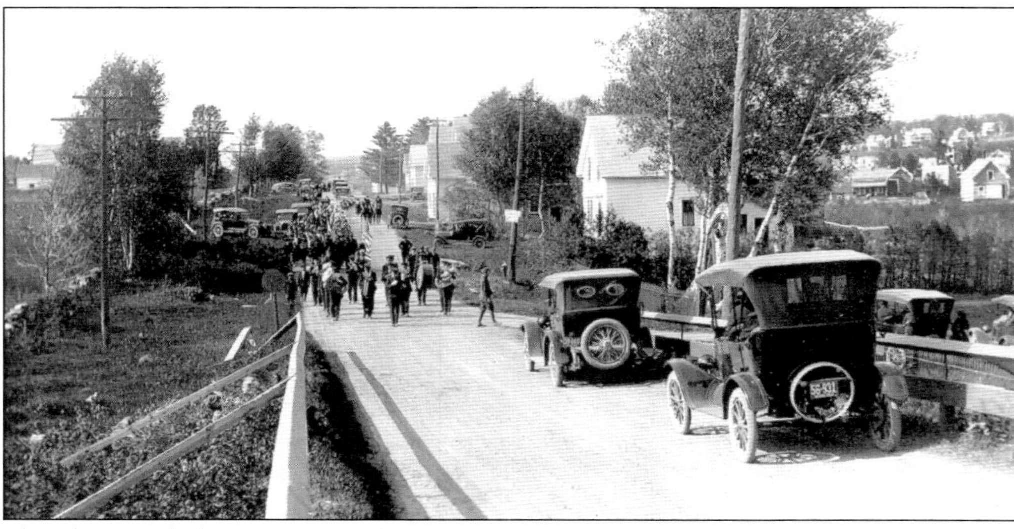

This photograph shows a Memorial Day parade in 1922 approaching the Greenville Cemetery. This was the old entrance to the cemetery. Main Street is now to the left of this photograph. The sign on the tree in the center shows the speed limit was 15 miles per hour. Members of the Greenville Marine Band are in the front of the procession to the cemetery.

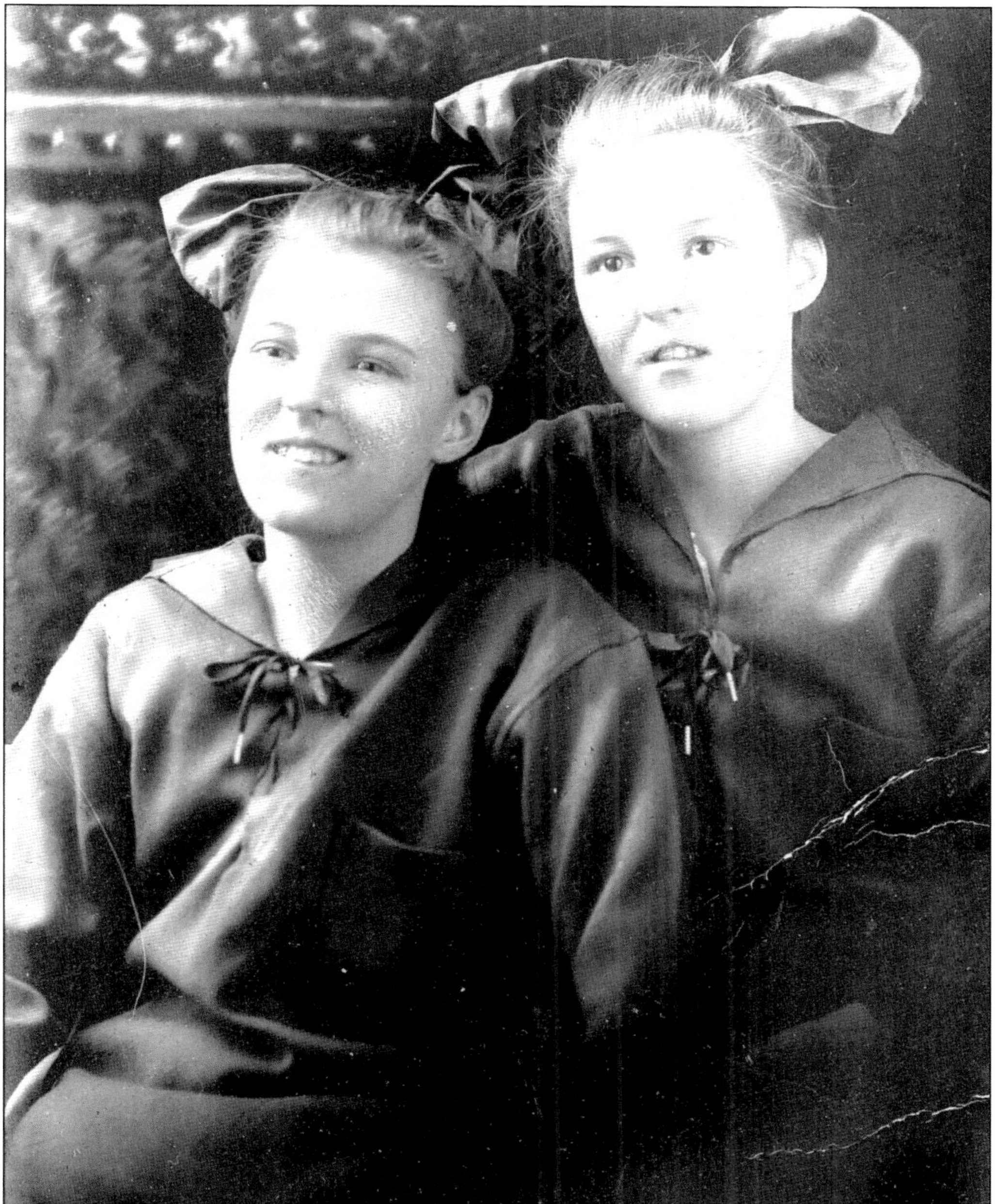

Elizabeth (left) and Elinor Hamilton were twin daughters of Irving and Laura Hamilton. They were born in Greenville on December 27, 1905, and lived in Kokadjo, and later in Seboomook, where their parents operated the Seboomook House. Elizabeth Hamilton Hartsgrove became a well-known author of several Maine history books, and Elinor Hamilton was a nurse, working closely with Dr. Fred Pritham in logging camps and lumbering operations throughout the north. She was also a decorated veteran of World War II and the Korean Conflict, retiring in 1965. Elizabeth died on March 15, 1986, in Bath, Maine, and Elinor died July 29, 1995, in Newburyport, Massachusetts.

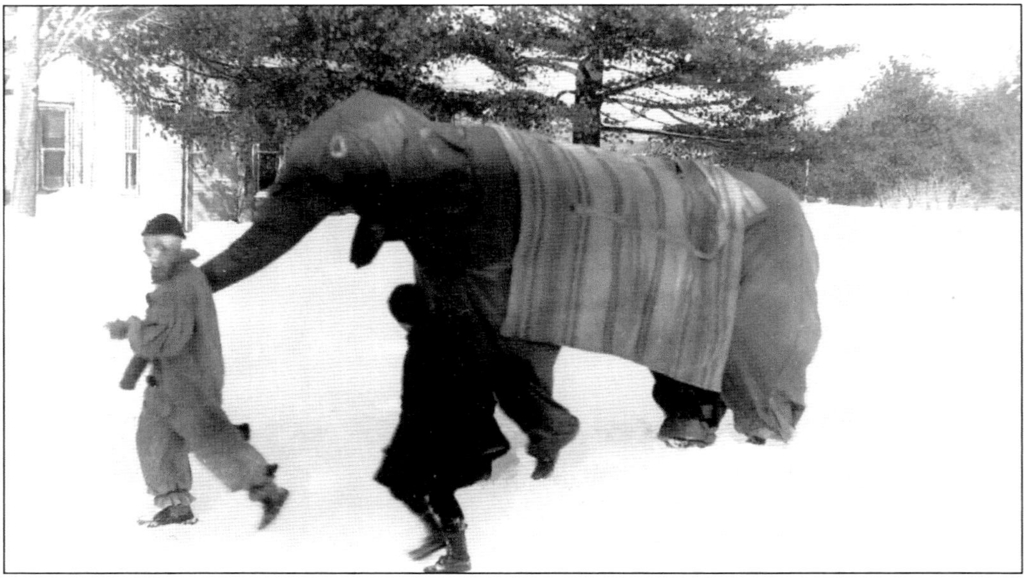

Greenville High School students sponsored an annual Rollicky-Pollicky Fair at the school for decades. Part of the festivities was a parade along West Street (now Pritham Avenue). This photograph, taken March 9, 1923, shows one student dressed as a clown and two others inside an elephant costume.

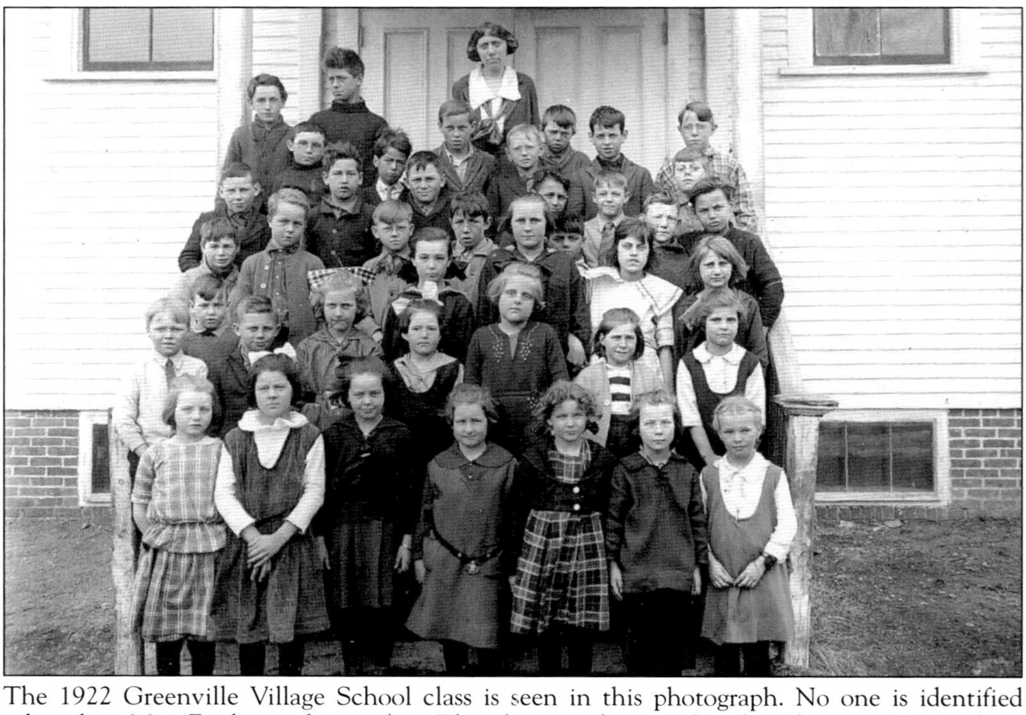

The 1922 Greenville Village School class is seen in this photograph. No one is identified other than Miss Erickson, the teacher. The photograph was taken by Clarence W. Meade, a Greenville photographer. This class, with over 40 pupils, was a large one for a single teacher.

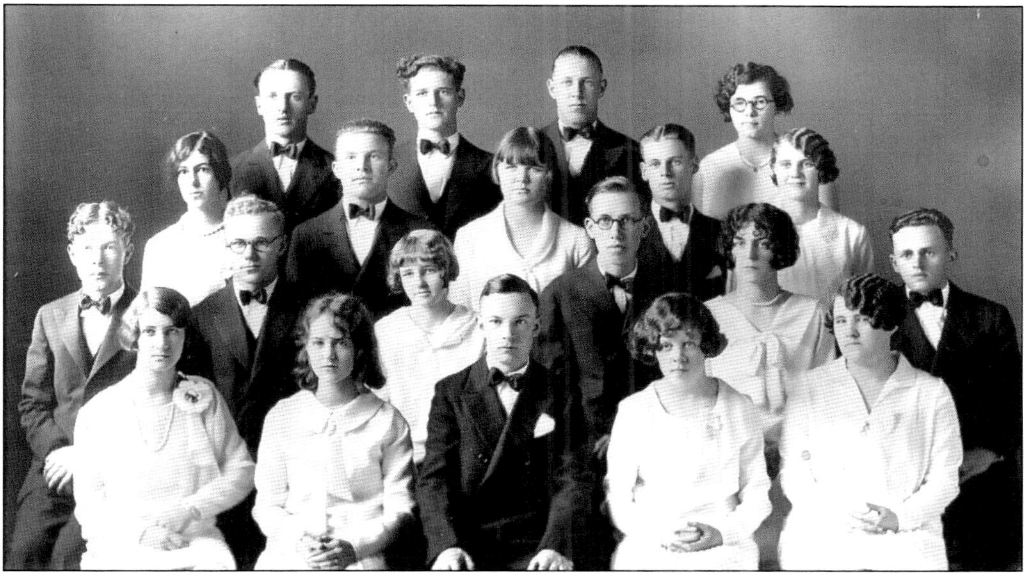

Here, the Greenville High School class of 1929 posed for a formal photograph. Shown from left to right are the following: (first row) Freda Potter Keirstead, Sarah Dean Fahey, Roy Davis, Arvilla Leet Sinford, and Annie MacDonald Carter; (second row) Russell Jardine, Perry Wortman, Charlotte Jardine Keirstead, Carl Moore, Ruth Duty Hamlin Anderson, and Phillip Keirstead; (third row) Katherine Masterman Young, Ellery Robinson, Louise Smith Jardine, Phillip Wilt, and Virginia Buck Chase; (fourth row) Benjamin Tyler, Woodrouffe Bartley, Rodney Brett, and Ethel Drew Meyers.

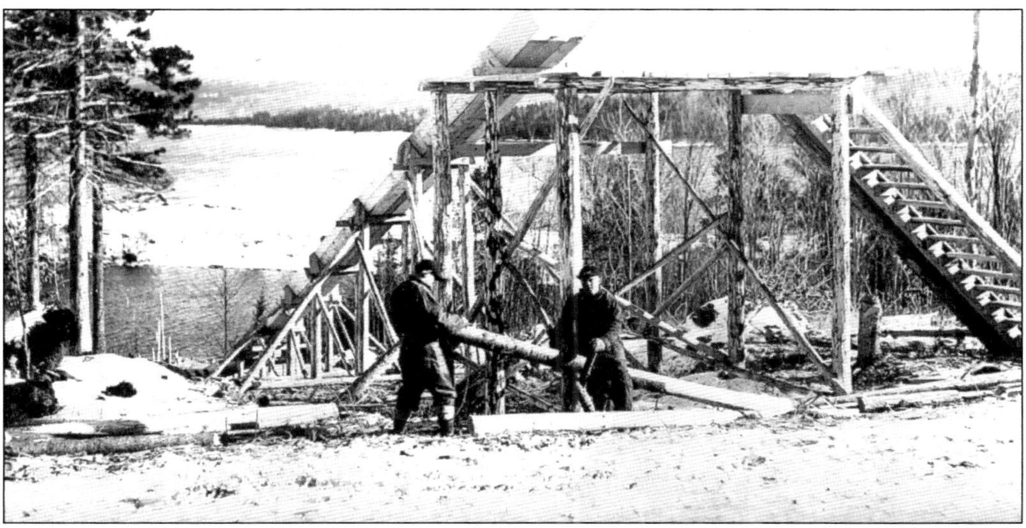

The Shadow Pond Recreation Area was a popular spot with locals and visitors alike in 1934, when this photograph was taken. Here, two men are at work on the toboggan chute. The site included both the toboggan chute and a ski jump. The site was cleared and the ski run constructed in the 1930s as a project of the Greenville contingent of the Civilian Conservation Corps.

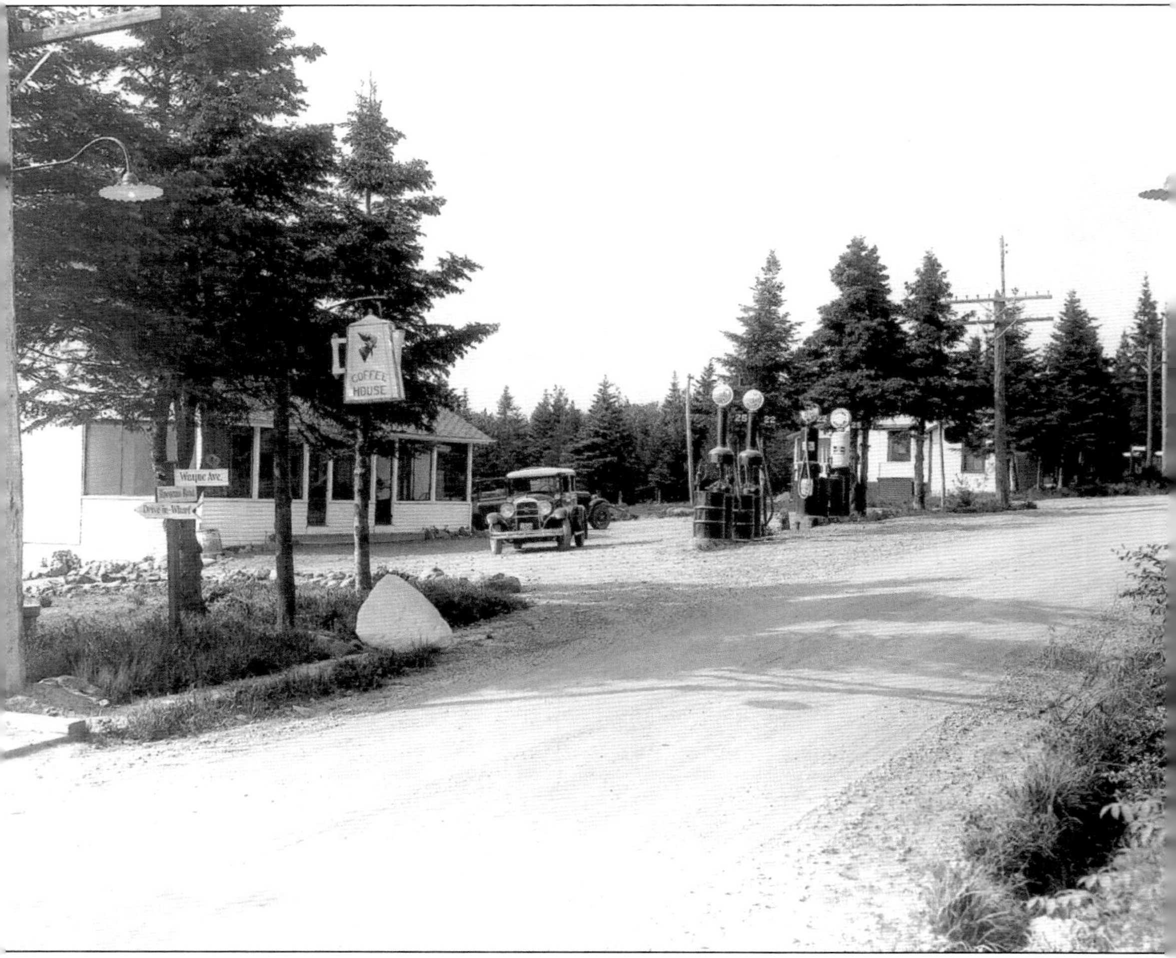

The Moosehead Coffee House was opened in 1928 by Lawrence and Edith Barney. It was a restaurant and gasoline service station on the Ripogenus Road (also known as the Kokadjo, or Rip Dam Road) on Blair Hill. Overnight cottages were soon added. When this photograph was taken in the summer of 1929, Gulf No-Nox gasoline was being sold for 22¢ a gallon for regular and 25¢ a gallon for high-test. The cook at this time was Marguerite Kinney, with Elaine Bartley and Ruth Duty serving as waitresses. The restaurant could seat 60 people, and there was a large screened porch on the front of the building and a sun deck on the rear. The business operated for many years, but the site is now a vacant lot.

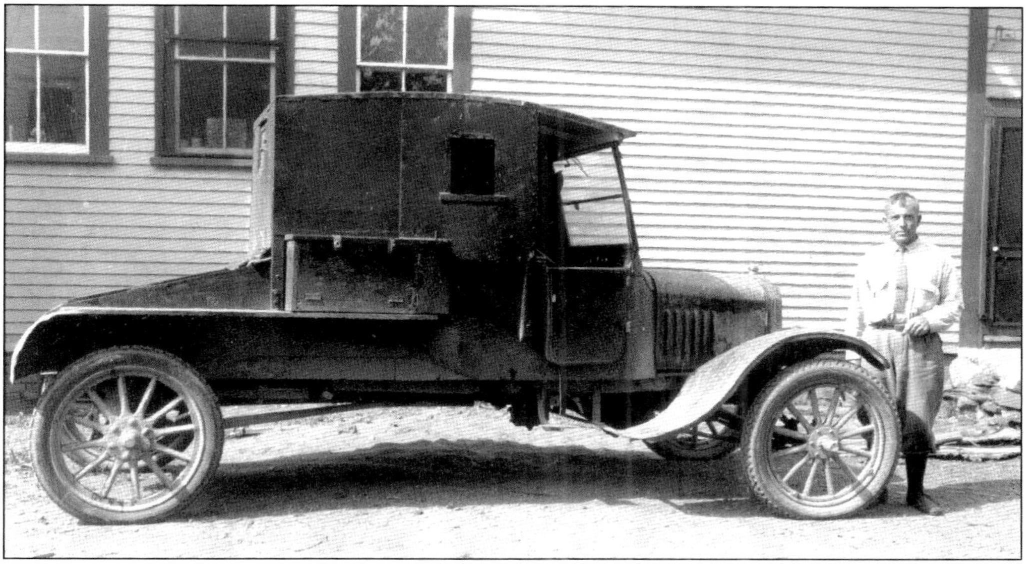

Dr. Fred Pritham was known as the wilderness doctor of the Moosehead region who could always be counted on in the days when physicians made house calls. His many tales of walking miles through snowdrifts to reach an injured woods worker or traveling by handcar on the Canadian Pacific Railroad in negative 40 degree weather to attend a sick individual made him a legend. His story was carefully preserved in Dorothy Clarke Wilson's book, *The Big-Little World of Doc Pritham*. Winter travel was always a problem for the doctor, so *c.* 1926 he converted his automobile, shown here, into a snowmobile so he could go where automobiles could not. He also had a tractor converted into a snowmobile.

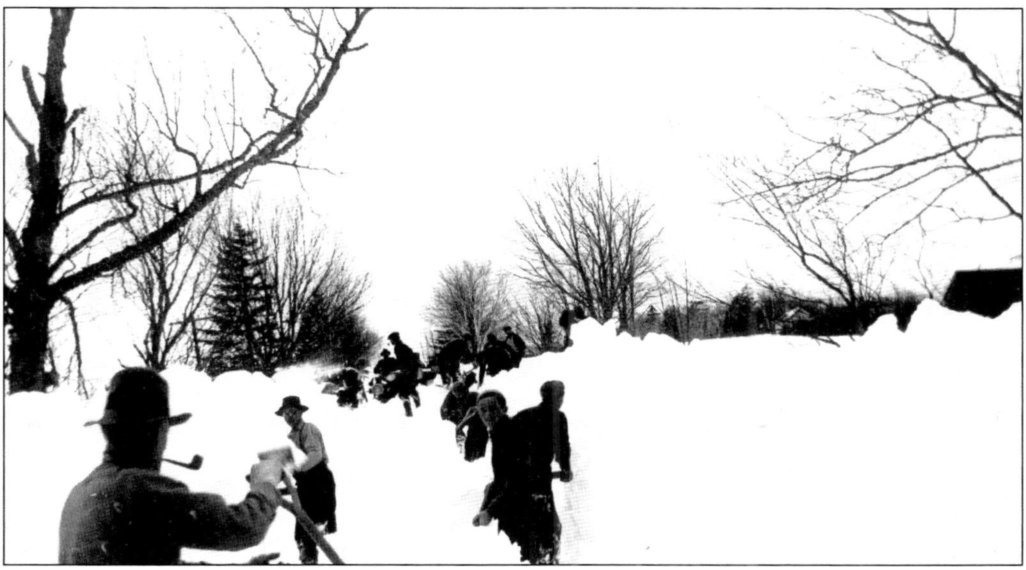

Snow was a real problem in the earlier days of the 1900s, when eight-foot drifts could block town streets. This photograph was taken in the winter of 1934 on Outer Pleasant Street near the Lonnie Rowe residence and shows men hard at work shoveling through drifts that blocked the roadway for days. In those days, snowplows did not have the power to break through drifts, and thus, a great deal of muscle power was needed.

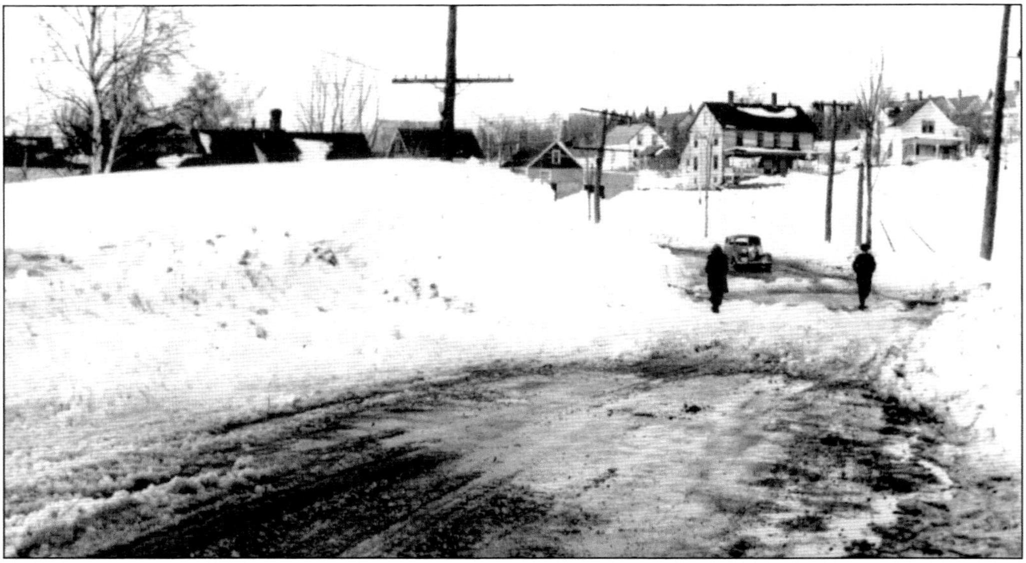

This photograph was taken in the 1930s looking north on Main Street near the site of the Shaw Public Library and what is now Fleet Bank. The snow had drifted in, blown by fierce winds across East Cove of Moosehead Lake, which is located to the left of the photograph, but not seen. Road travel was much more difficult in this earlier period.

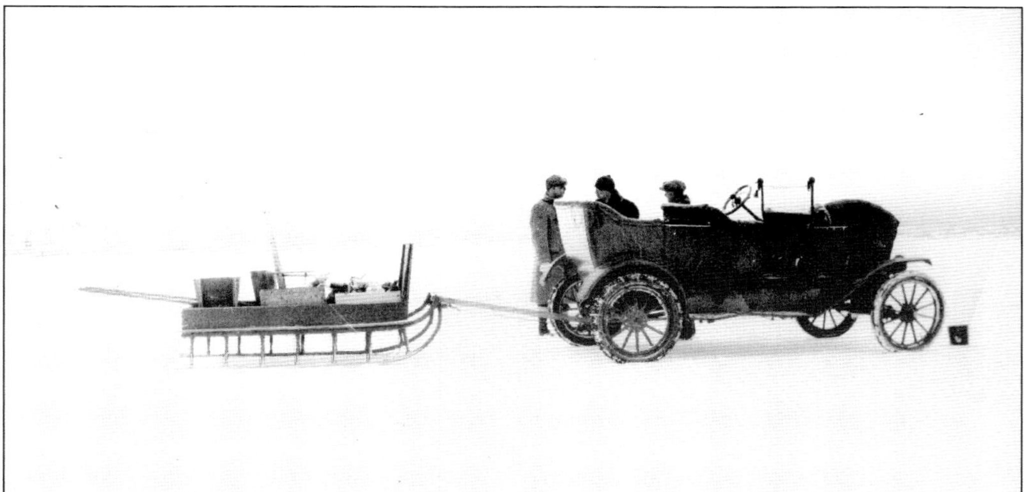

This automobile was pulling a sled across the ice of East Cove of Moosehead Lake when it apparently broke down (notice the man working under the hood at the right). It appears the men in this *c.* 1930s photograph were on an ice fishing expedition.

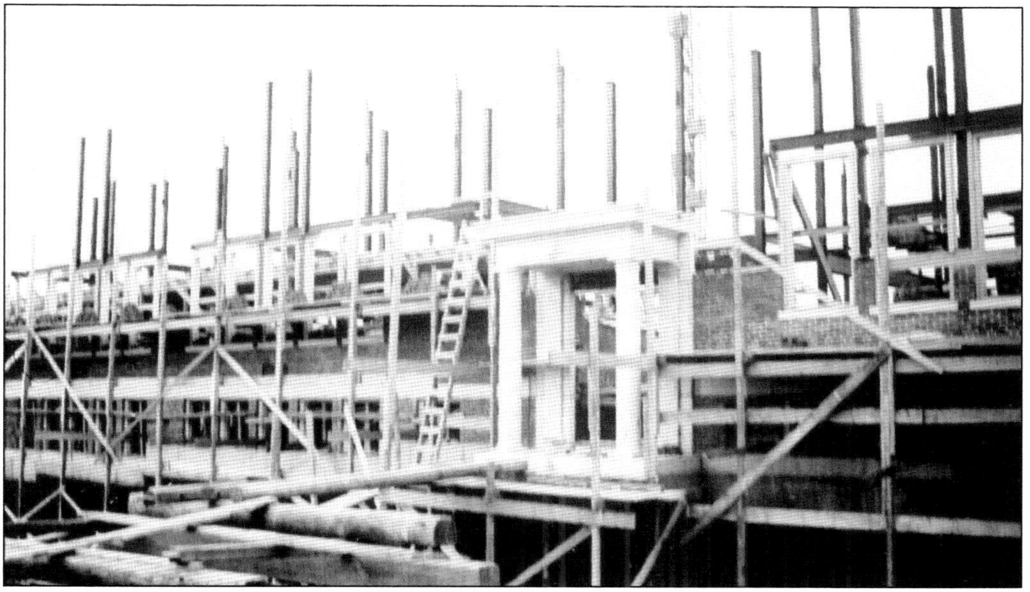

The new and enlarged Greenville Consolidated School was completed and dedicated in 1935. It was constructed on West Street (now Pritham Avenue), near where the old school had been located. This photograph shows part of the construction of the building, likely the rear entrance.

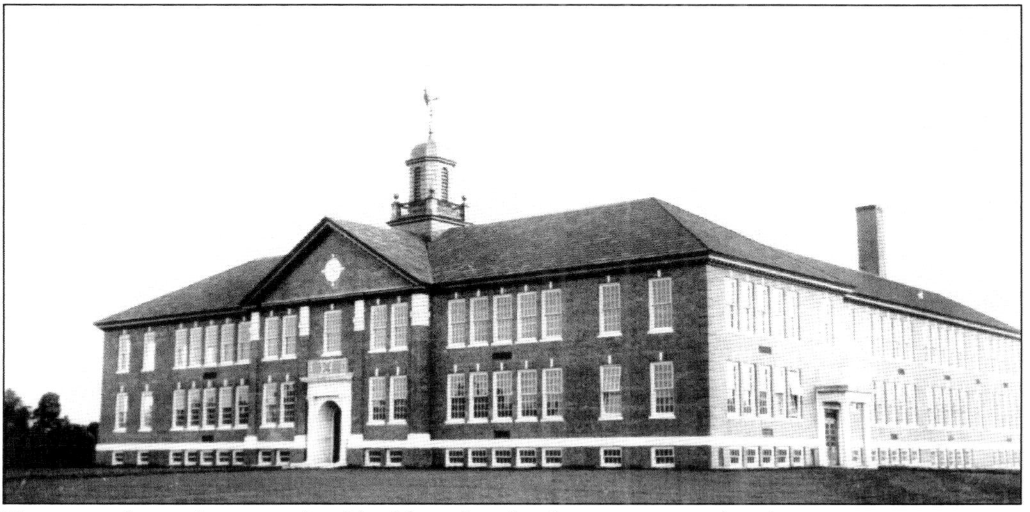

This view shows the new school building shortly after it was completed.

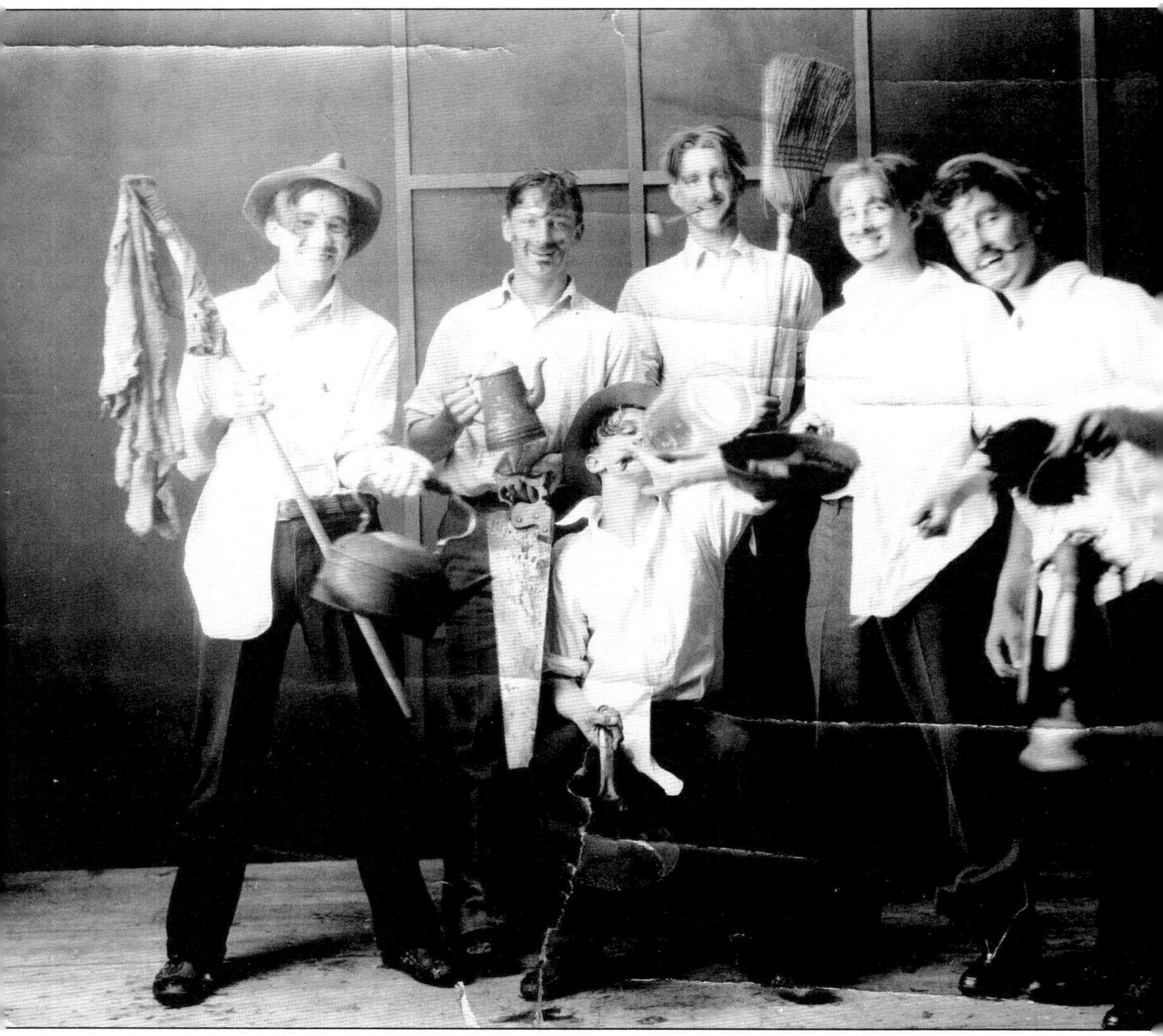

This group of young men was hamming it up when Dave Curtis took this photograph at his studio on the East Road. Bill Johnson is on the stool in front. The other individuals are, from left to right, Bob Smith, Herb Hanson, Hubert Templeton, Earl McEachern, and Llewellyn "Gus" Wortman. The group may have been in costume for a talent show or Halloween party.

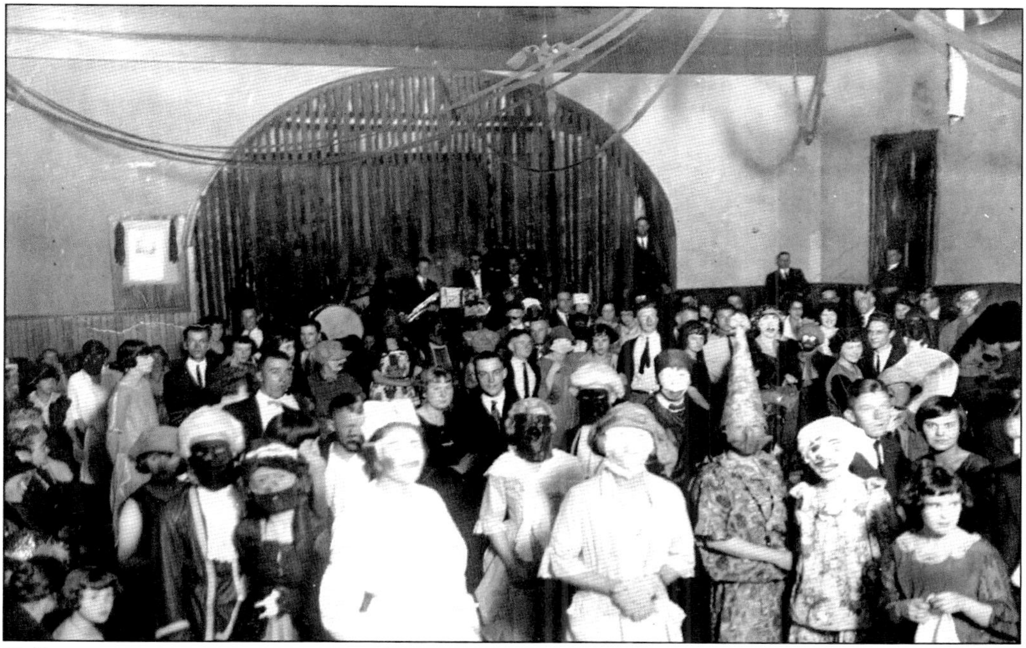

Halloween parties were a very popular event during the first half of the last century. This group gathered at the Shaw Block's upstairs meeting hall for a party in the 1920s.

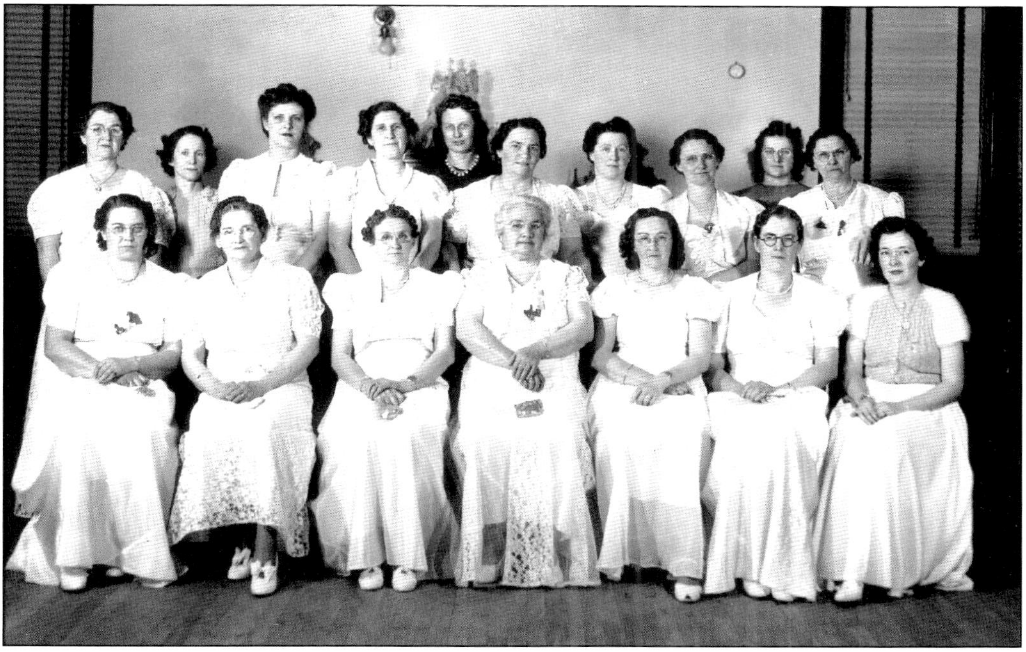

The 1941 degree staff of Lakeside Rebekah Lodge is shown here in a formal photograph. Shown from left to right are the following: (first row) Lena McEachern, Ruby Goven, Ola Mason, Christine Murray, Lottie Graham, Marguerite Gray, and Ruby Brett; (second row) Mollie Canders, Edith Roberts, Ida Best, Emma Cole, Dorothy Smith, Ozella Carter, Velma Finley, Margaret Moran, Veronica Champeon, and Evelyn Graham.

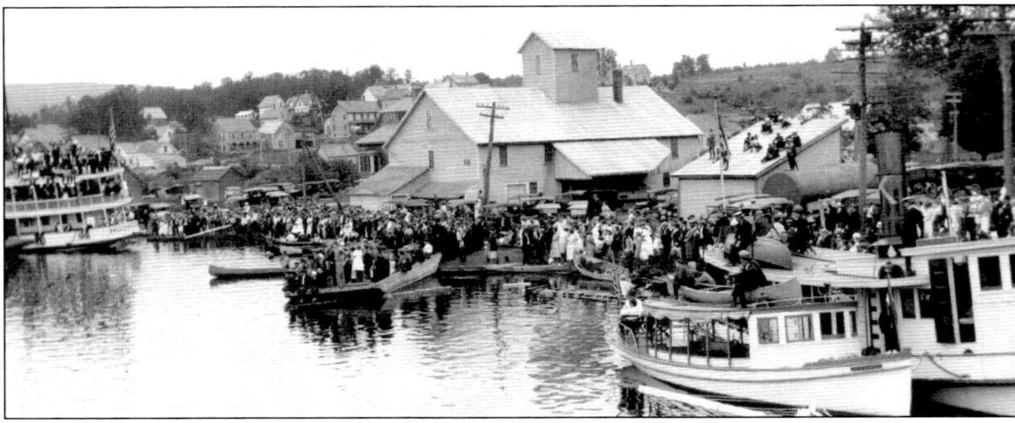

Water sports have always been popular on Moosehead Lake. Swimming races, boating races, rowing competition, bateau races, and steamer races were among the most popular activities. This event on East Cove of Moosehead Lake during the 1930s drew a huge crowd, so many in fact that some even sat on the roof of a building next to the old grist mill (tall building in center). The stern of the steamer *Moosehead* at the far left is also full of people.

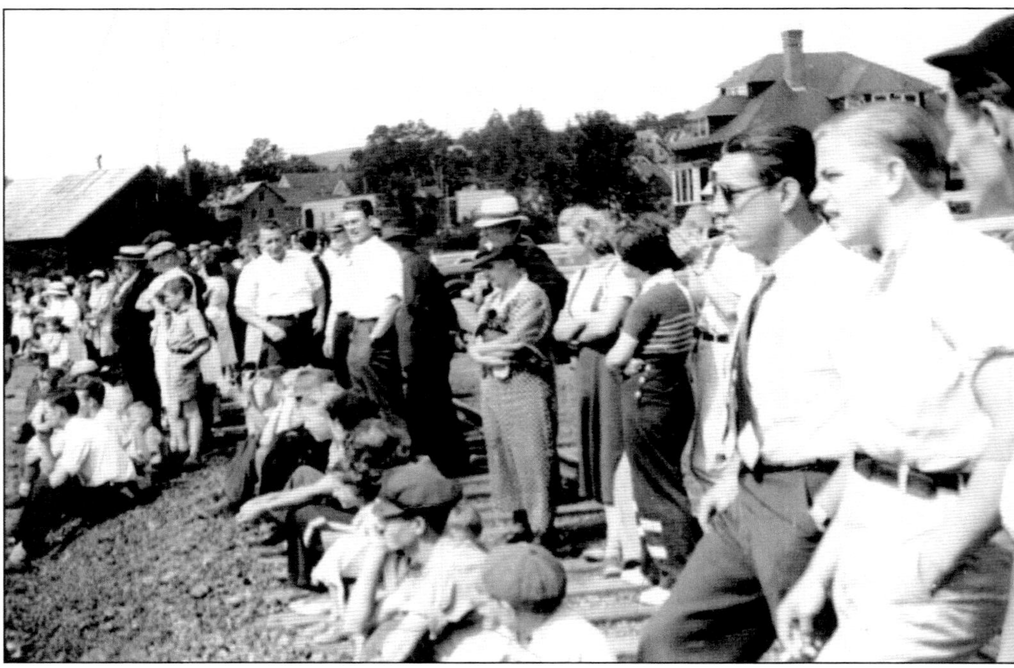

This photograph shows the same area of East Cove but a different event. It was taken on July 4, 1937, and shows people lined up along the shoreline in the same spot as the previous photograph. A portion of the former Lake House (then the Green Parrot) is visible at the upper right.

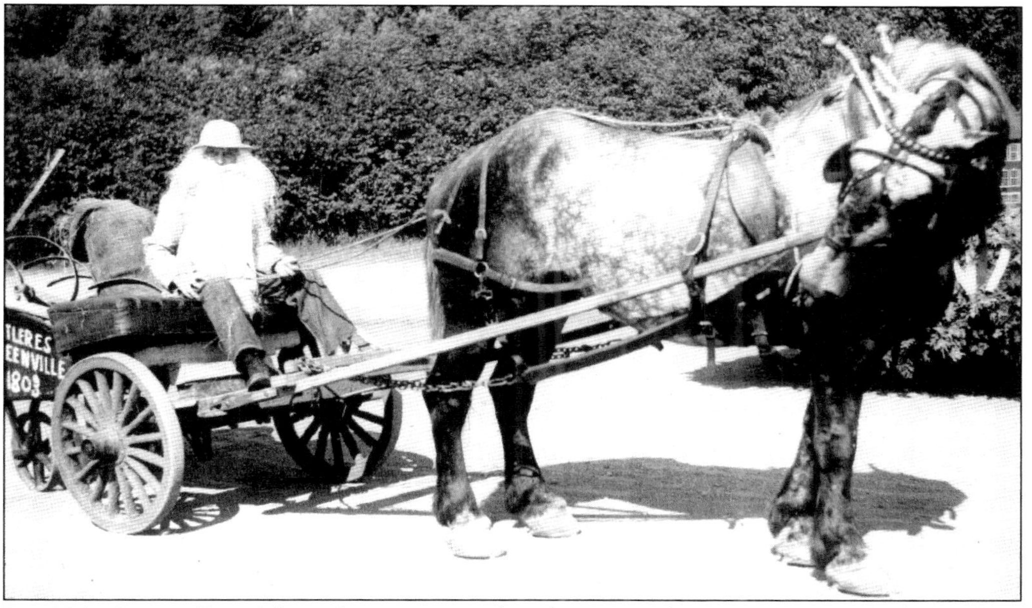

In 1936, Greenville celebrated its centennial with summer-long activities, including one of the longest parades to date. This man depicted an early settler with his long (obviously fake) beard and horse-drawn wagon. The sign on his wagon states "Settleres Greenville 1803." Unfortunately, his date was off; the settlement began in the 1820s, leading to incorporation as a town in 1836.

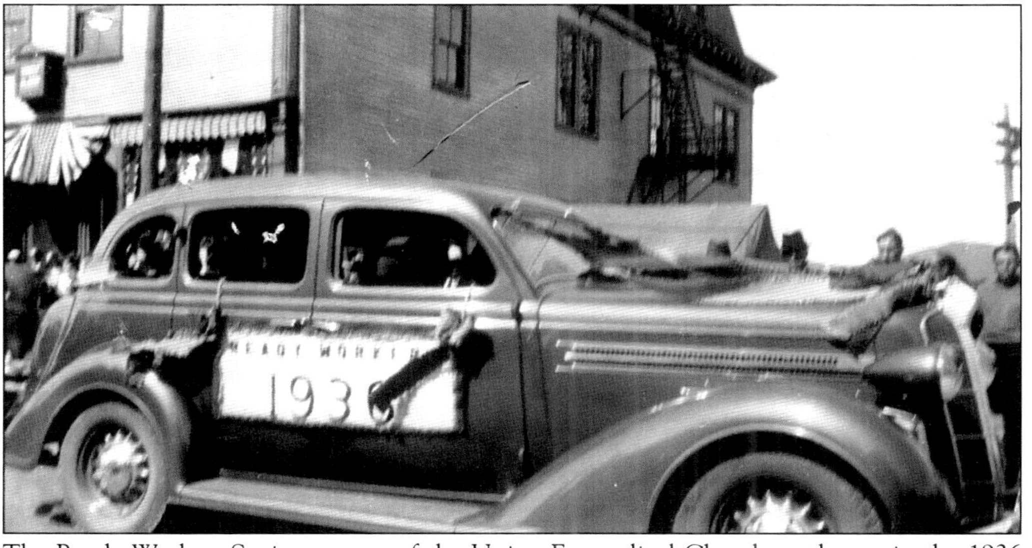

The Ready Workers Society, a part of the Union Evangelical Church, took part in the 1936 centennial parade. The Shaw Block is in the background in this view along Main Street.

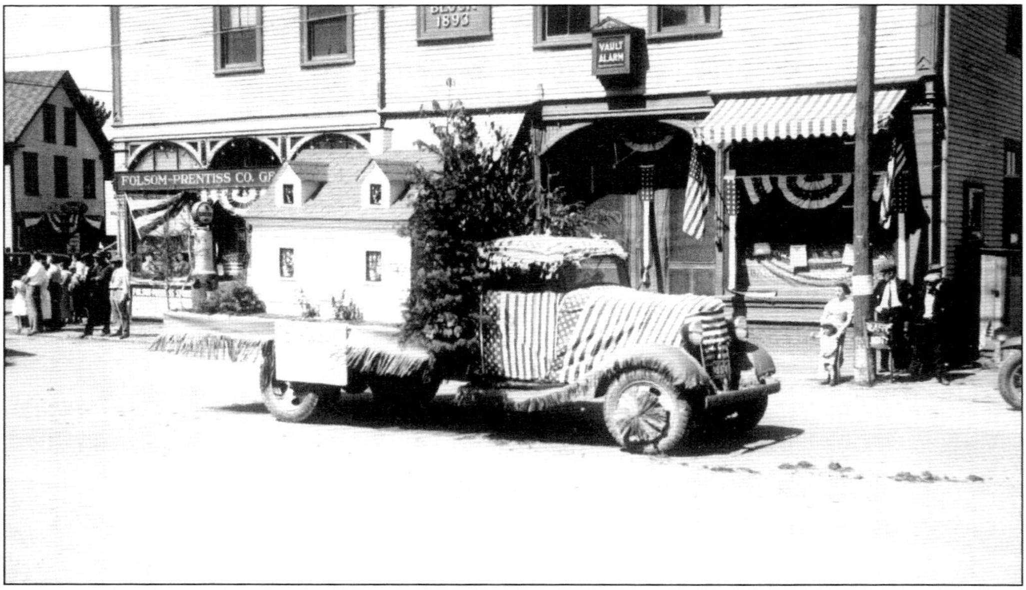

Parades are always special to Moosehead region people, and the Fourth of July is always a good time to have one. This 1930s photograph shows a float sponsored by D. M. Ward Contractors and Builders, according to the sign on the side of the truck bed. The float featured a miniature house. The photograph was taken in front of the Shaw Block on Main Street.

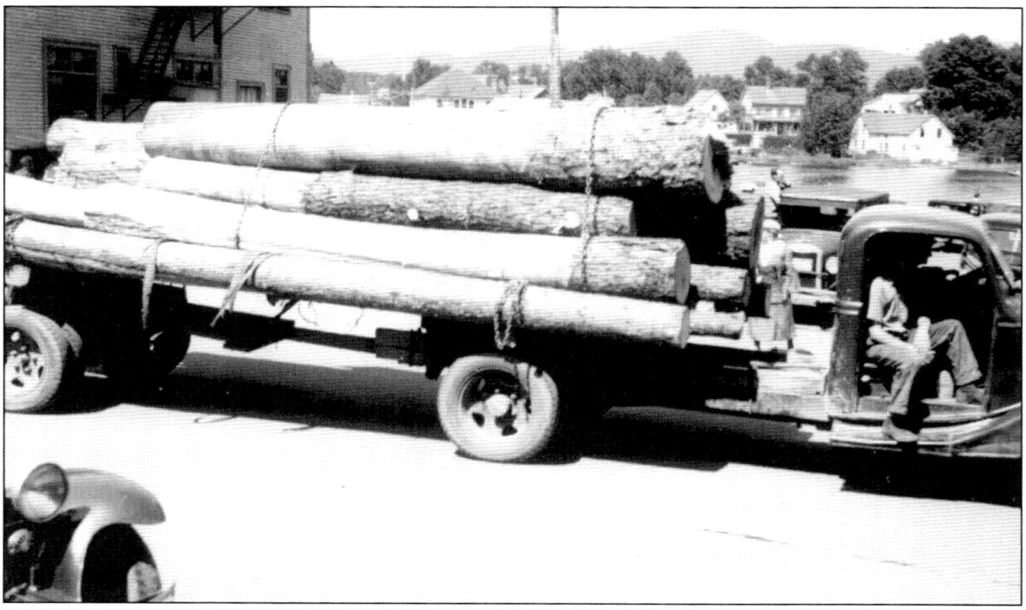

The lumbering industry is always a part of Greenville parades. The exact date in the 1930s is not known, but this photograph may be of the 1936 centennial parade. Shown is a truck pulling a load of long logs. Compare this load with the much larger ones pulled by trucks today.

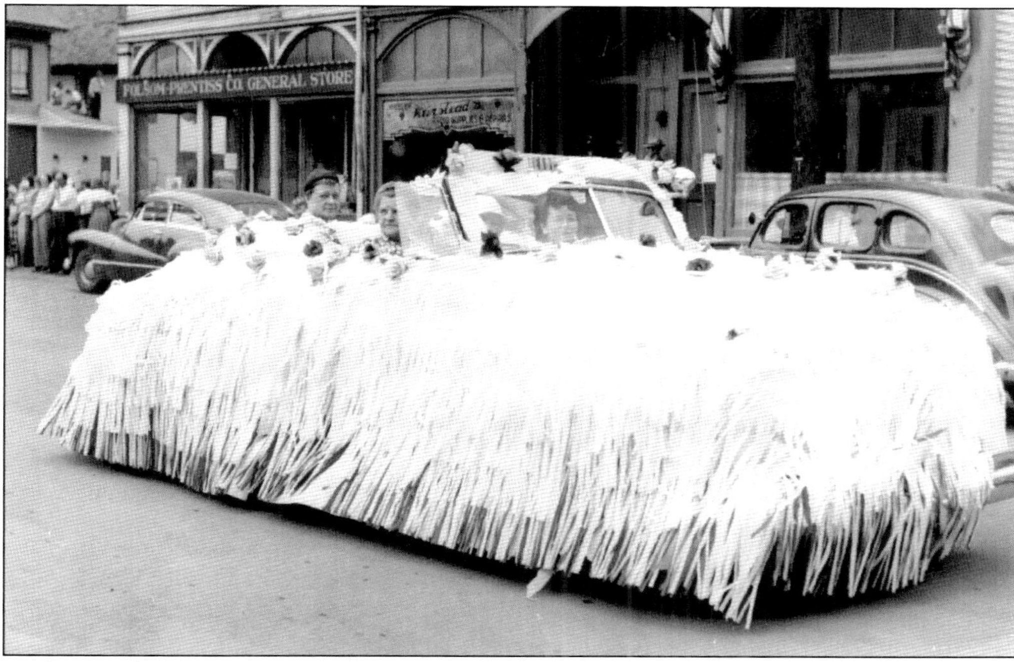

Nothing indicates when this photograph was taken, but it is likely a Fourth of July parade in the 1930s or 1940s. It is likely that the car was decorated as a float, perhaps for the Moosehead Information Center, a precursor to today's Moosehead Lake Region Chamber of Commerce. Ruby Brett, who ran the information center for years, is the driver. Others shown are Louisa Sawyer, Faith Harvey, Deltha Hanson, and Clara Buck.

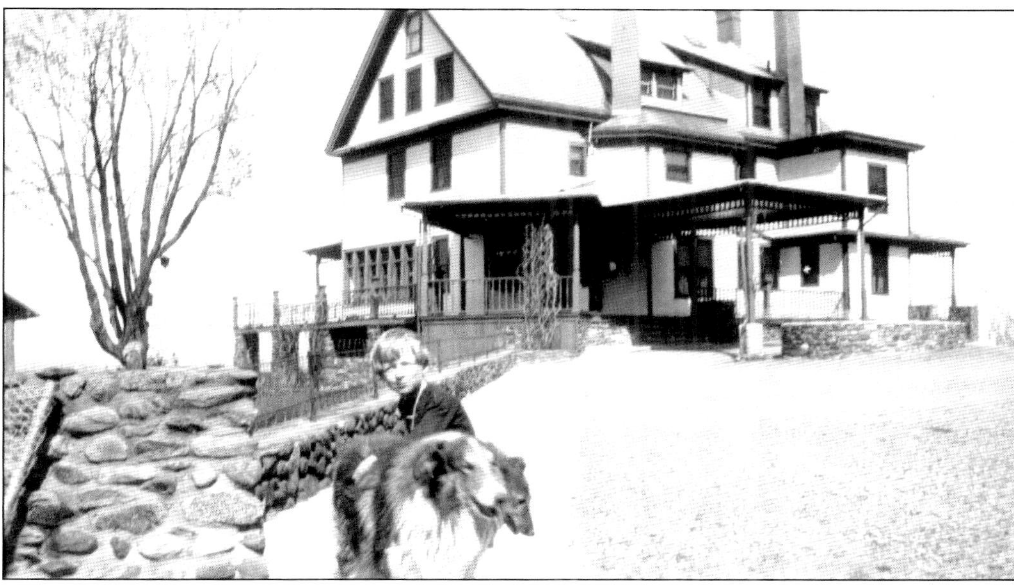

Frederick H. Bigney is shown in front of the Lyman Blair home on Blair Hill c. 1936. Bigney graduated from the University of Maine (class of 1951) and was active in the forest industry for 31 years. He later was a construction inspector and real estate broker in Maine and New Hampshire.

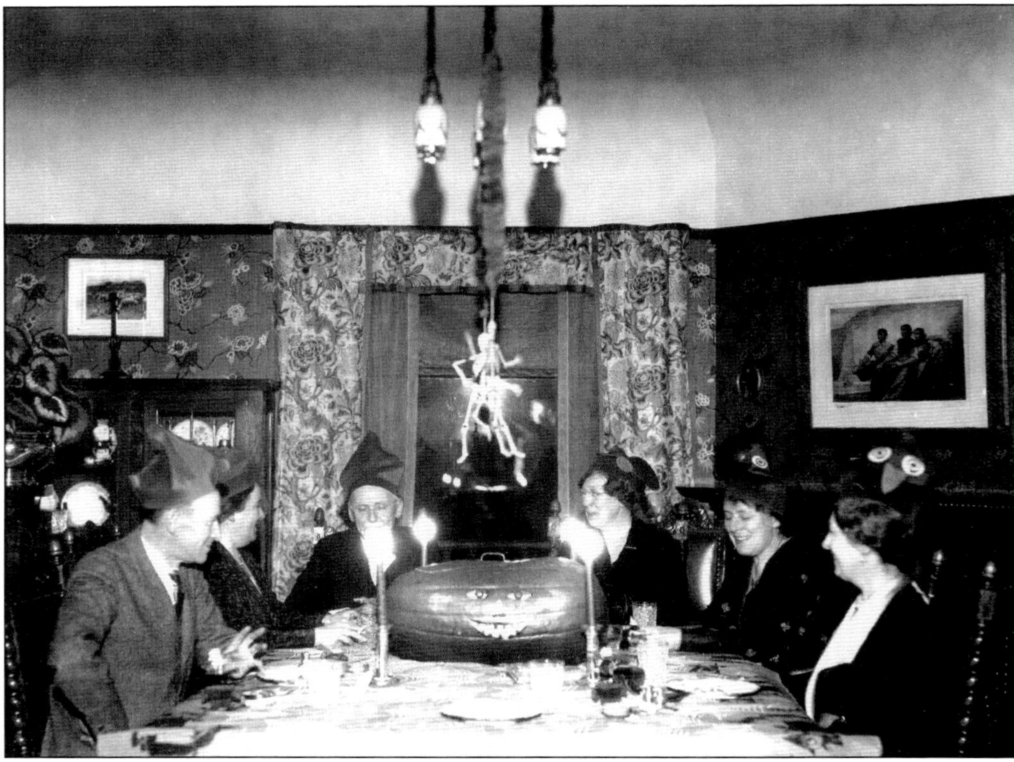

Lyman Blair and his wife often hosted dinner parties at their Blair Hill home. This photograph shows Cornelia Blair (second from the left), Lyman Blair (third from the left), and Mildred Bigney (fourth from the left) with others at a Halloween party in the 1930s. Notice the large squash in the center of the table decorated as a jack-o'-lantern.

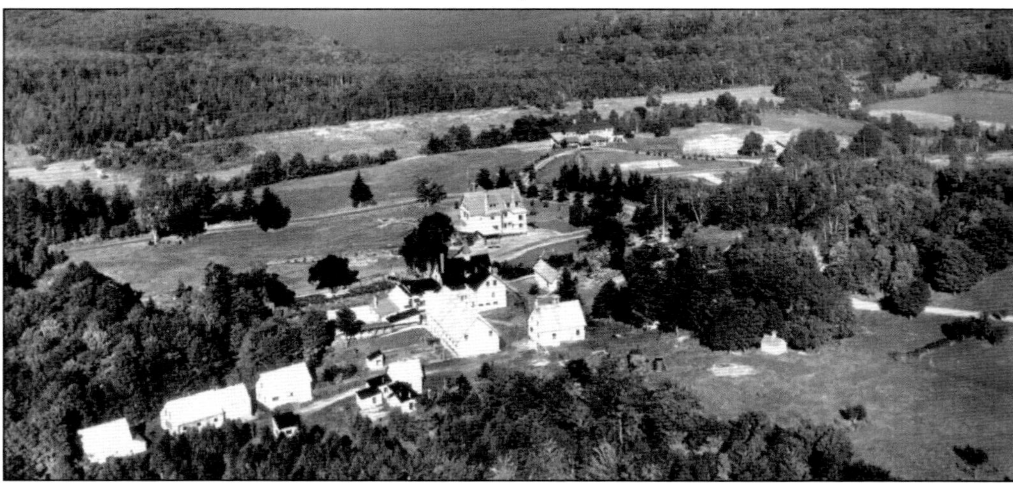

This 1930s aerial photograph shows the Blair estate on Blair Hill. The impressive set of buildings was also known as Hillside Gardens and Hillside Farms at various times and is now the site of the Blair Hill Inn and Restaurant. Several of the buildings shown in this photograph are no longer standing. The photograph was taken by the Curtiss Wright Flying Service, Aerial Survey Division.

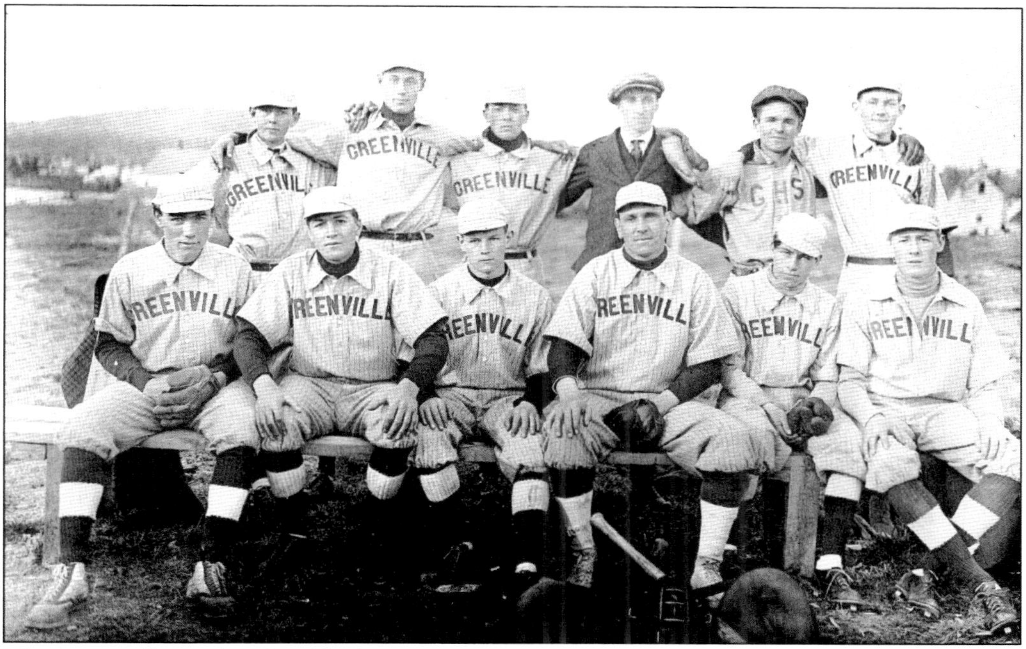

The Greenville High School had an active baseball team during the 1930s. Unfortunately, no one is identified in this photograph.

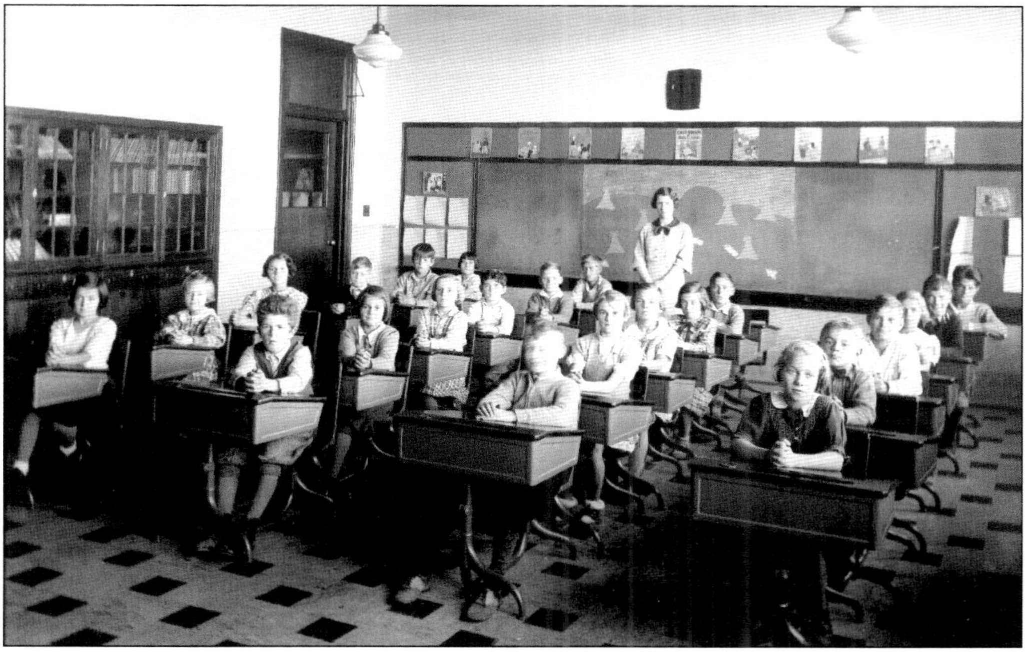

The exact date is unknown, but this photograph shows Louise Parent and her class of pupils at the Greenville Elementary School. Only a few are identified: Eunice Graham, Joyce McEachern, Lionel Breau, Gladys Deveaux, Vella Ryder, Durward Canders, Don Grant, Bill Gleason, Margaret Murray, Nadia Sullivan, Thelma Roberts, Charles Deveaux, and John Richards.

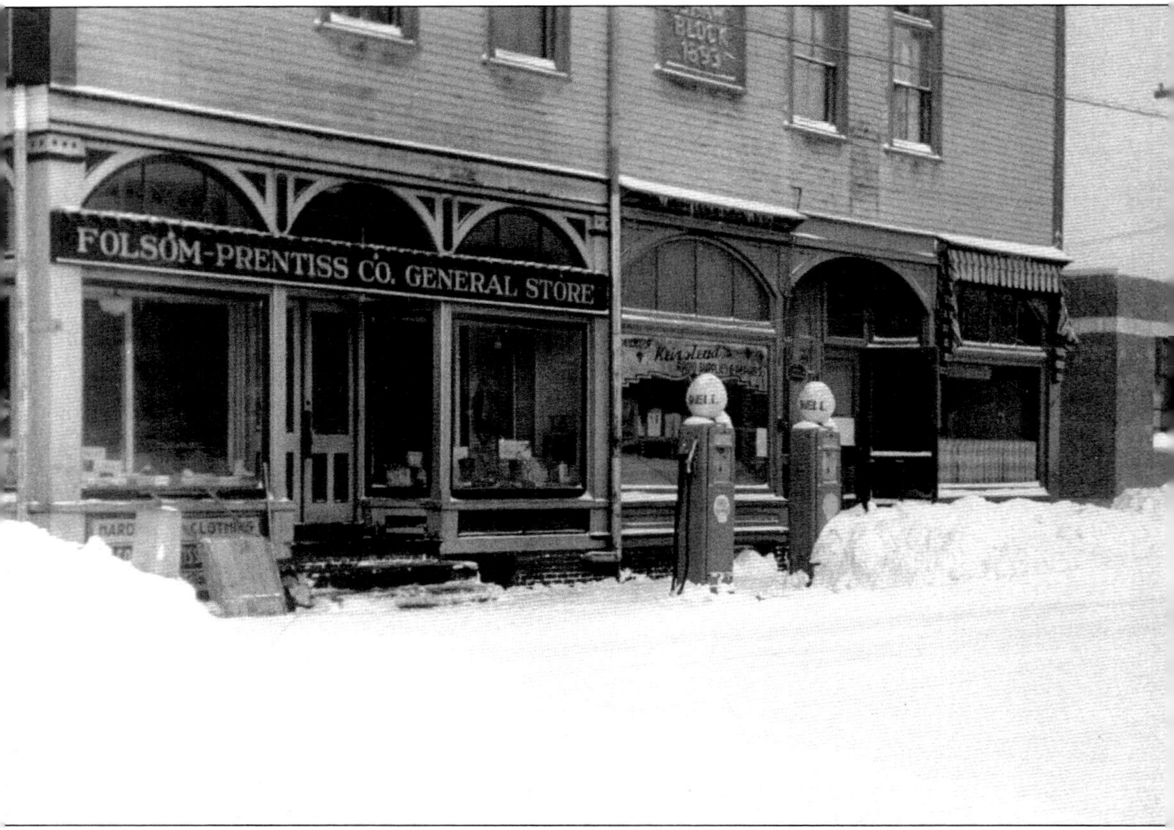

The Shaw Block at the intersection of Main Street and West Street (now Pritham Avenue) was constructed in 1893 and has been a centerpiece of Greenville village. At various times it housed a number of businesses and is the original site of the town library. This 1930s photograph shows two businesses that occupied the ground floor during this era. The Folsom-Prentiss Company General Store is shown at the left and Keirstead's Jewelry Store is at the right. Keirstead's sign also advertised radio supplies and repairs. The separate building at the far right is the Guilford Trust Company. Both buildings remain to this day, although the Folsom-Prentiss Company and Keirstead's are long gone.

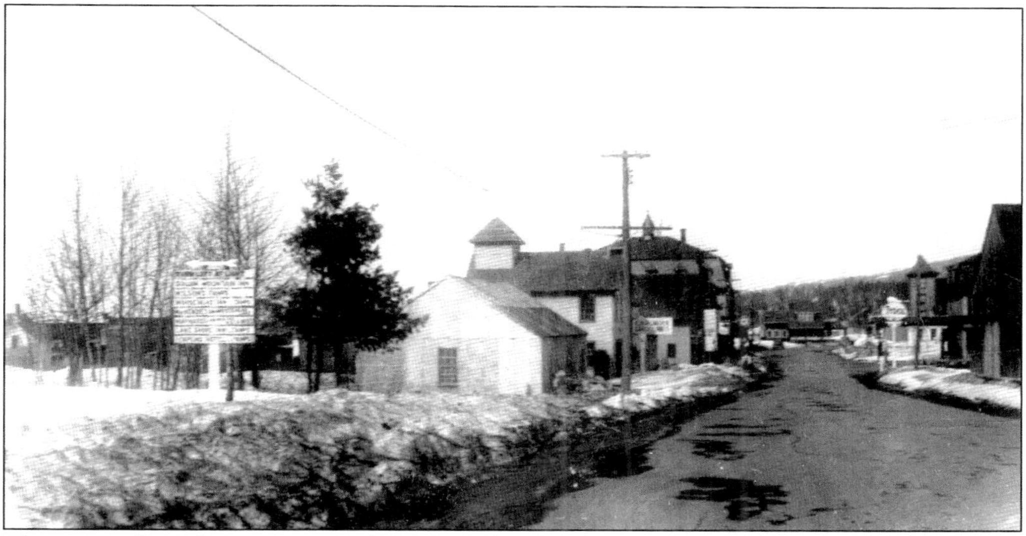

This view of South Main Street dates from the 1930s and shows the Sanders Store (tower in the right center background) and other buildings, several of which are no longer standing. The sign located in left center directs motorists to the Squaw Mountain Inn, Squaw Mountain, and locations in Rockwood.

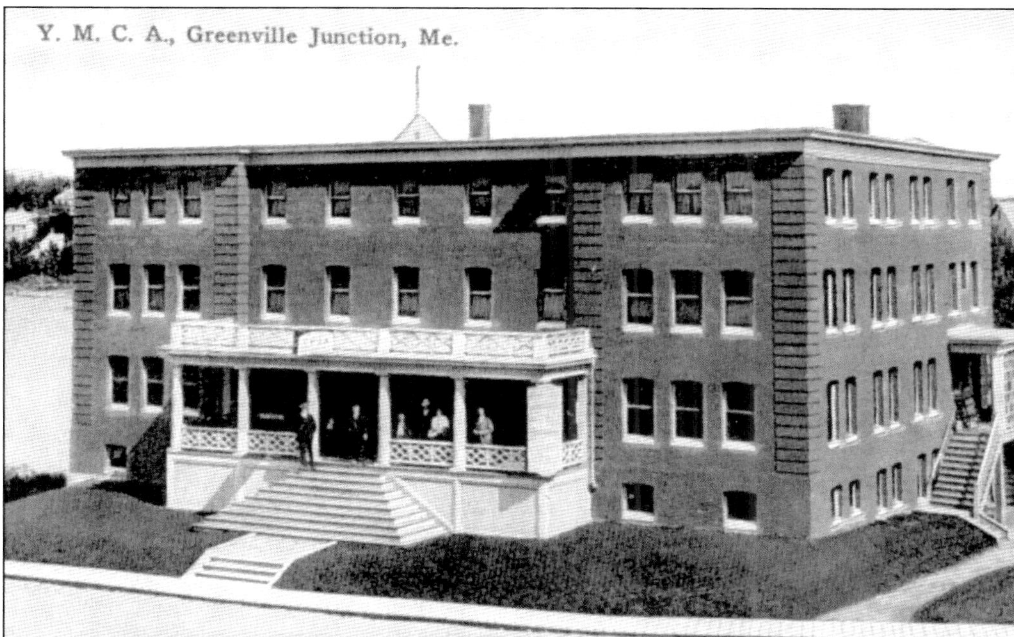

The YMCA building was located on the Junction Wharf in Greenville Junction for many years. The upstairs was the first hospital in Greenville and served the needs of local patients until a real hospital was constructed during the World War I era. This building eventually went into disuse and was burned. Today the site is a parking lot for the Junction Wharf.

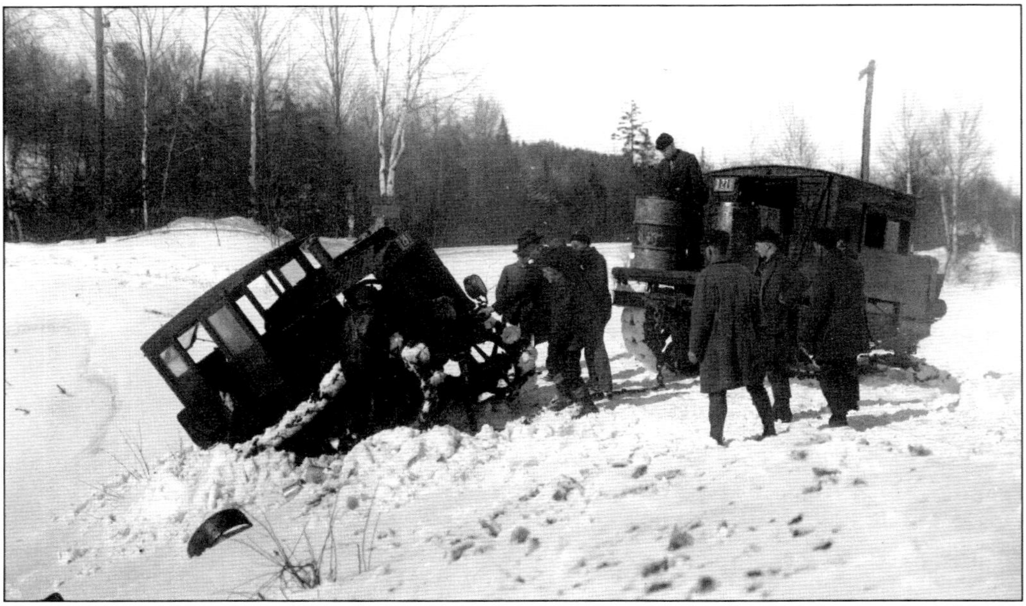

Tractors were used a lot during the early 1900s for snow removal in Greenville, but even tractors were not immune from slipping off the road occasionally. This early 1930s photograph shows men trying to pull one tractor out of a ditch with the aid of another.

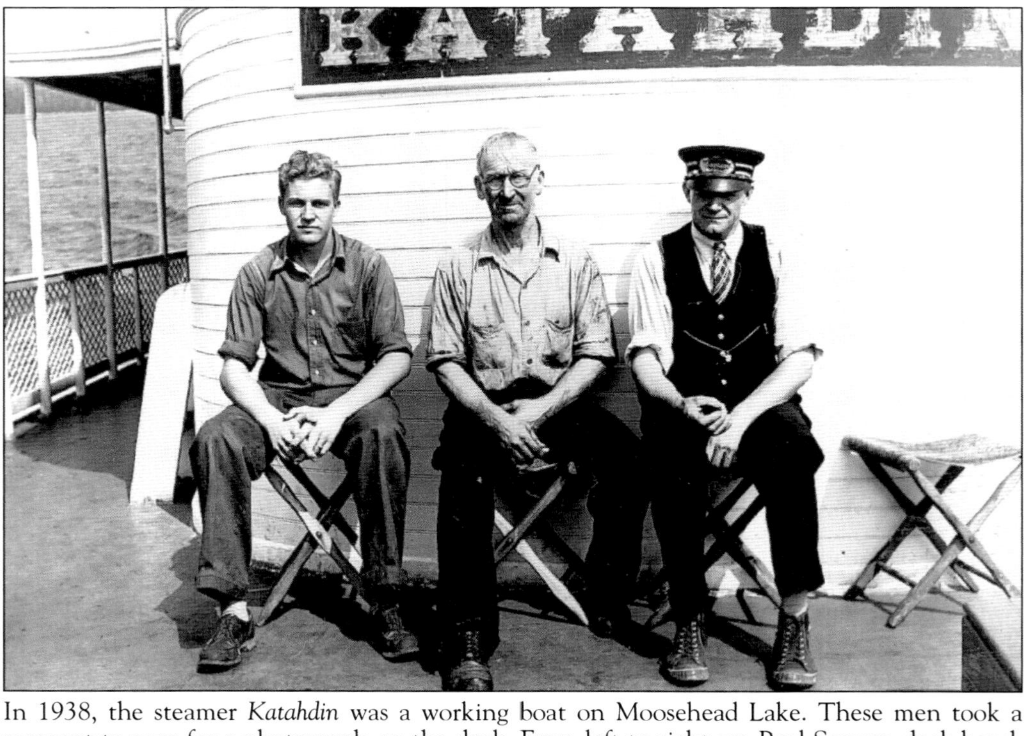

In 1938, the steamer *Katahdin* was a working boat on Moosehead Lake. These men took a moment to pose for a photograph on the deck. From left to right are Paul Sawyer, deck hand; Bert Colby, engineer; and Capt. Cliff Sawyer. The photograph was taken by Charles M. Sawyer of Greenville.

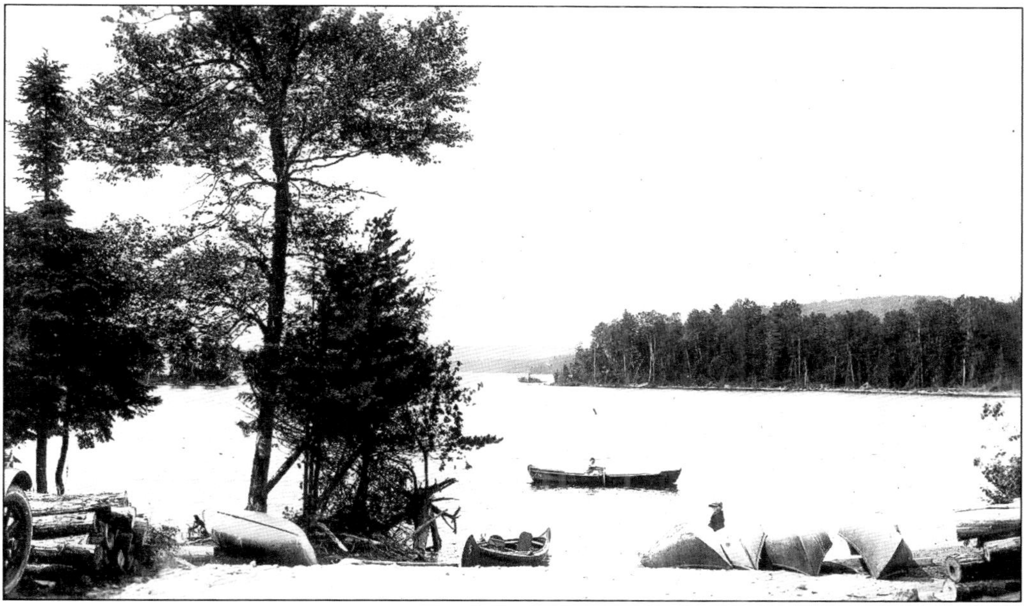

The Beaver Creek Tenting Ground was located north of Greenville on the shore of Moosehead Lake. The site later became the Lily Bay State Park. This scene from the 1930s shows the sandy beach with a number of canoes on the shore.

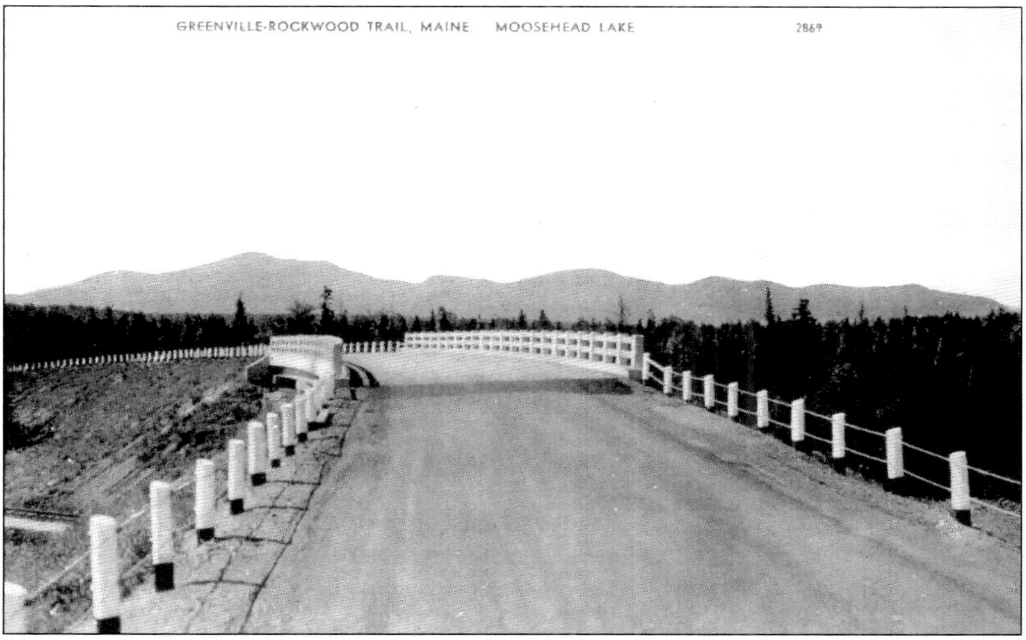

This view shows the new overpass over the Canadian Pacific Railroad between Greenville and Rockwood in the late 1930s. The road was constructed during the 1930s, and this view was photographed just after the new roadway opened. Prior to the roadway, now Route 15, the only way to reach Rockwood from Greenville was by railroad or boat.

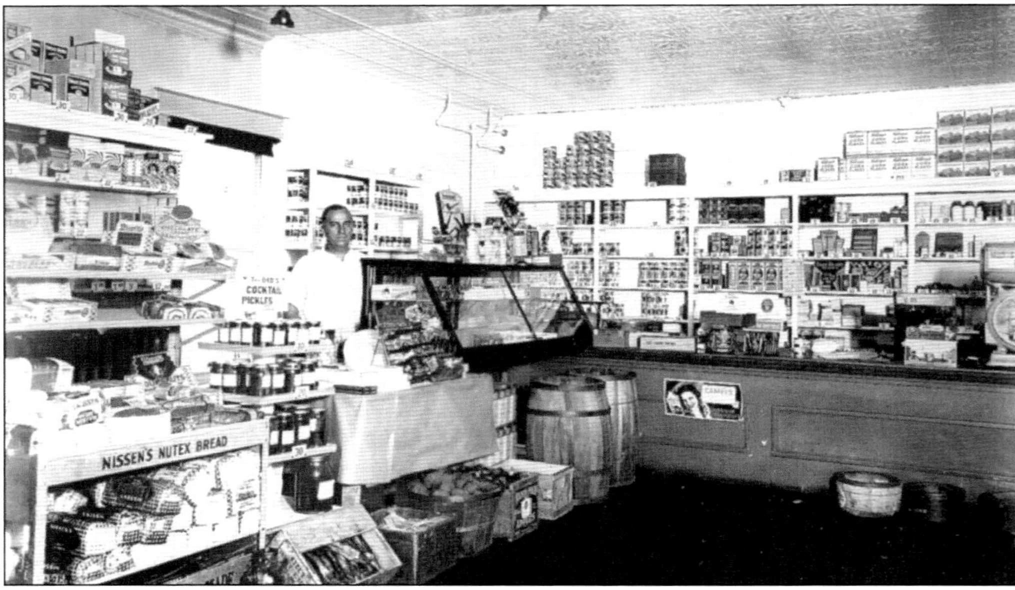

Harold "Nig" Graham worked at the A. A. Crafts Store in Greenville Junction and was later chief deputy of the Piscataquis County Sheriff's Department. He was well known throughout the Moosehead region. He and his wife, Mary McIntosh Graham, also owned and operated the Log Cabin Restaurant in Greenville Junction from 1947 through 1951. Graham was a town selectman for 17 years and Greenville fire chief for two decades.

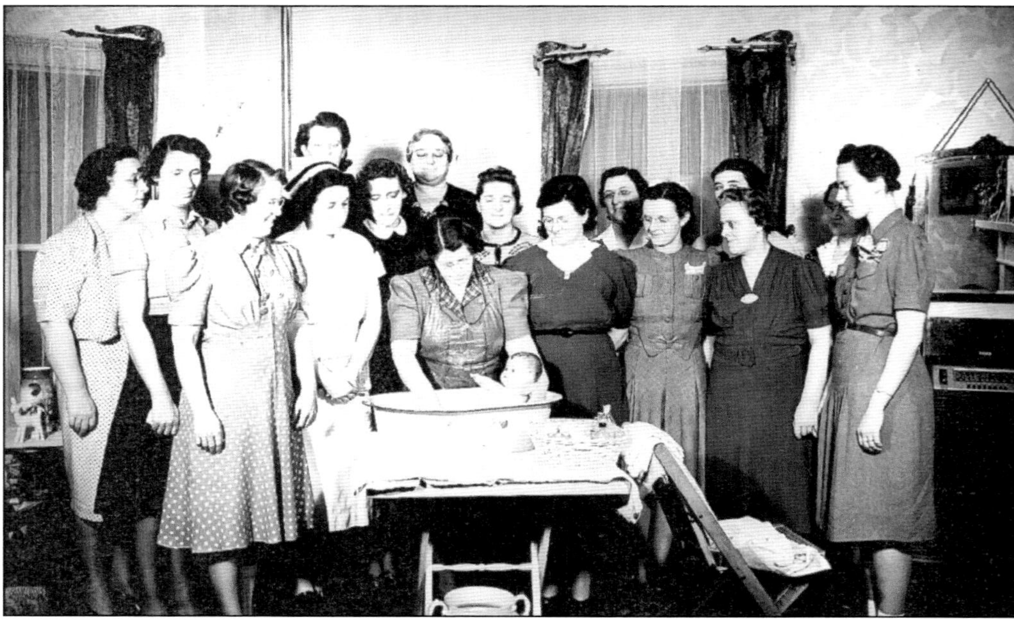

During the era of World War II, the American National Red Cross taught a home nursing training program throughout Maine. The course in Greenville was offered in June 1942, and several local women took part. This photograph shows a group of 16 ladies participating in the program, apparently regarding the care and washing of infants. The instructor, center, is using a doll for the demonstration.

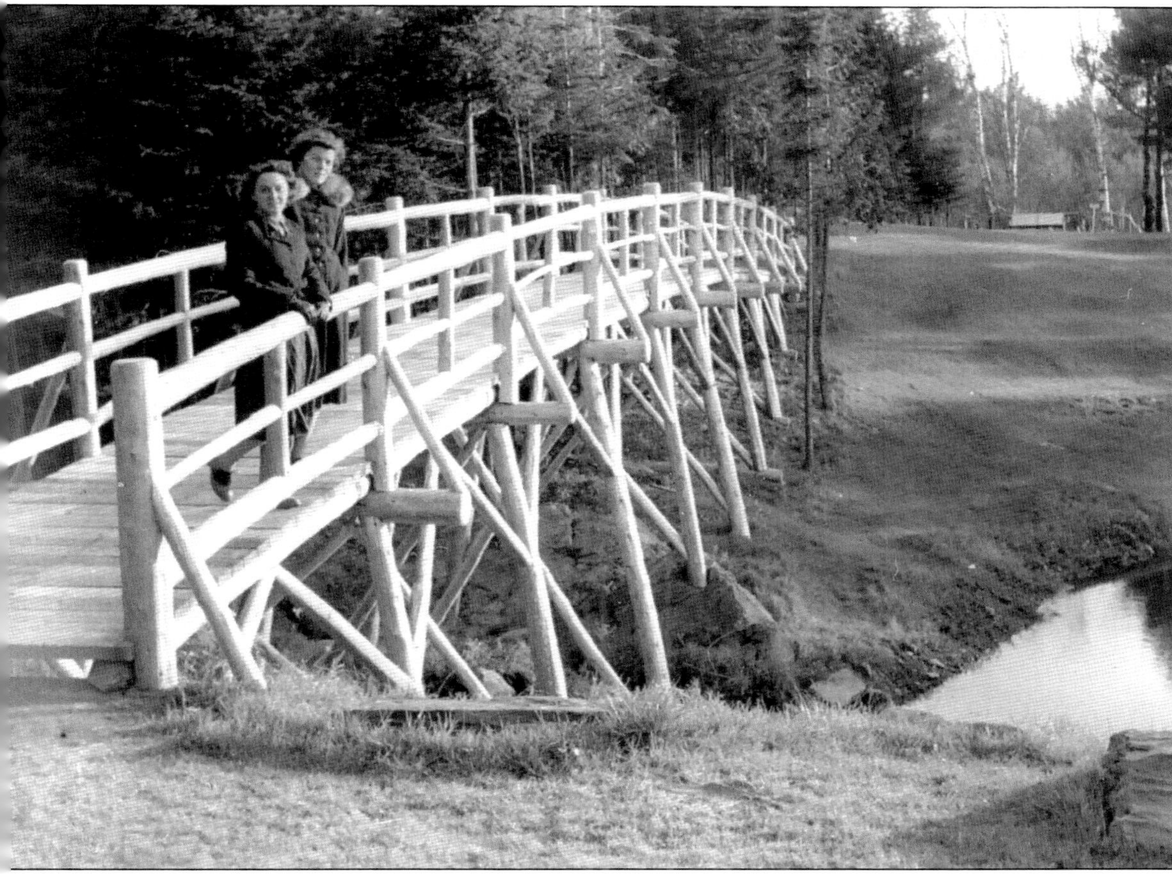

Although the location is not known, this photograph shows Phyllis Tompkins and Roberta Harris, both of Greenville, on a footbridge during the 1940s.

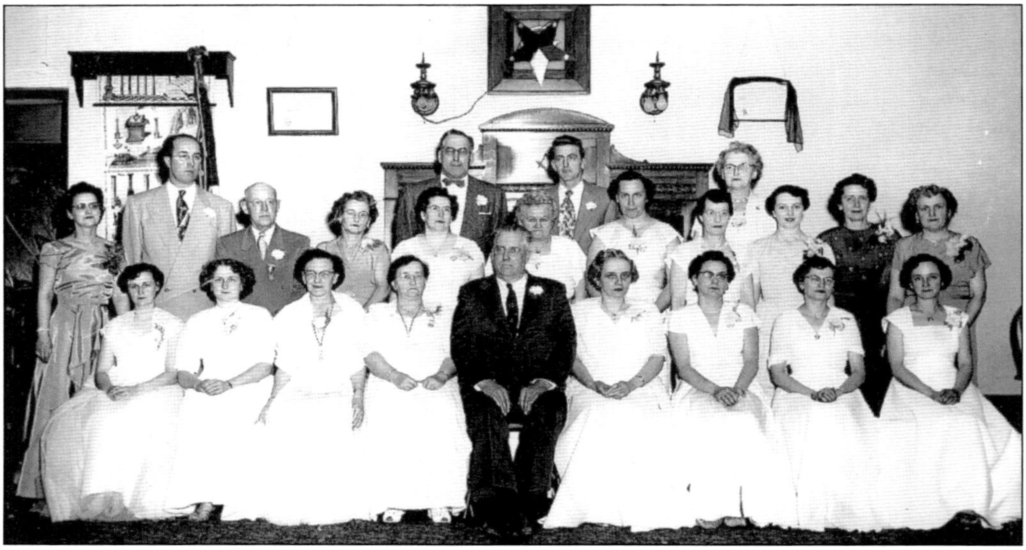

A large group posed for a formal photograph during an activity of the Eastern Star held at the Masonic Temple during the 1940s. No one is identified. The photograph was taken by Wilson Studio in Dover-Foxcroft.

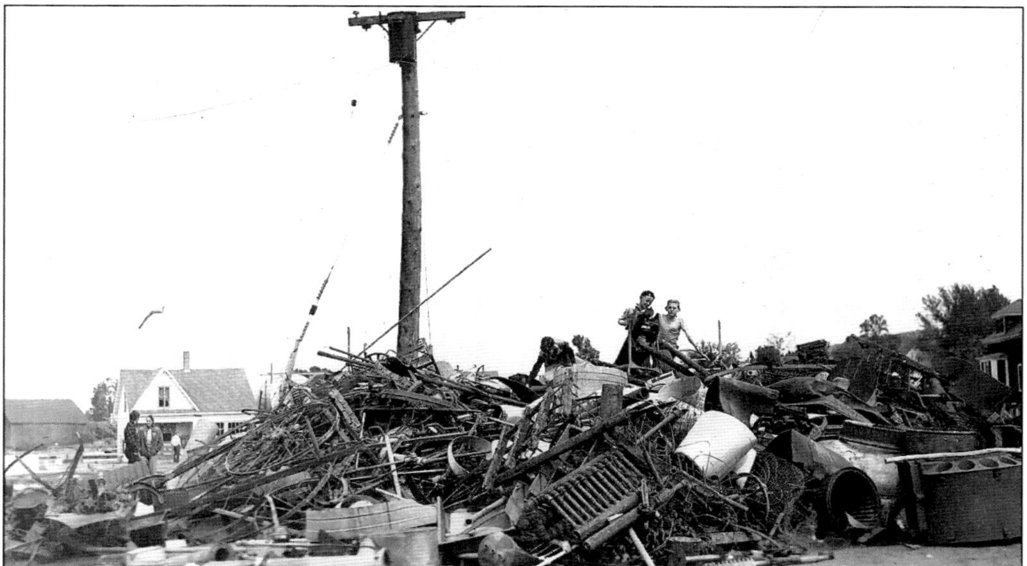

Scrap metal was important to the wartime efforts during World War II, and communities throughout the United States collected as much as possible for processing. This pile of metal was collected in the municipal parking lot across from the Shaw Public Library c. 1942.

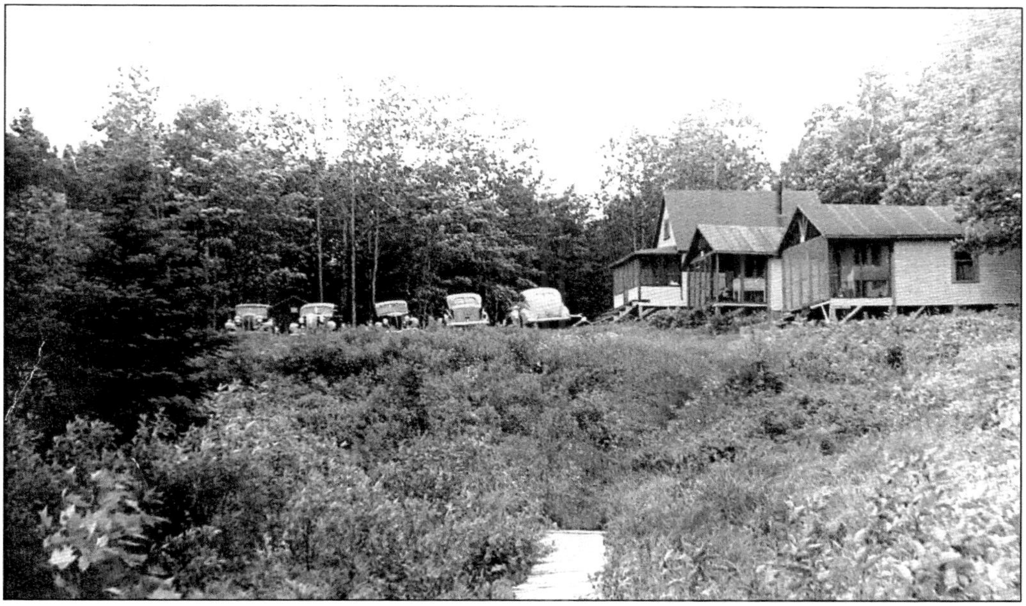

Lawrence Hall's Camps on Blair Hill was a popular destination for summer tourists during the 1940s. The site is now known as the Highlands, but during the World War II era, it offered swimming in Moosehead Lake and a dock in the water.

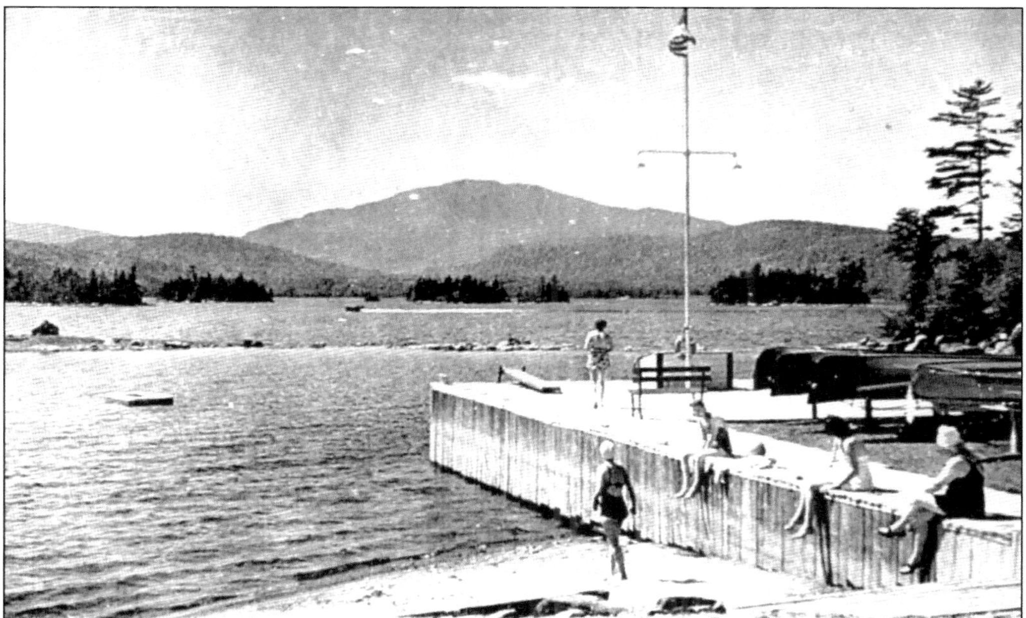

During the post–World War II era, Hall's Landing on Blair Hill was a popular spot for residents and tourists alike. Moosehead Lake's cool waters, even during the hottest part of summer, are inviting for a refreshing dip. Squaw Mountain can be seen in the background.

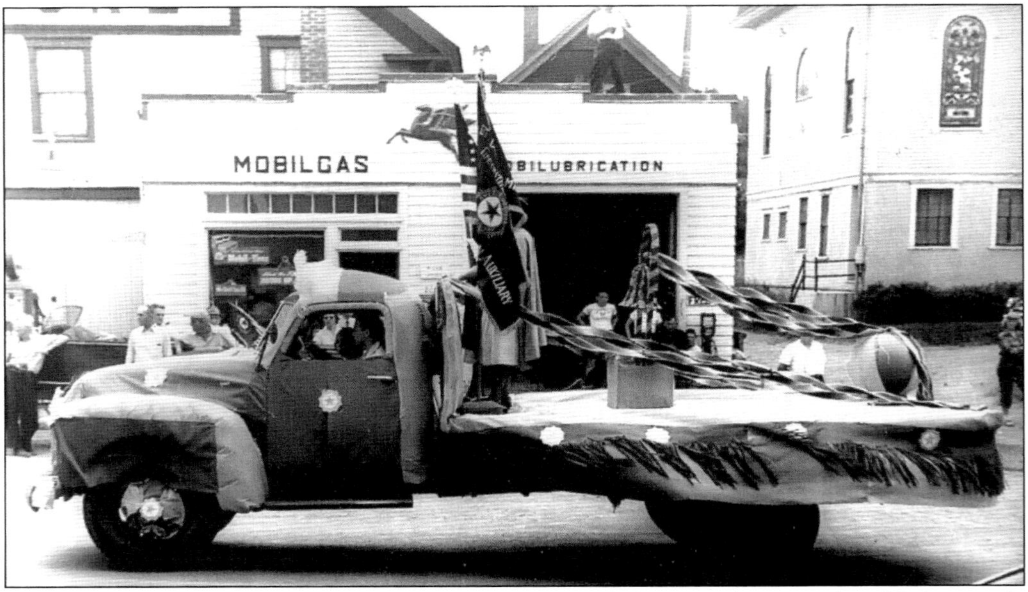

The American Legion Auxiliary entered a decorated float in this Fourth of July parade around 1950. The American Legion has had an active chapter in Greenville for decades. This photograph was taken on Main Street at the intersection with West Street (now Pritham Avenue). The Union Evangelical Church is on the right, and the Mobil gas service station was later owned by Ralph Murray before it was converted to an office.

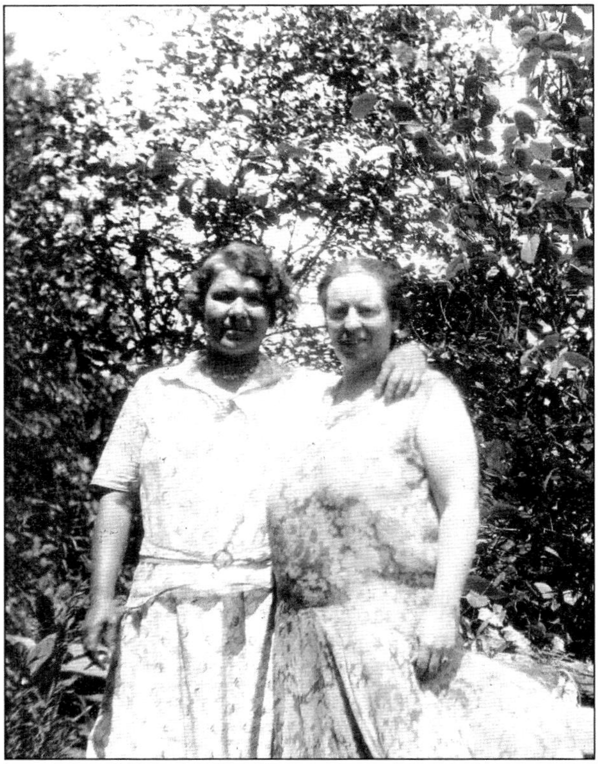

Wanna Eagle (right) was a well-known Penobscot Indian. In her youth she joined touring Wild West shows and traveled throughout the United States and Canada with groups such as the 101 Ranch. She also appeared at New York's Coney Island with such attractions as Dreamland and the World Circus Sideshow. In addition to being a skilled horsewoman, she was an accomplished swimmer, having appeared in aquatic exhibitions at the fabled Hippodrome in New York. Her aquatic work with handicapped children was saluted widely by medical and educational authorities, and she ran a swimming camp on Sugar Island in Moosehead Lake. Married to Henry Perley (Chief Henry Red Eagle), she is shown with her friend Maude Bolduc of Greenville.

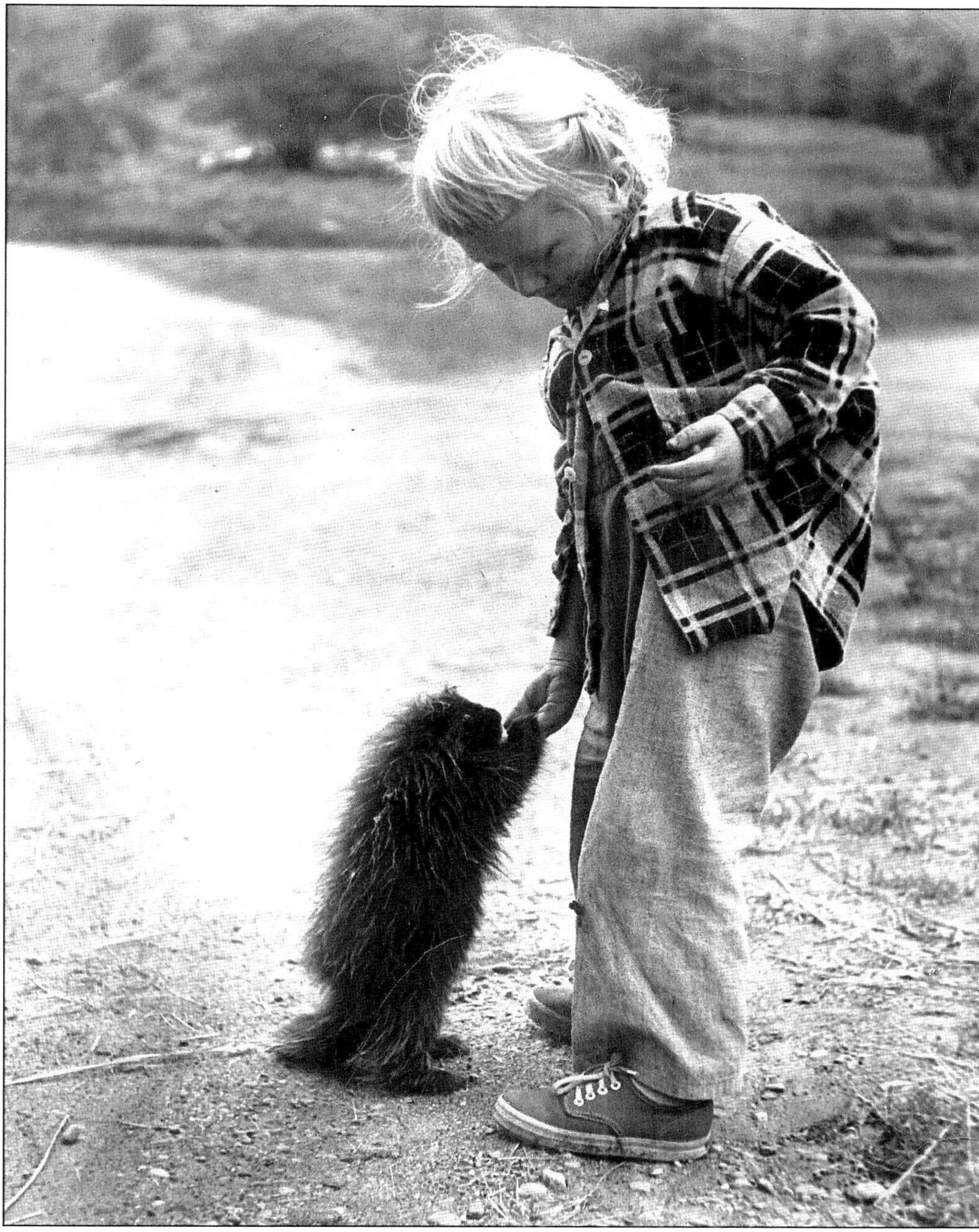

Most people might not think of a porcupine as a pet, but Eileen Later of Greenville enjoyed the companionship of this porky that ate out of her hand. The undated photograph was taken by Greenville photographer Walford H. Budden.

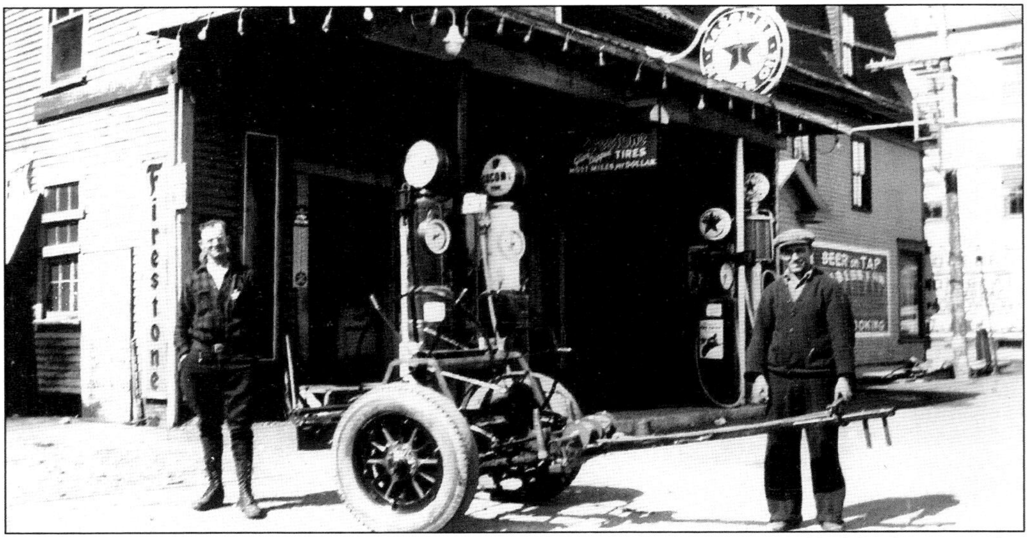

Greenville's first firefighting equipment was this two-wheel machine pulled by horses. This photograph shows Newton "Cy" Porter (left) and Web Cole displaying the equipment in the 1930s. Belmont's Restaurant, then a three-story building, is shown at the near right. The top floor burned in the 1950s, and the building is now the Corner Shop. Porter's Garage is seen behind Porter and Cole.

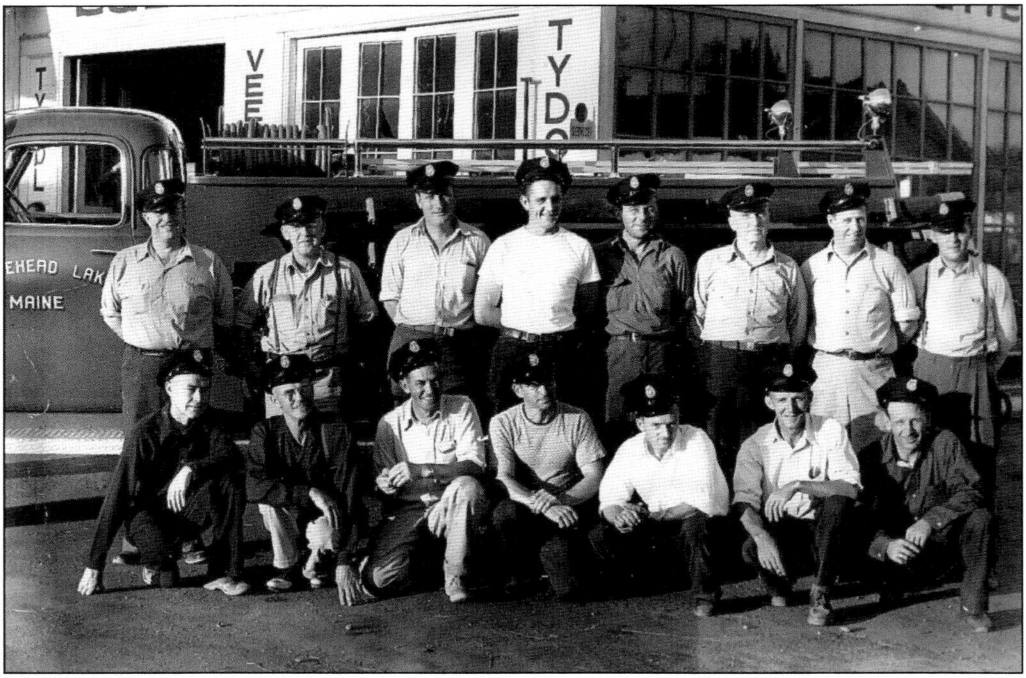

Members of the Greenville Fire Department pose for a photograph *c.* 1950. From left to right are the following: (first row) Chief Nick Hanson, Jake Hanson, Paul Budden, Lewis "Beanie" Champeon, Carl Snow, Web Cole, and Ervin "Peanut" Howe; (second row) Norman Thombs, Ted Bement, Charles Rogers, Earl Budden, Howard York, Harry Hubbard, Rodney Brett, and Gus Harris.

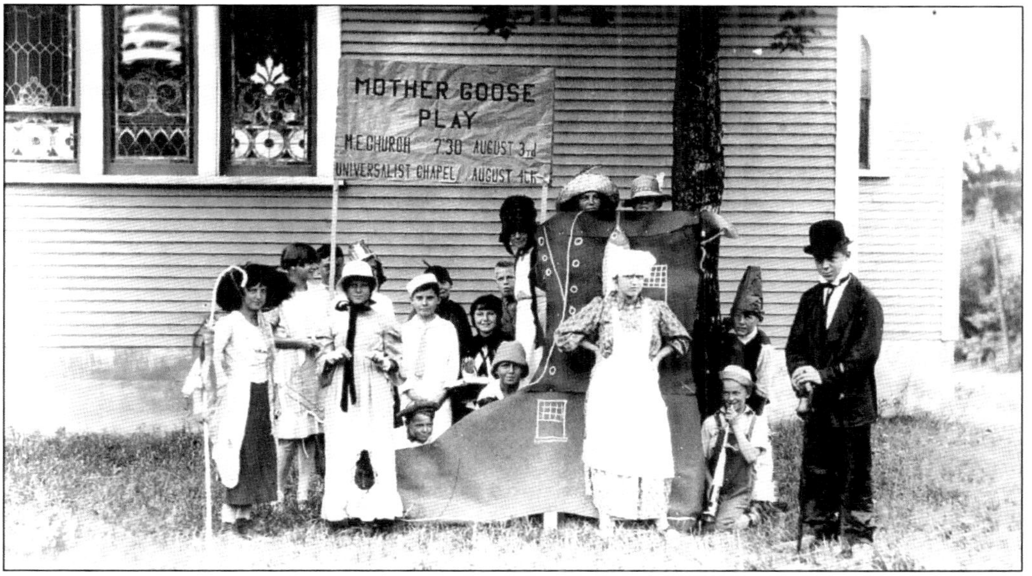

The Ready Workers Community House (also known as the Greenville Community House) was originally a Universalist church. Over the decades, the community house has been the site of many plays and skits performed on the second-floor stage. This photograph shows a group of children who participated in an undated version of the *Mother Goose Play*.

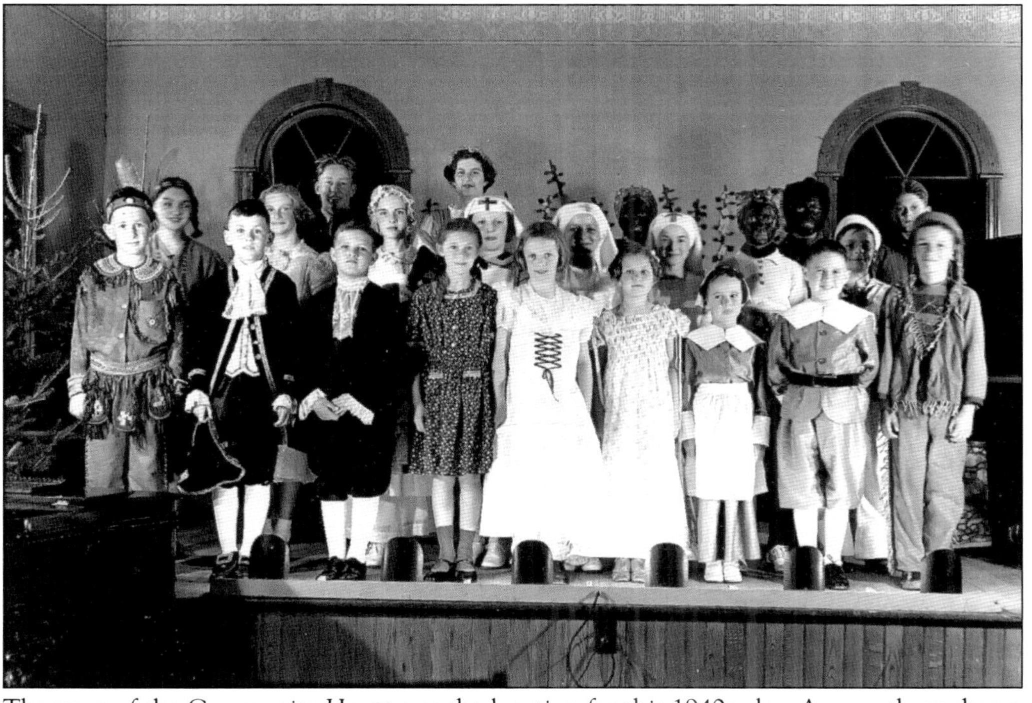

The stage of the Community House was the location for this 1940s play. Among those shown are Jim Bement, Robert MacFadden, Fred King, Virginia Nickerson, Pat Landerkin, Charlotte Cole, Joan Hathaway, Arthur Hathaway, Ted Hanson, Nancy Hall, Ellen Rose Nickerson, Joyce Stanhope, Ginny Knowlton, Doris Libby, Pinky Ells, David Duke, and Sonny Bartlett.

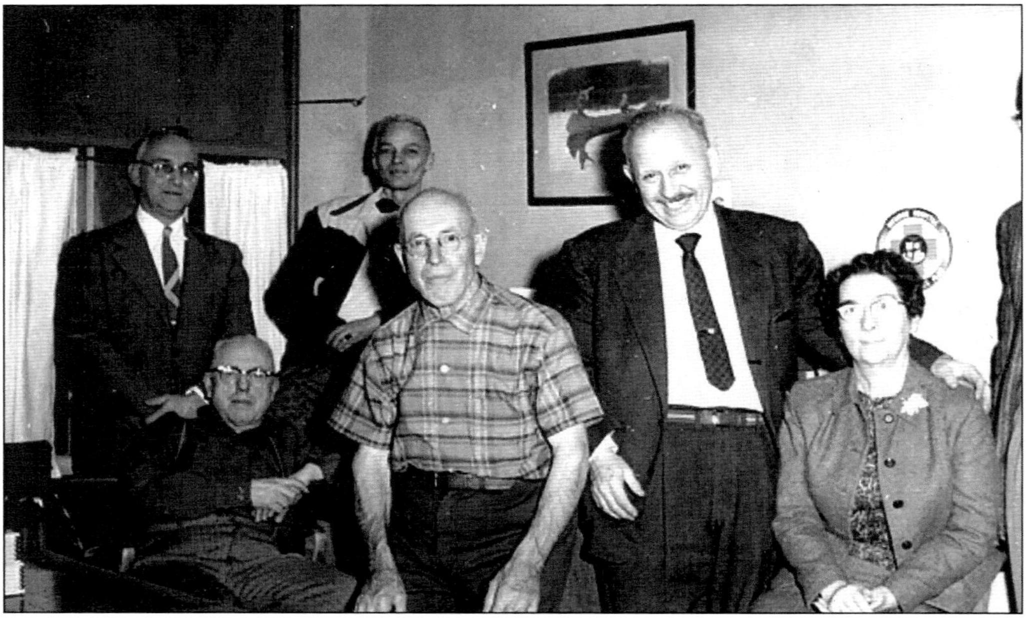

Many of the Moosehead region's medical doctors have become legends. This photograph shows three of them together. From left to right are the following: (first row) Dr. Norman Nickerson, Dr. Fred Pritham, Dr. Isaac Nelson, and Nurse Nellie Morrell; (second row) Llewellyn Wortman and Maurice Anderson.

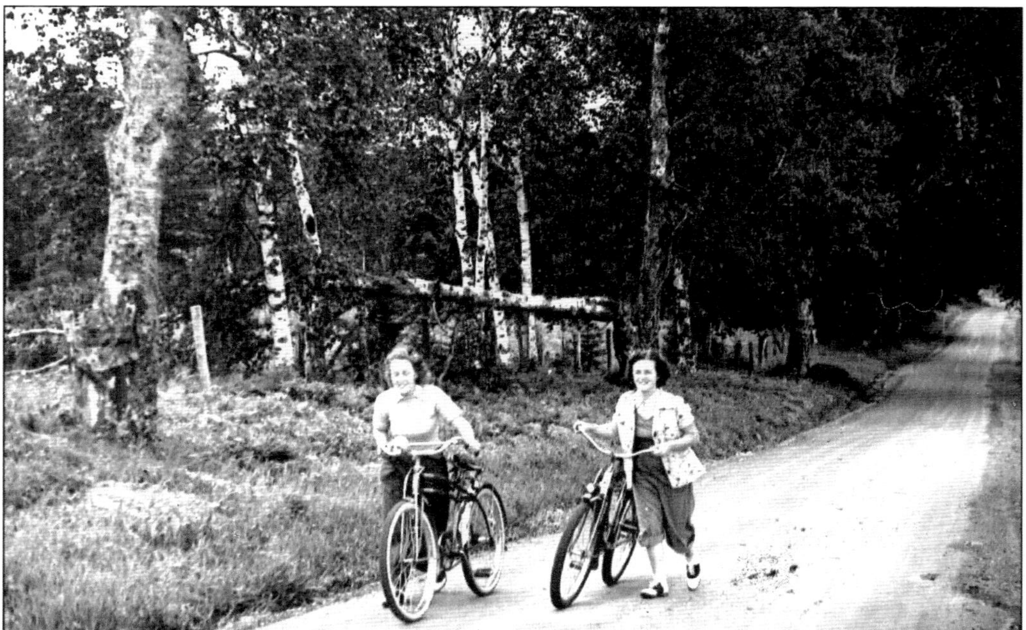

A long bicycle ride in the country was a delight for Octavia Sanders (left) and Hortence Graham shown in this c. 1940s photograph.

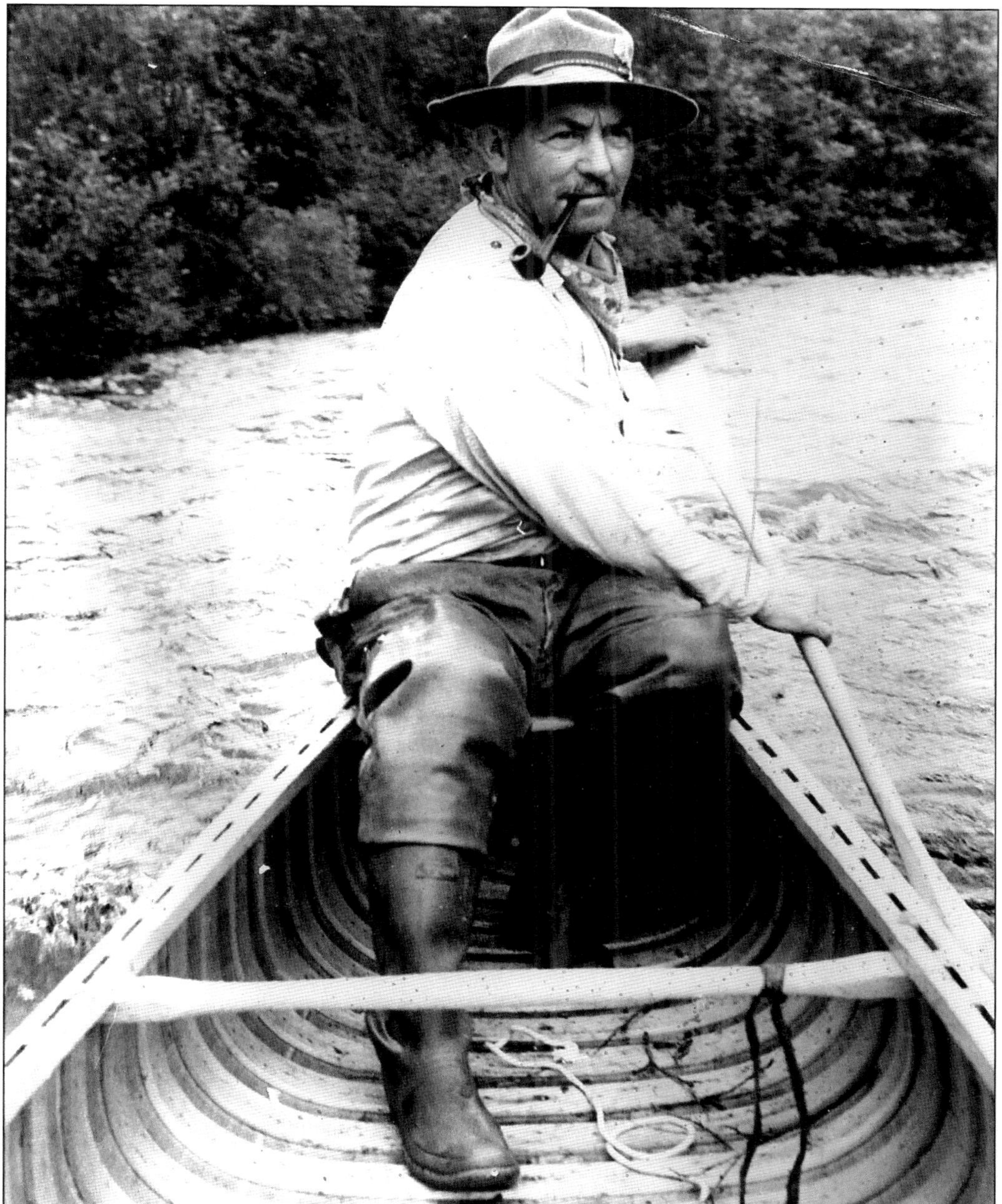

Bert Duty was a well-known guide and game warden. Born in Greenville, he was perhaps best known as the legendary warden of Roach River at Kokadjo, north of Greenville. His exploits in the remote areas of northern Piscataquis County are legendary. This photograph shows Duty in a canoe with his ever-present pipe. He was likely guiding at the time.

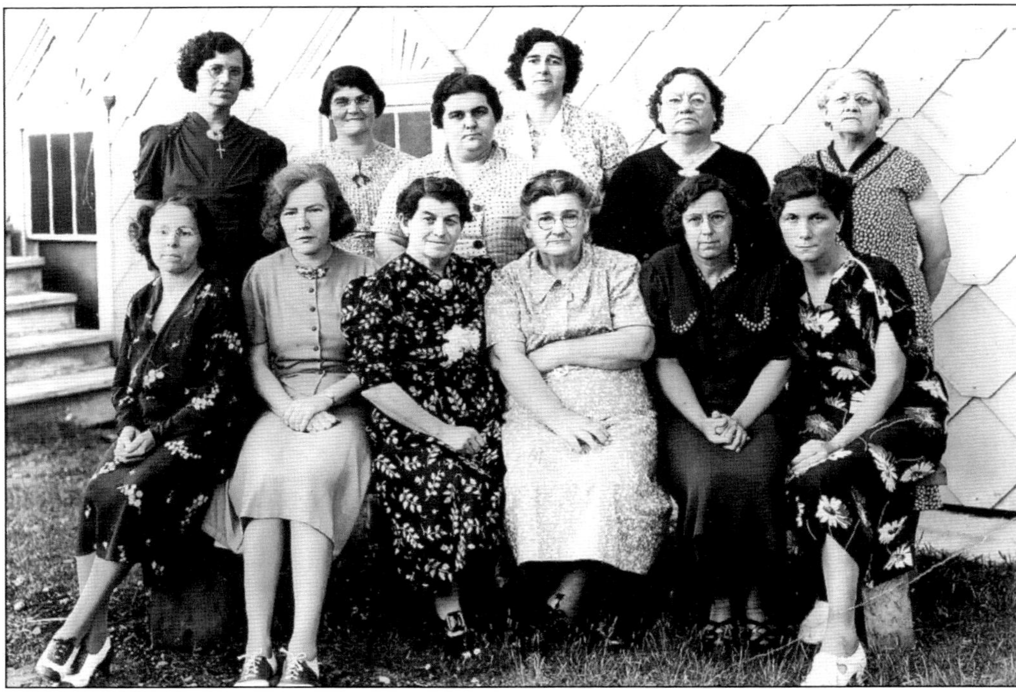

This group of ladies gathered for a photograph outside the Holy Family Catholic Church in the 1940s. From left to right are the following: (first row) Mrs. Littlefield, Mrs. Smith, Mrs. Devoe, Mrs. King, Mrs. Breau, and Mrs. Shufelt; (second row) Mrs. Genest, Mrs. Boucher, Mrs. Harris, Mrs. Hennesy, Mrs. Clark, and Mrs. Sawyer.

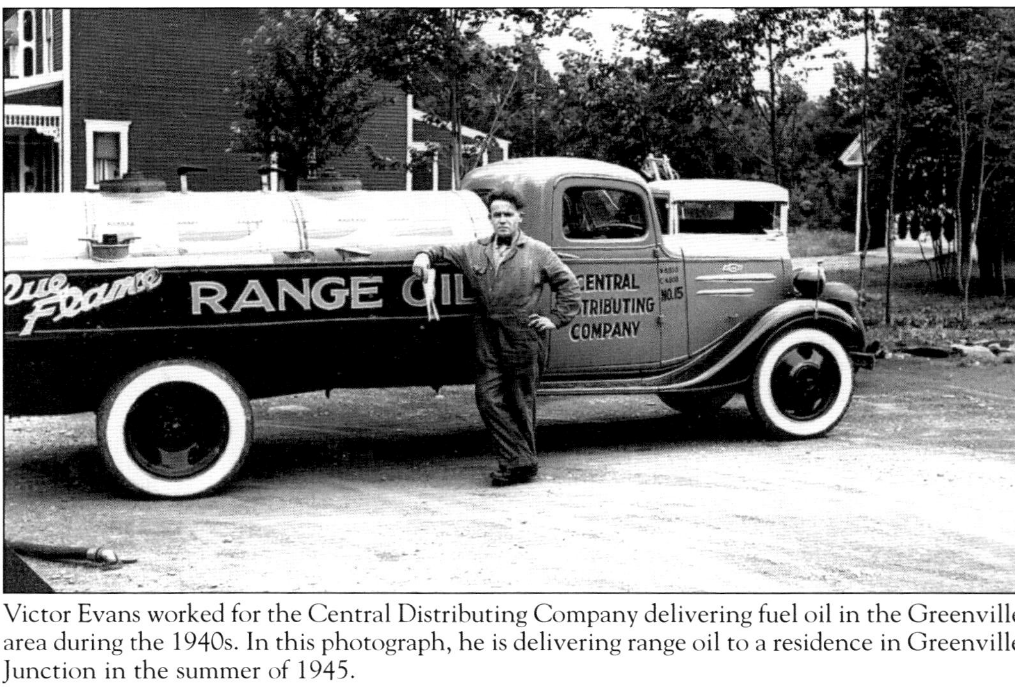

Victor Evans worked for the Central Distributing Company delivering fuel oil in the Greenville area during the 1940s. In this photograph, he is delivering range oil to a residence in Greenville Junction in the summer of 1945.

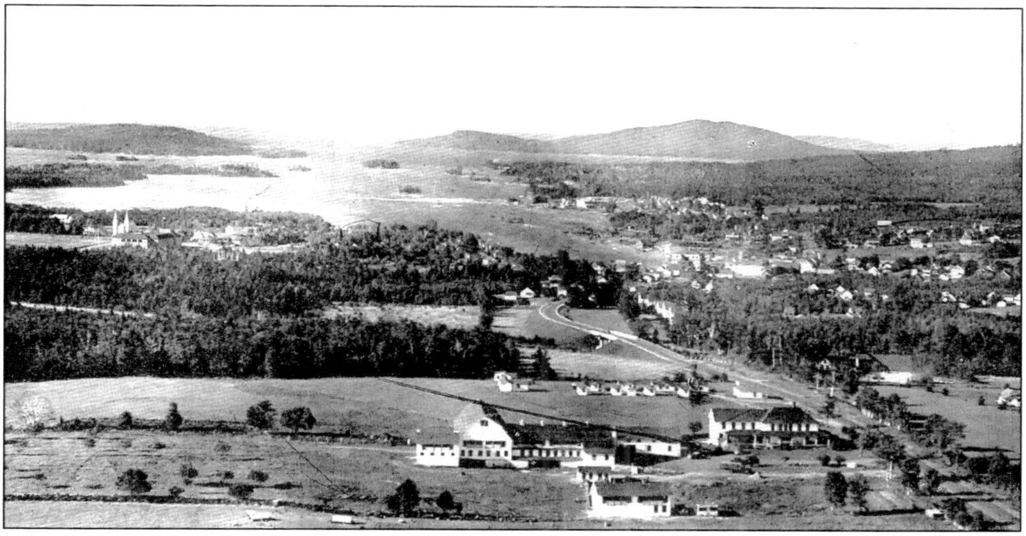

The Indian Hill Farm was one of several farms serving the Moosehead region in the early 1900s. This aerial view was taken likely in the late 1940s and shows the farm, which included the Indian Hill Dairy, and tourist camps that were operated by the Muzzy family. Although the farm buildings are gone, the farmhouse remains in the Muzzy family today, and the tourist camps are now the Indian Hill Motel. This photograph, taken looking north, also shows East Cove of Moosehead Lake. The twin spires at the far left center are of the Holy Family Catholic Church.

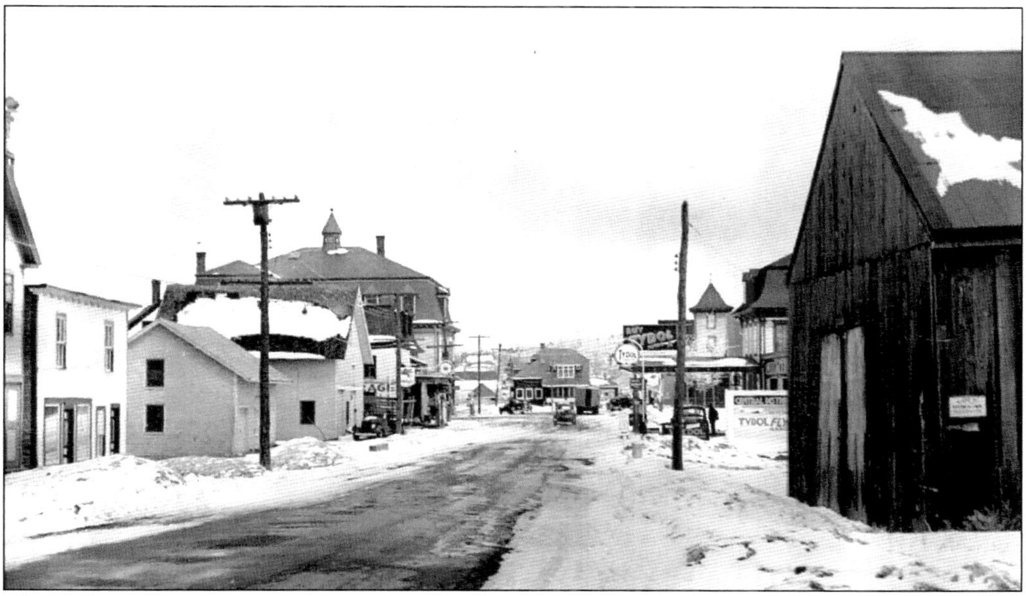

This 1940s view looking north shows South Main Street. The building on the right is now gone, as is the Tydol service station (the former D. H. Whitney garage). Also on the right, the tower to the right of the utility pole was at Sanders Store, and although the store itself remains, the tower is gone. The building on the left with the flat roof was later home to the Boom Chain Restaurant. Porter's Garage is located just past the truck. The Shaw Block is the tall building, and in the center is the Lake House (by then the Green Parrot).

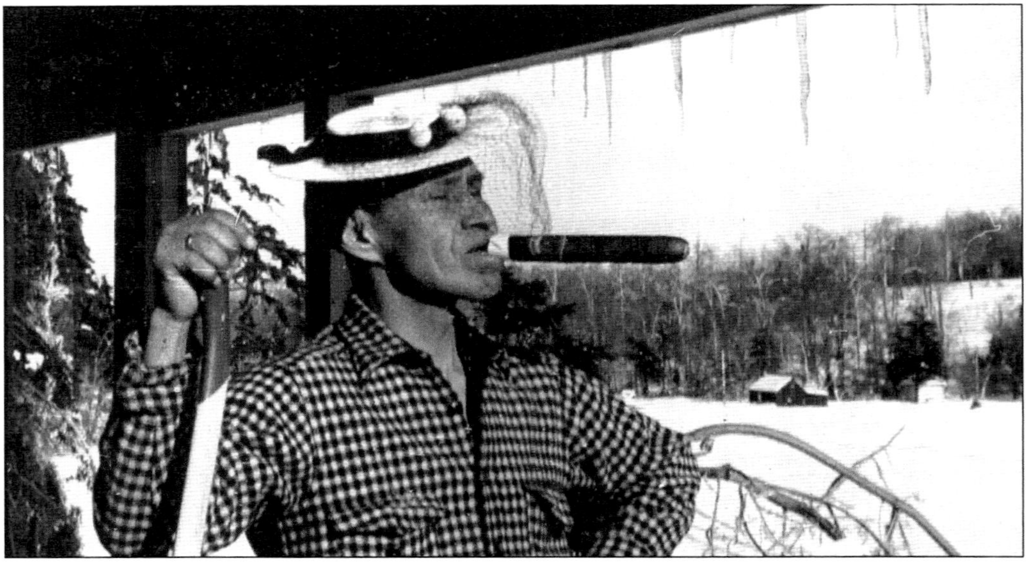

Henry Perley was a Penobscot Indian born in Greenville. Known as Chief Henry Red Eagle, Perley was not only the first Native American to graduate from Greenville High School but also valedictorian of his class. He was a well-known entertainer and author of hundreds of articles of North Woods lore. Having equal billing with Mary Pickford and other early stars, he also appeared in silent movies. Perley is shown here hamming it up with an oversized cigar and a hat with a veil. He died in 1972 and is buried in the Greenville Cemetery.

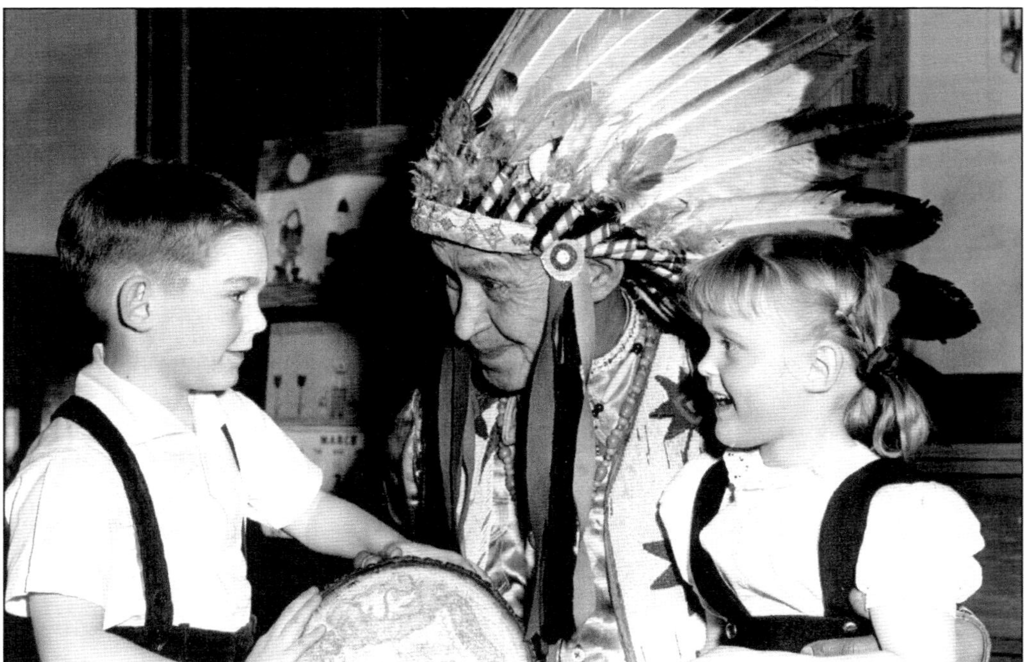

Chief Henry Red Eagle represented the Moosehead Lake region at many trade shows in Massachusetts and New York City over the years. This photograph, likely from the 1940s, shows him with two children. He is wearing the full headdress and regalia of the Penobscot Nation.

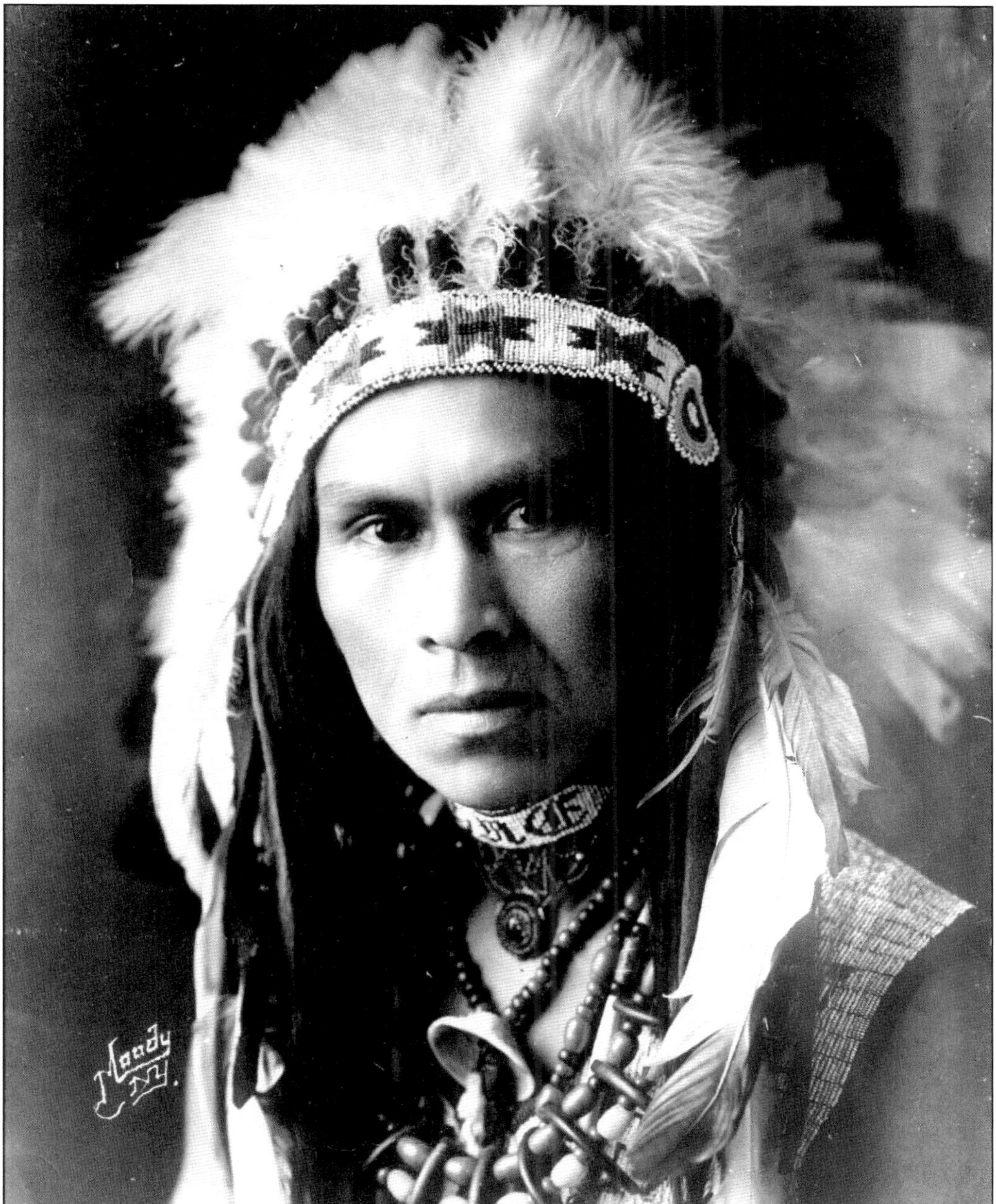

This formal portrait of Henry Perley (Chief Henry Red Eagle) was taken likely for publicity purposes. It is the work of New York City photographer William Shilling.

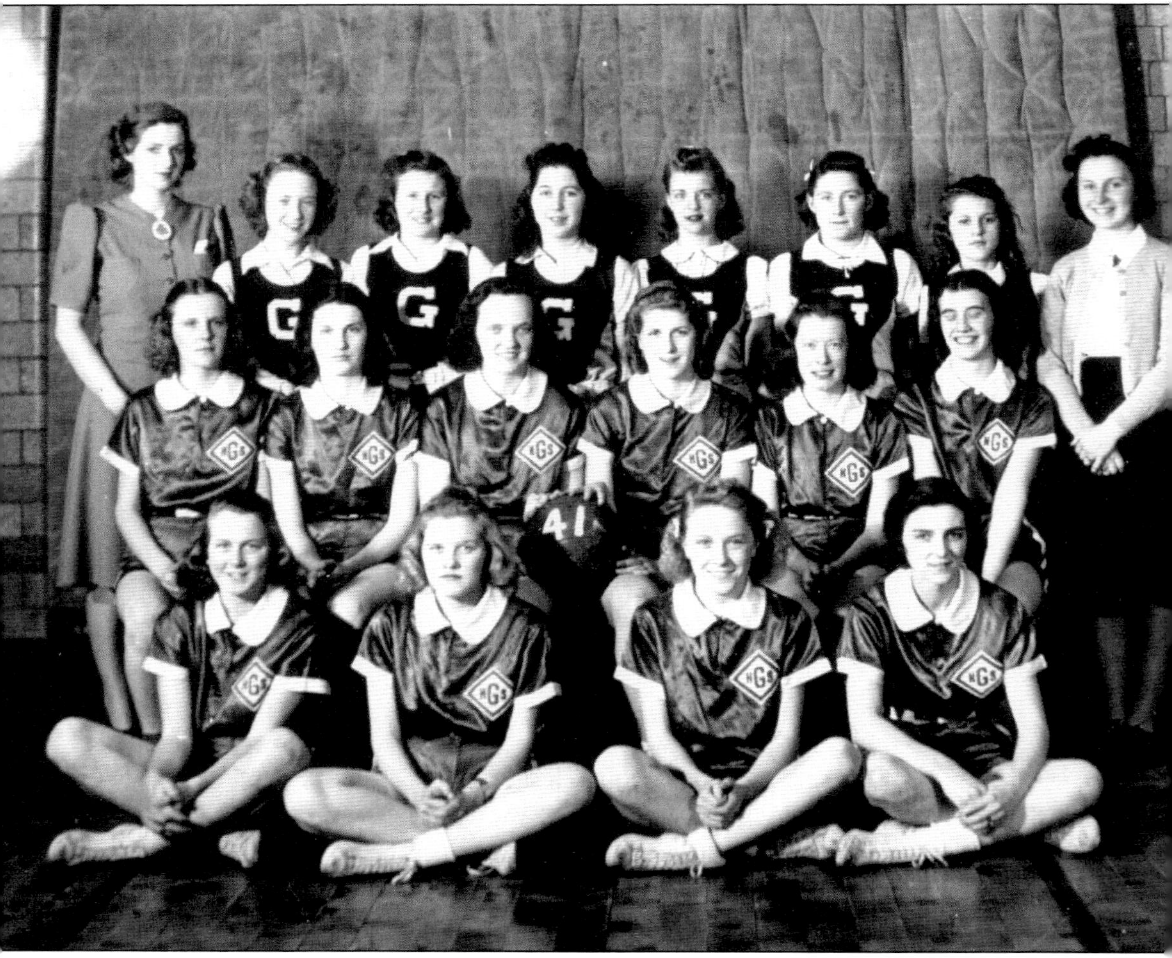

This photograph shows members of the Greenville High School girls basketball team in 1941. Members are, from left to right, as follows: (first row) Mary (Mason) Ryder, Vera (Leet) Canders, Betty Jardine, and Bernice (Smith) Canders; (second row) Mary (Ryder) Genest, Muriel (Graham) Noyes, May Faulkner, Helen Stacey, unidentified, and Helene (Conley) Aucoin; (third row) Dora Stacey (coach), Norma Graham, Barbara (Chadburn) Colgan, Charlotte (Finley) Steeves, Nina (Ward) Crossman, Rose (Deveaux) McIver, Connie Ward, and Florence Craig (manager).

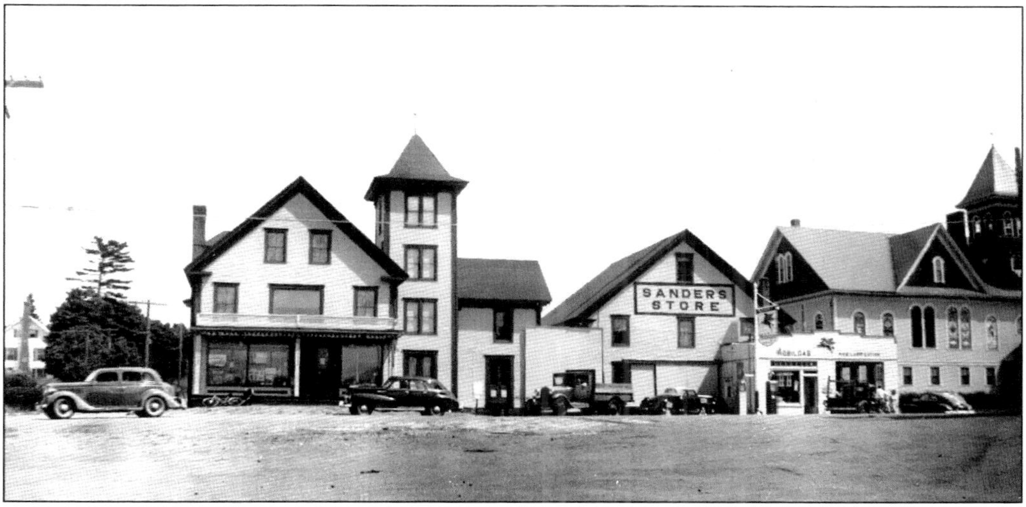

This view of part of North Main Street was taken in the late 1940s from the municipal parking lot on East Cove of Moosehead Lake. Shown on the right is the Sanders Store and Mobil gas service station; at the far right is the Union Evangelical Church. Behind the car on the far left is Pleasant Street.

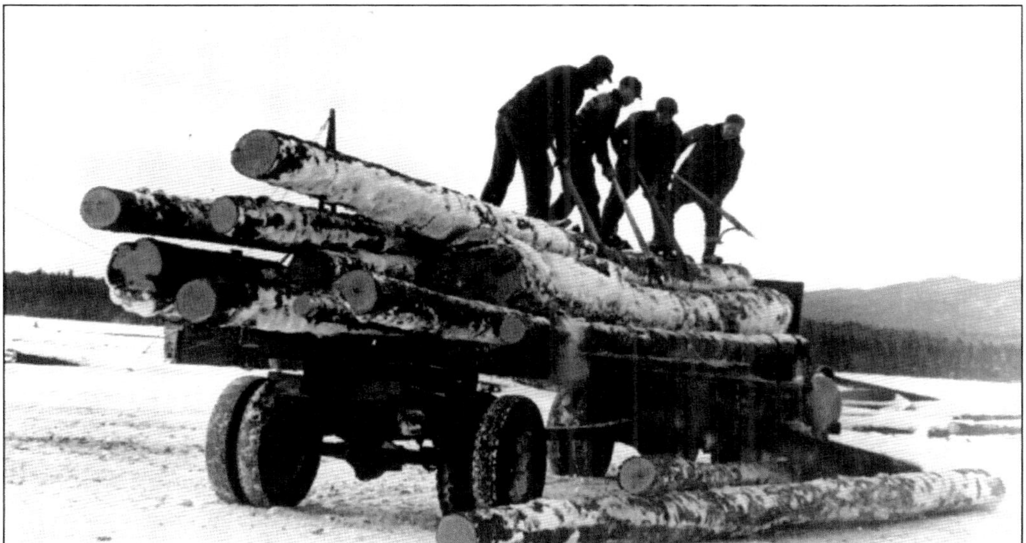

Unloading long logs at a sawmill in the 1940s required a lot of muscle. These men, armed with peaveys for rolling the logs, are hard at work unloading at the Atlas Plywood Mill.

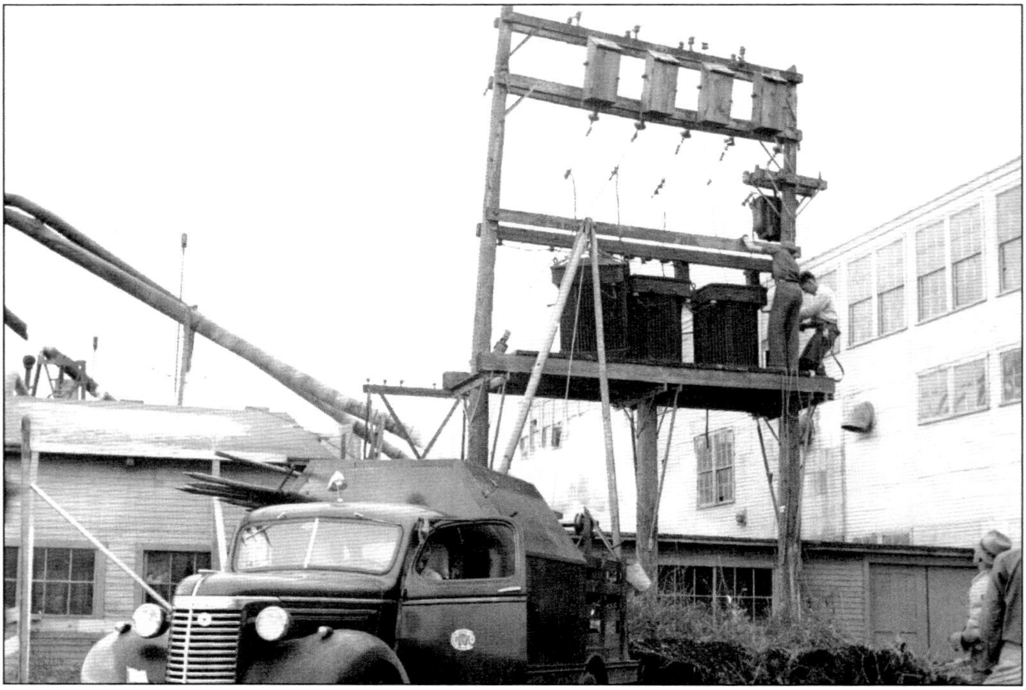

This 1947 photograph shows workmen making repairs to electrical equipment at the Atlas Plywood Mill. The mill, also known as the veneer mill, milled logs into plywood and paneling for many years before closing. The site, located off North Main Street, is now vacant. The logs were transported to the mill by truck or hauled down Moosehead Lake in booms.

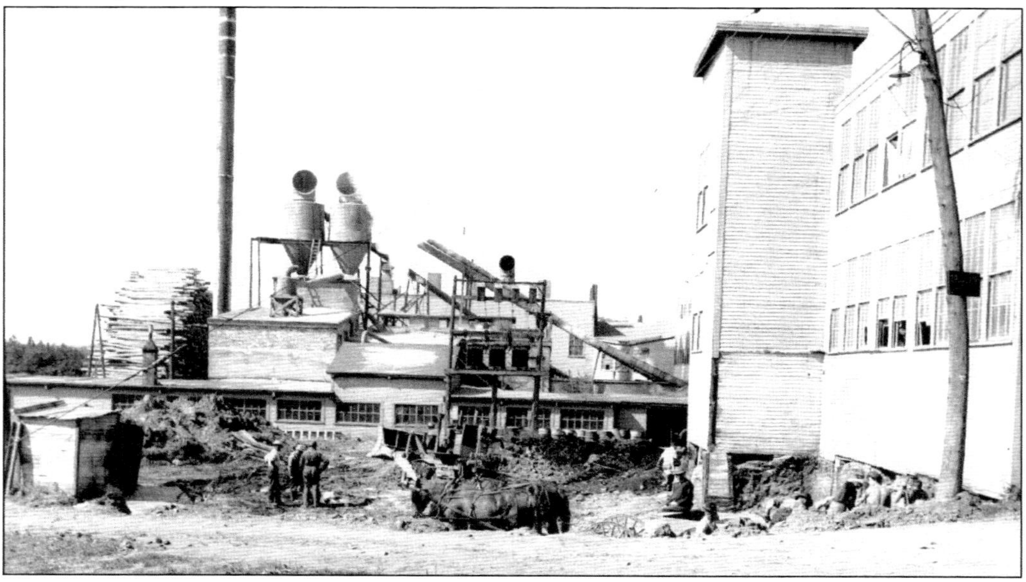

The Atlas Plywood Mill employed scores of Greenville men in 1947. Here, two eras of manual labor are depicted. In the center foreground, a team of horses and a wagon are used for foundation work (workmen are partially hidden by the roadway), and just behind them, a bulldozer is working. Notice also the huge pile of logs at the left ready for milling.

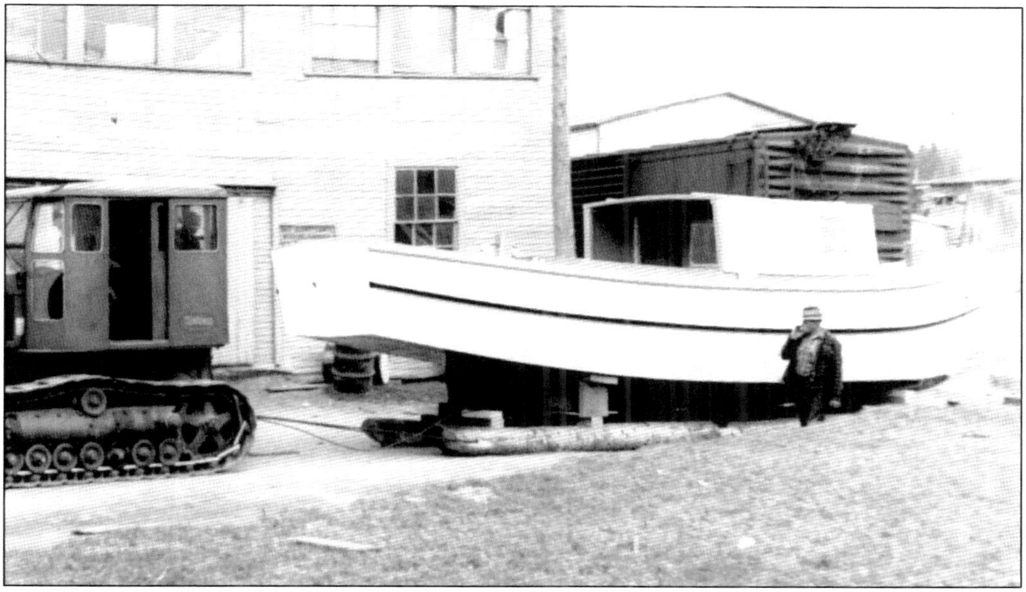

The Atlas Plywood Mill had a small boat that was used for moving logs in Moosehead Lake at the mill. The boat was constructed by the Templeton Canoe Company and had one-inch thick oak planking with a transom six-inches thick. Volney Roberts is shown operating the tractor at the left in this late-1940s photograph.

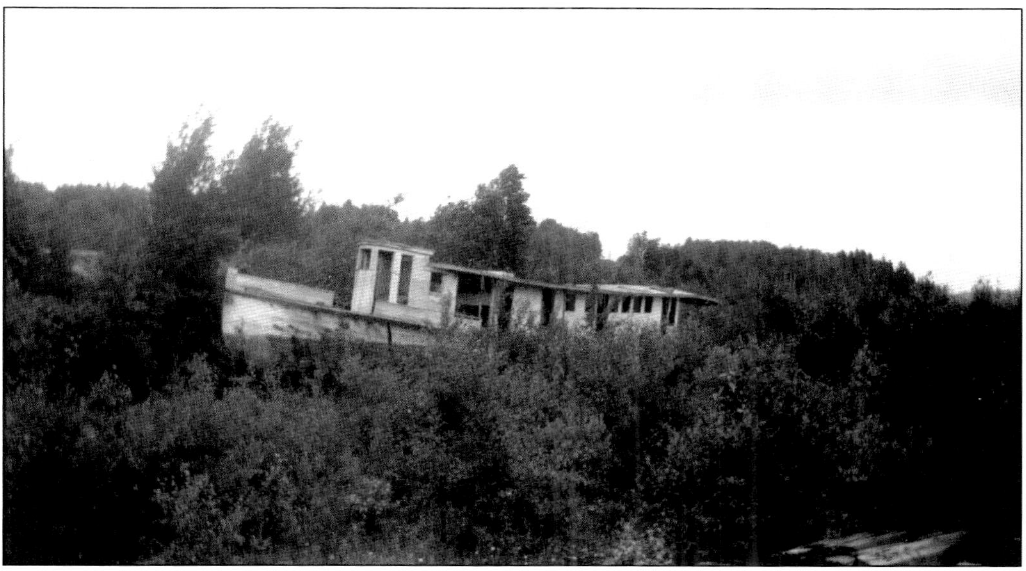

Many of the steamers that once operated on Moosehead Lake were abandoned on shore when they were no longer of use. Here, the steamer *Louisa* is shown at Scott Beach, north of Greenville Junction, in a photograph taken on July 11, 1950. Over the decades, scores of boats were abandoned in this way.

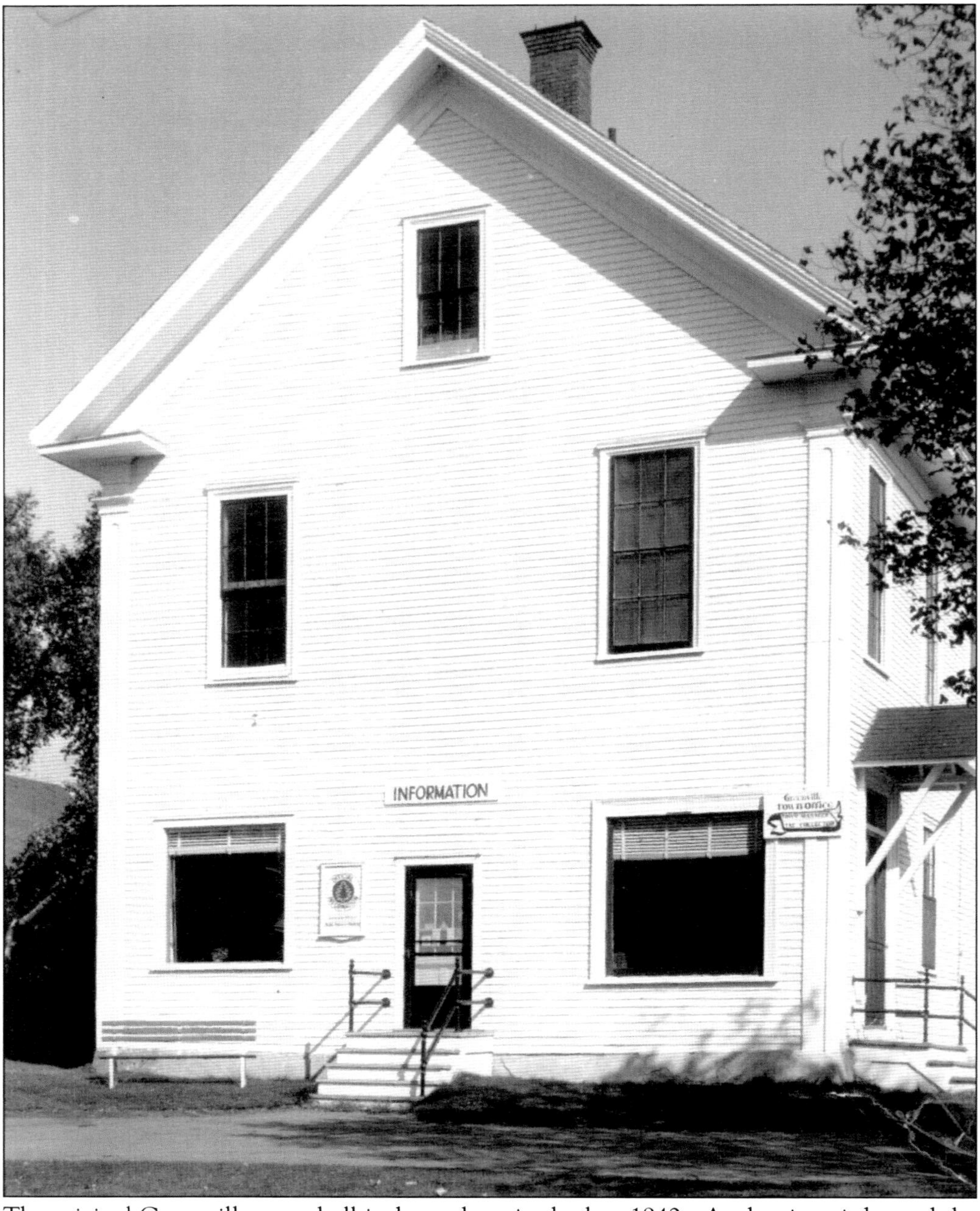

The original Greenville town hall is shown here in the late 1940s. At the time, it housed the Greenville town office and the Moosehead Information Center. The sign on the front door indicates it was the Greenville branch of the Maine Publicity Bureau. The building, which stood on the south side of the Union Evangelical Church, was constructed in 1869 by Benjamin S. Bigney, and also served as the village school at one time. The building was torn down in later years to make way for a new town office and a police and fire department building, as well as a parking lot.

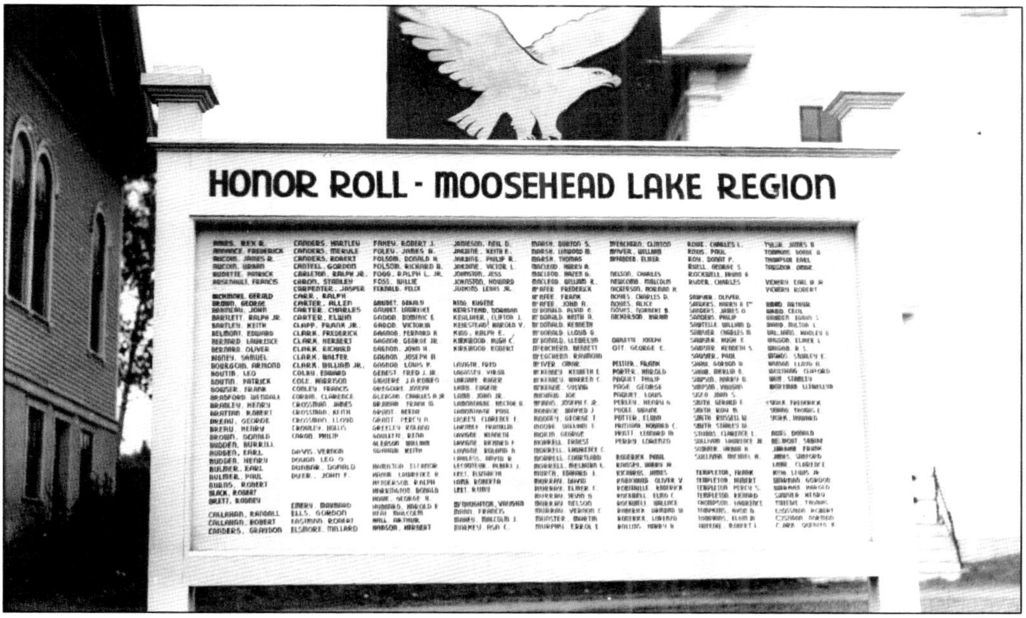

The old Greenville Honor Roll was located in front of the Greenville Town Hall in the late 1940s. The Union Evangelical Church is located at the far left. This honor roll, constructed of wood, was later removed and a new one with lighting was constructed near the corner of Main and Minden Streets.

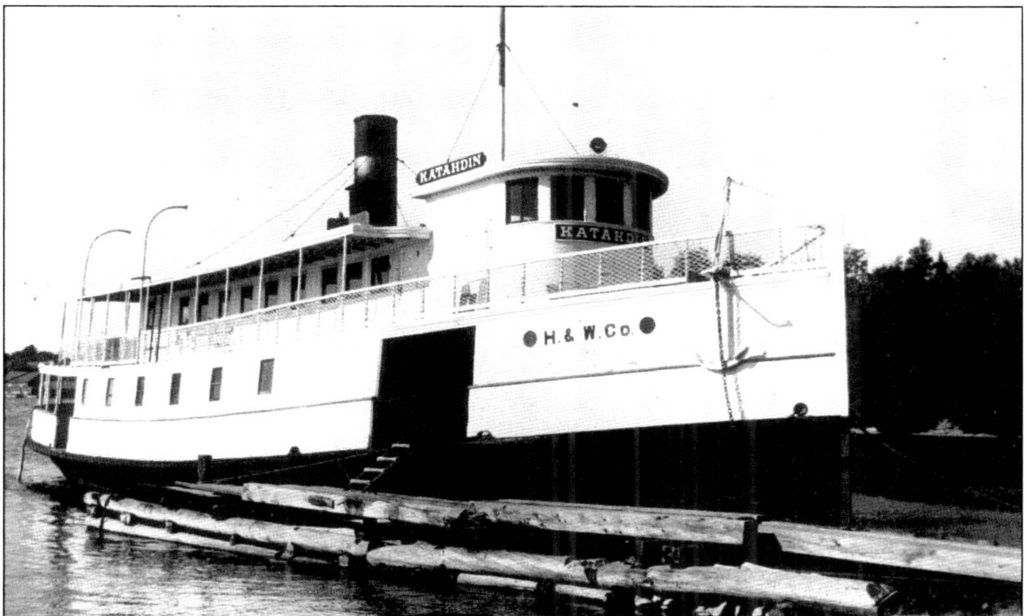

The steamer *Katahdin* is shown at dock during the time she was owned by the Hollingsworth & Whitney Company. The Hollingsworth & Whitney Company later became Scott Paper Company. During this era, the "*Kate*" was used for hauling booms of logs on Moosehead Lake.

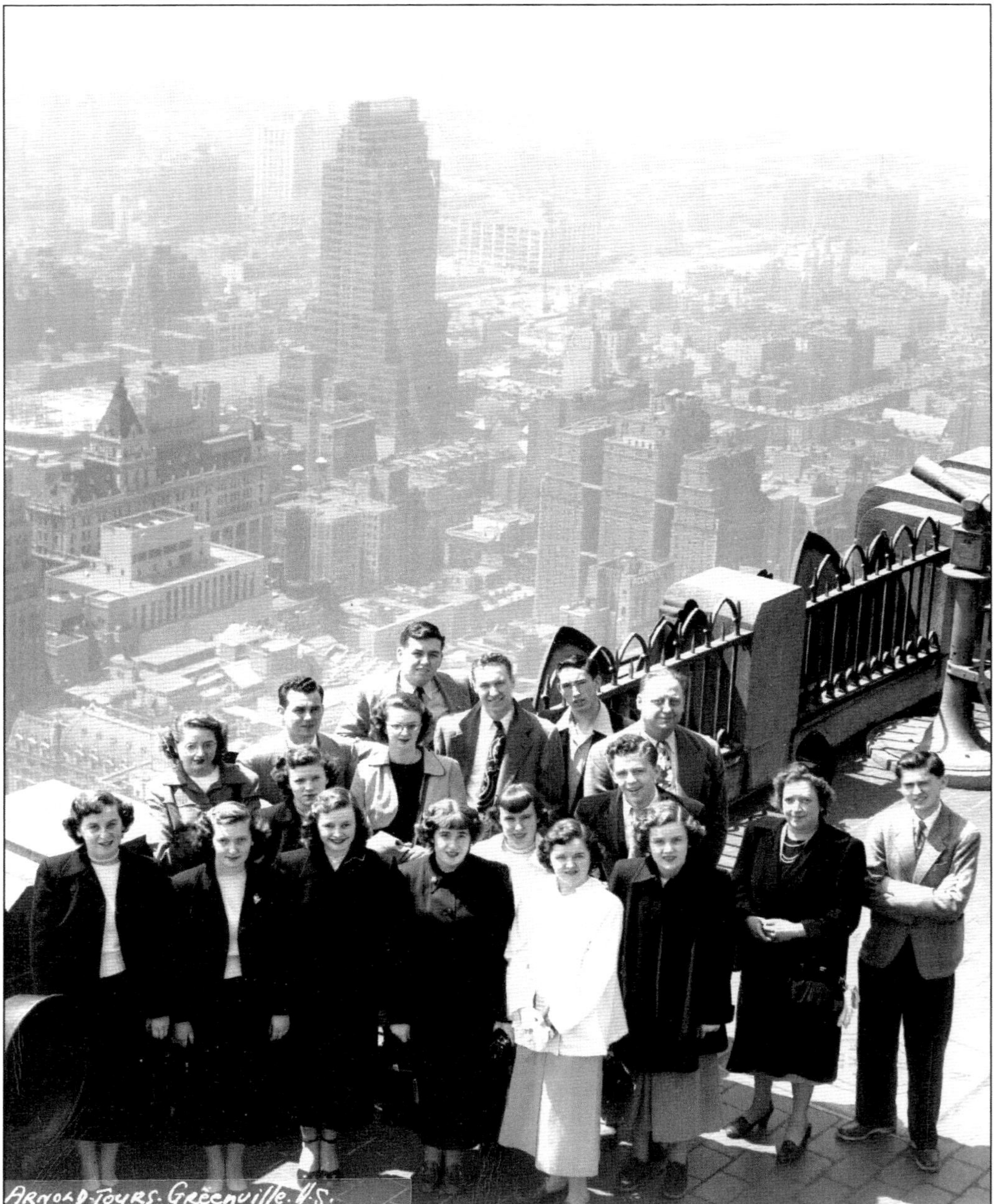

The Greenville High School class of 1950 was one of the first to travel to New York City for a senior trip. The group is shown here at the Rockefeller Center building on April 19, 1950.

Two

SHIRLEY

The question is often asked how the town of Shirley (more accurately, Shirley Mills) got its name. It was named by J. Kelly, a member of the Maine legislature who suggested it after his hometown, Shirley, Massachusetts. The township was incorporated in the spring of 1834. The name selected by a number of inhabitants was Somerset, but that was rejected by the legislature because of other places with similar names, such as Somerset County. Shirley lies to the south of Greenville and was originally part of the so-called "Million Acres" of the Bingham Kennebec Purchase. Over the years, the land was subdivided by hardy settlers. Shirley is one of 43 named townships that were created from the Million Acres. The headwaters of the Piscataquis River are found in Shirley Township. An excellent flowage from Shirley Pond, in the heart of the village, saw light industry in the form of mills in years past. The first settlement was created *c.* 1825, when Joseph Mitchell and Eben and David Marble settled on a lot in the east side of what was to become the town. A post office was established under the name True's Mills in 1830, named after Jabez True, one of the early settlers. The name was changed to Shirley in 1834.

A number of houses were constructed along Shirley Pond, along with a church and school buildings on a knoll. Over the years, Shirley has remained much the same. The town hall is still used for community functions and is also the home of Shirley Grange No. 413, which was organized in 1903. A quintessential Maine general store can be found next-door, complete with a wood stove where locals gather on cold mornings and a small post office in addition to groceries and other essentials. Today, Shirley has a population of less than 200 people. The Bangor & Aroostook Railroad, which once ran through town, is long gone, as are businesses such as the Shirley Lumber Company and Shirley Industries.

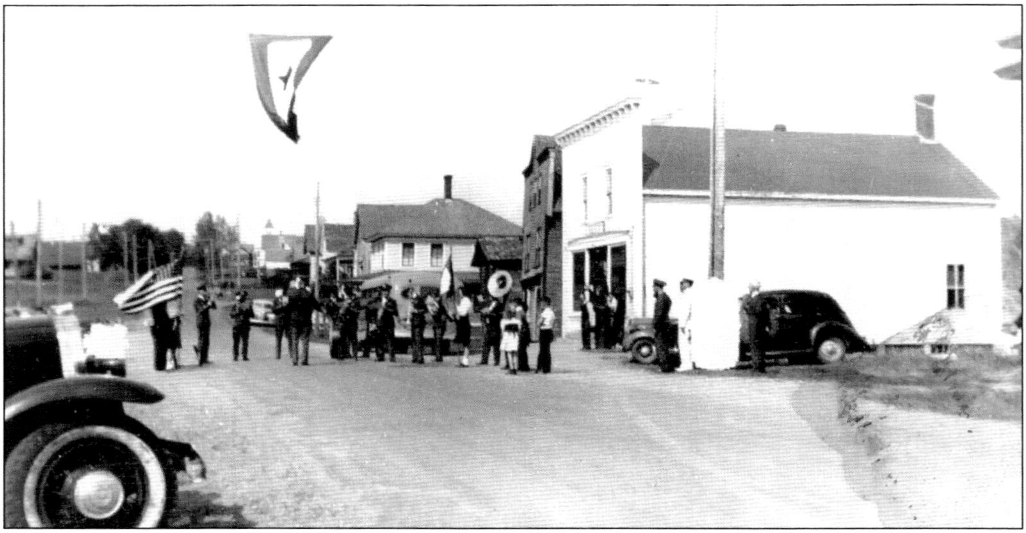

In 1940, a Memorial Day ceremony was held in front of the Shirley Honor Roll. Shirley Town Hall is just to the right of the photograph, and the Shirley General Store is the white building at the right.

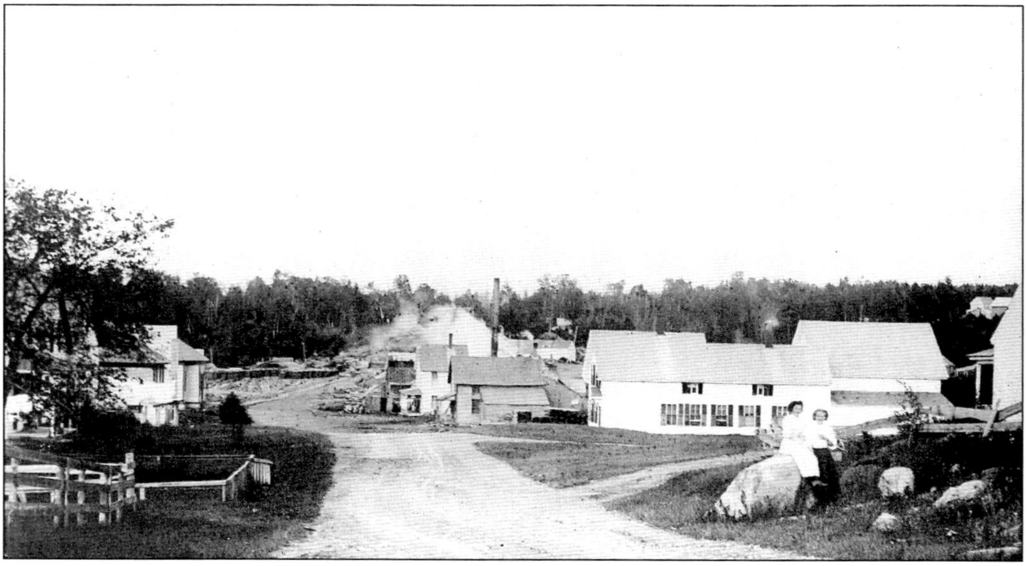

This is a view of Main Street *c.* the 1920s. The town hall and general store are partially seen at the left center, and the Shirley Lumber Company is in the distant center. The buildings in the center of the photograph past the white house are now gone, and the Shirley Fire Department building is now located there.

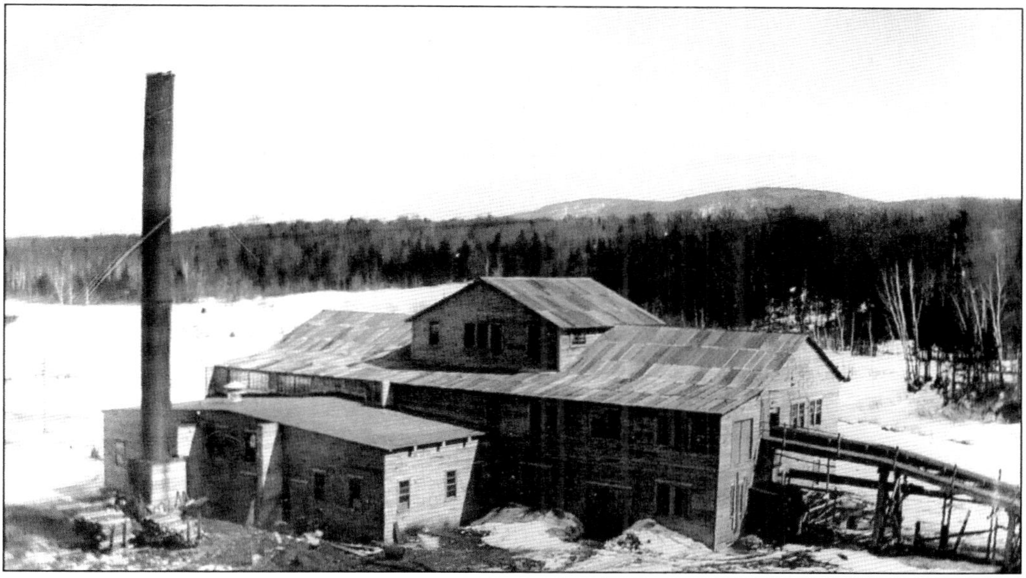

The Shirley Lumber Company was a major industry in the town of Shirley for many years. The mill was located on the shore of Shirley Pond, not far from the village district.

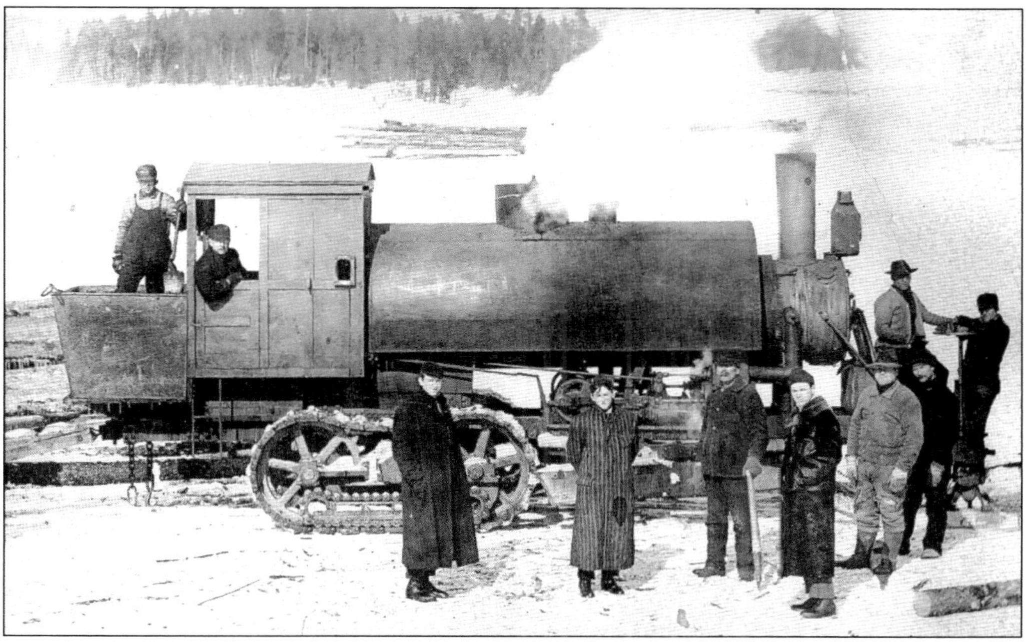

This Lombard Steam Log Hauler was used to transport logs to the Shirley Lumber Company in its early days of operation on the shore of Shirley Pond. No one is identified in this c. 1920 photograph.

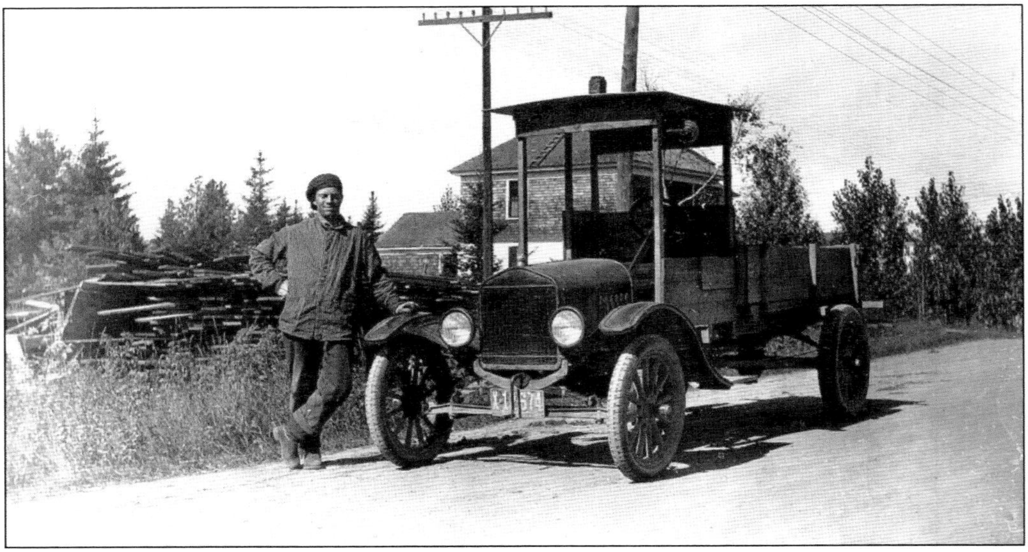

Wilson Ward Sawtelle of Shirley is shown in 1922 with his new truck. The truck featured an open cab and a small body for transporting goods. The location is believed to be the Shirley-Greenville Road in Shirley.

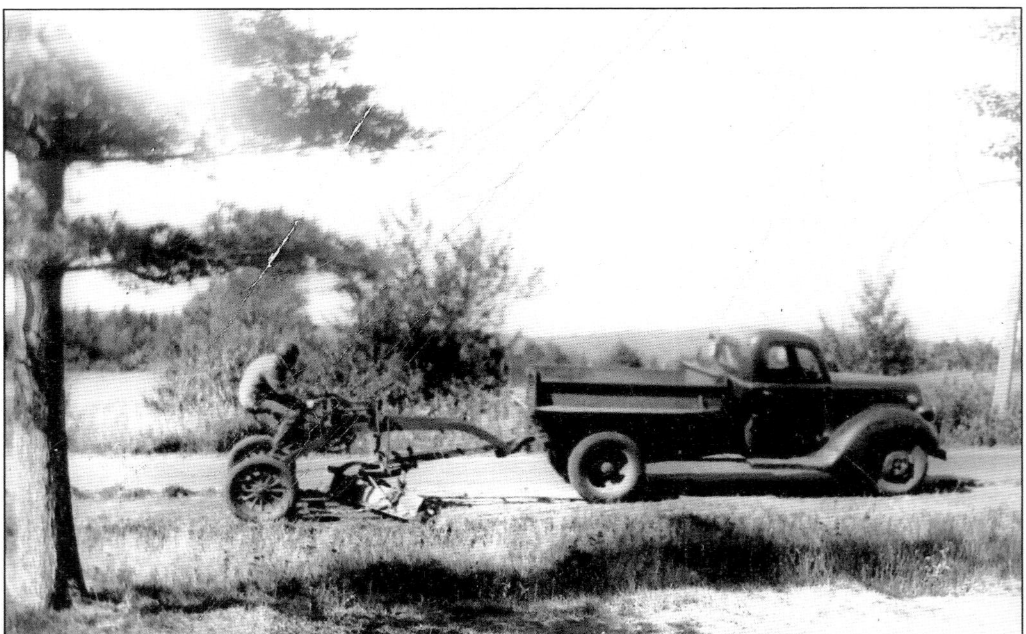

Roscoe "Rusty" Cook Jr. is driving the 1939 Ford pick up truck that is pulling a road grading machine operated by Arthur Bumpus in this early 1940s photograph. It is believed that the photograph shows the Shirley-Greenville Road.

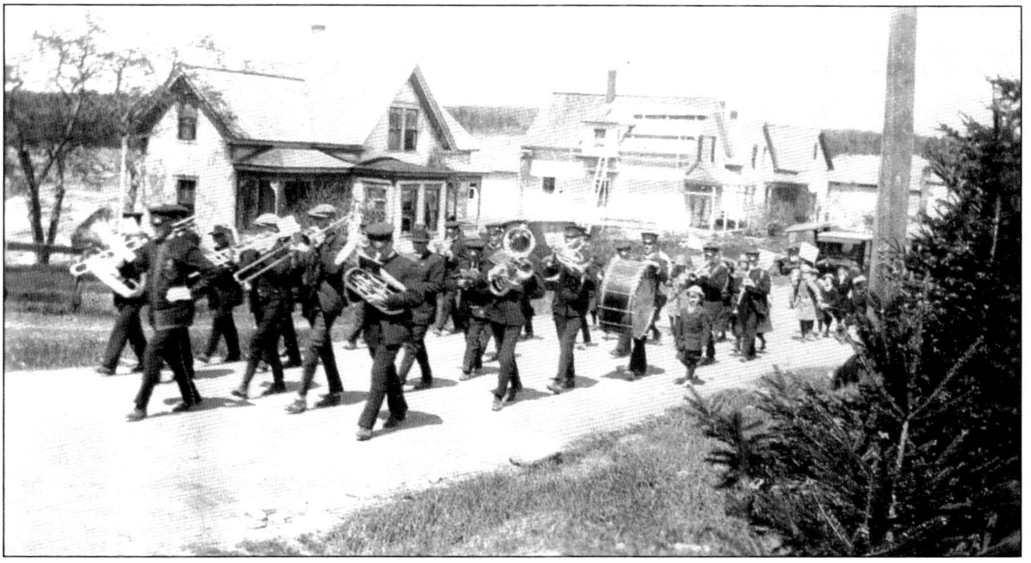

The Greenville Marine Band took part in this Memorial Day parade in the 1920s. This photograph shows the band marching on Main Street toward the Shirley Cemetery. Shirley Pond is visible beyond the houses in the top center of the photograph.

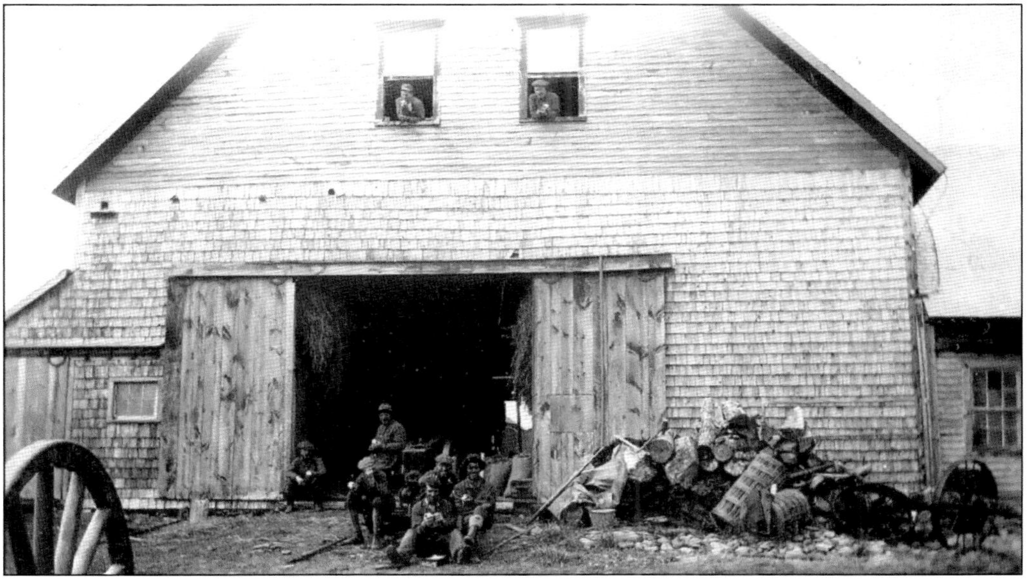

A threshing crew is taking a break in this c. 1915 photograph taken in front of the W. W. Sawtelle barn. Unfortunately, no one is identified. In this era, many farmers helped each other with harvesting duties in the fall of each year.

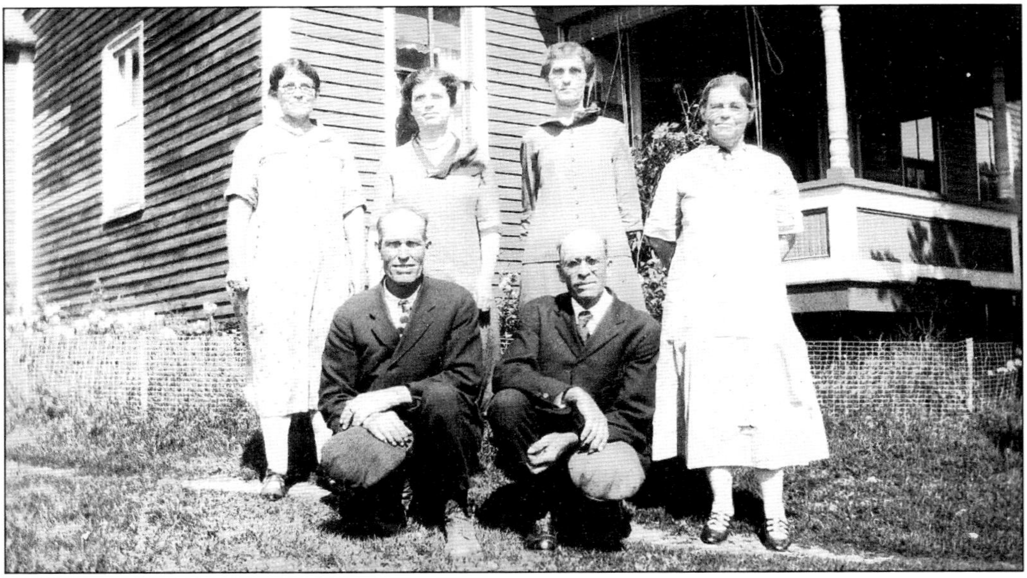

Here, the Sawtelle family of Shirley poses for a photograph in the early 1900s. From left to right are the following: (first row) Costello and Elledge Sawtelle; (second row) Myrtle, Ada, Annie, and Willie Sawtelle. The photograph was taken in front of the Sawtelle home. This was the family of Wilson W. Sawtelle, who fought in the battle of Gettysburg and other Civil War battles.

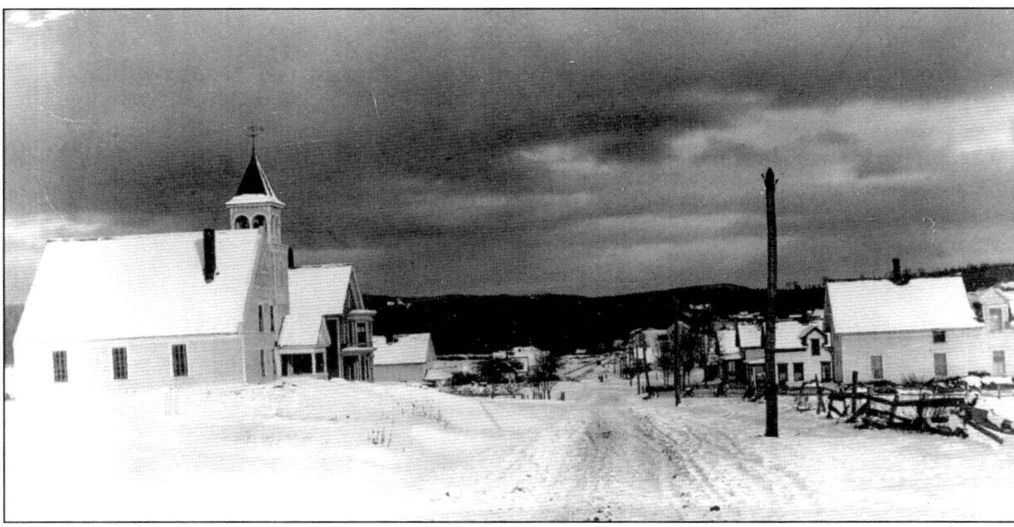

This is a winter view of Shirley taken in 1921. The Shirley Methodist Church (now United Methodist) is shown at the left. The view looks toward the village. The Shirley Cemetery is behind the fence at the right, and the Shirley Elementary School is just beyond the picture at the left.

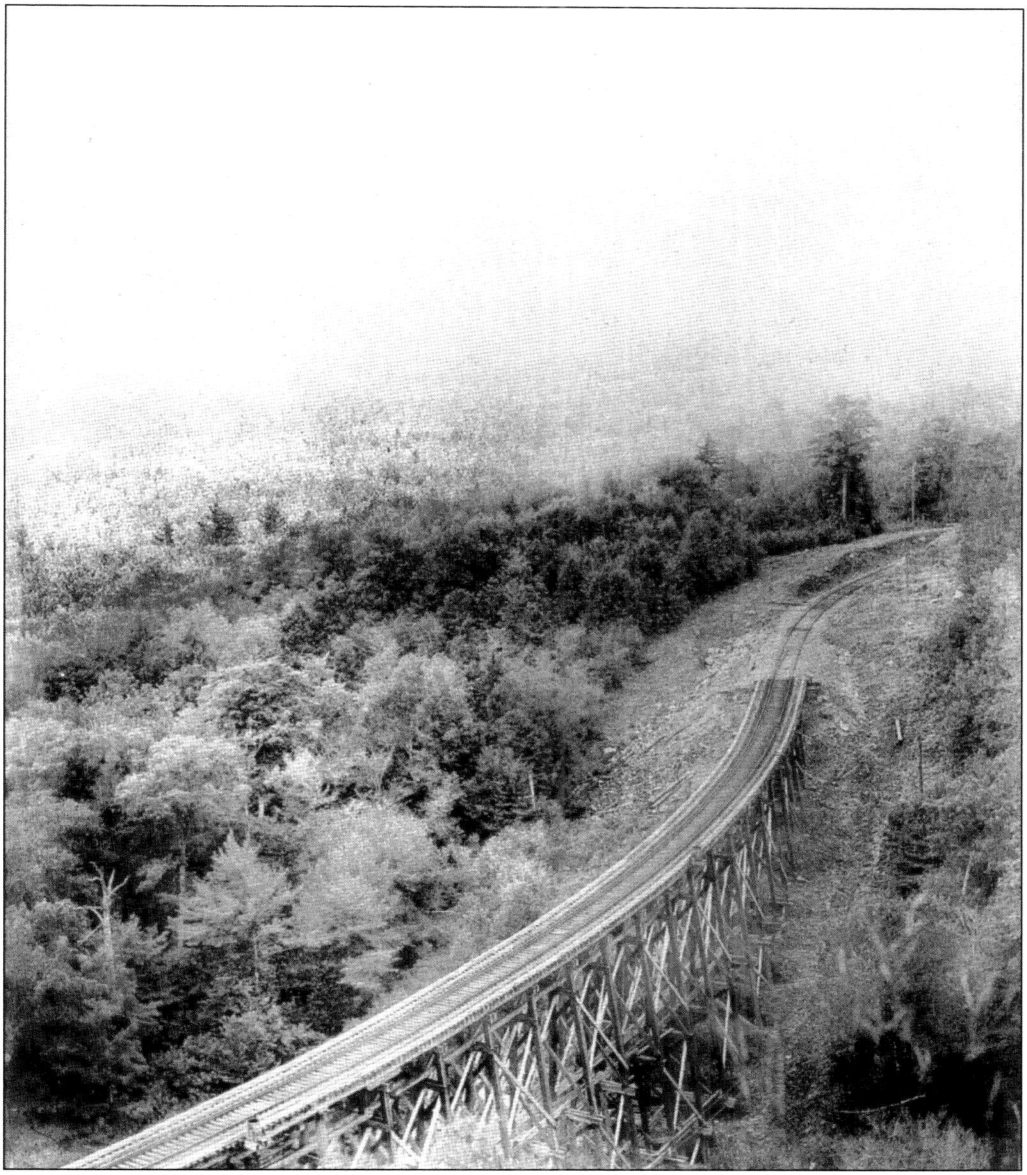

This rare view of the Bangor & Aroostook Railroad trestle between Shirley and Blanchard was captured *c.* 1910. Concrete abutments are all that remain of the trestle now. The Bangor & Aroostook Railroad tracks were removed after the line was abandoned later in the 1900s.

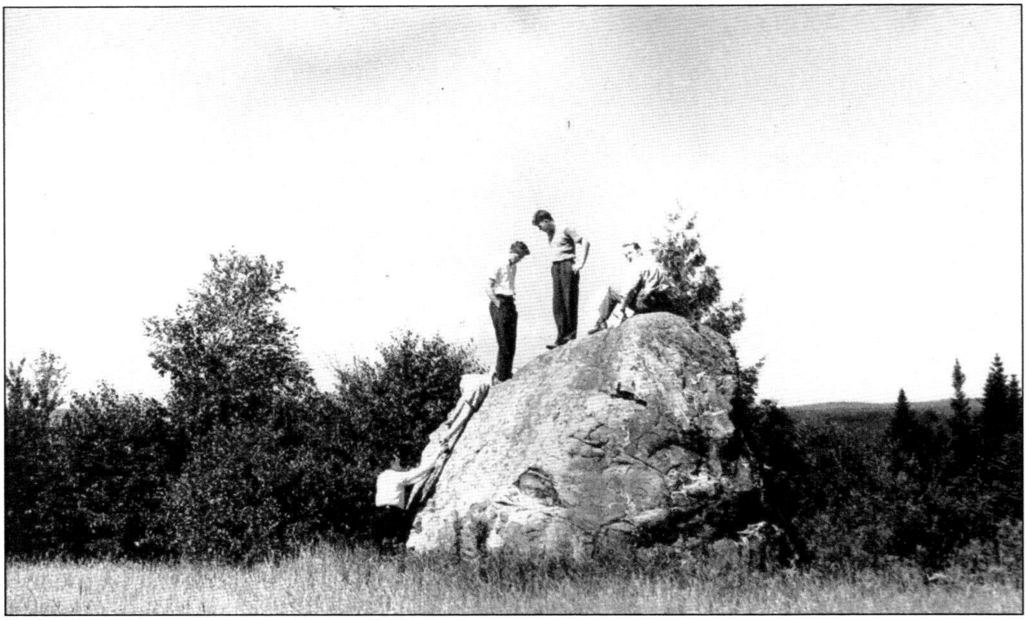

The C. B. Allen family was early settlers in the Shirley area. This huge boulder on the Allen family farm was a magnet for children because the top offered sweeping views of the area. This late-1940s photograph shows several children atop the rock. Charles Davis is helping Colleen Davis Ashe climb down.

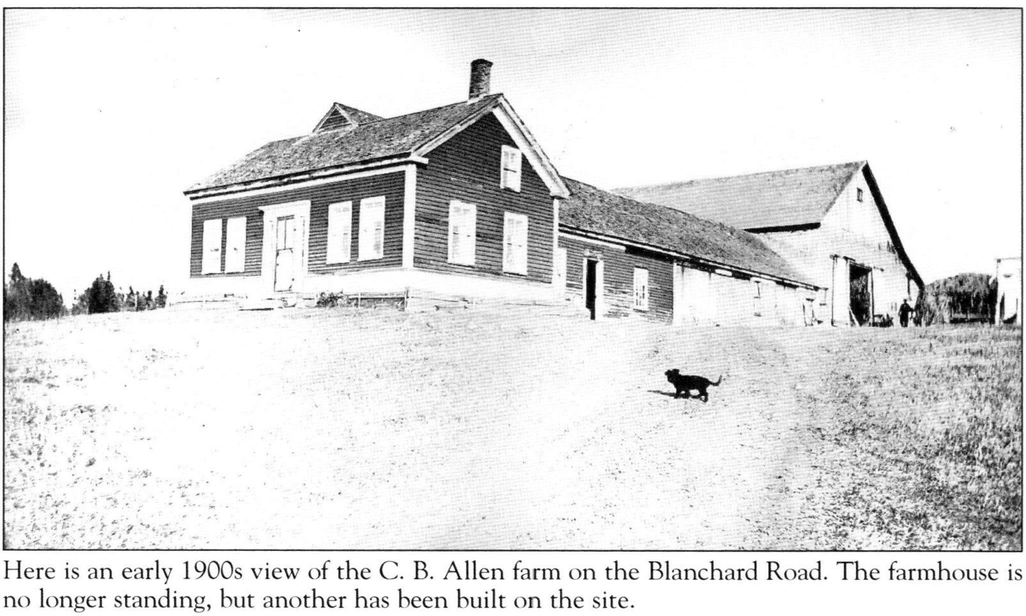

Here is an early 1900s view of the C. B. Allen farm on the Blanchard Road. The farmhouse is no longer standing, but another has been built on the site.

Three

KINEO

Native Americans have been coming to the Kineo Peninsula for thousands of years. Archaeologists and anthropologists have been studying the fruits of excavations for decades, and the results of their studies have added greatly to our knowledge of the so-called Moosehead Lake Indians. Most visitors today get their first view of Mount Kineo from the Greenville-Jackman Road (Route 15) as it tops a gentle slope near the Rockwood Elementary School. It is an impressive sight with an almost sheer cliff that rises more than 700 feet from Moosehead Lake. But aside from its scenic value and service as a gathering place for Native Americans, Kineo has had a long and colorful history as a resort. The first building on the peninsula was a log tavern constructed in 1844. Five hotel buildings have been located there, the last of them was the famous Mount Kineo House, which could accommodate more than 500 guests. Most people arrived at Kineo by way of the Maine Central Railroad's Kineo branch. They unloaded at the Kineo depot building in Rockwood and were transported across the mile or so of open water by steamboat.

Once at the hotel, many people spent three months relaxing and enjoying hunting and fishing or sightseeing excursions. But improvements to the automobile, particularly after World War I, brought the eventual demise of the hotel. Many people believe Kineo is an island, though it is actually a peninsula; to reach the area by automobile in the old days required a trip of more than 100 miles over rough gravel roads. By the 1930s, people were using cars to reach the Moosehead region, and they usually stayed for a week or two rather than long periods. This drastic decline in business saw the elimination of the Maine Central Railroad branch in 1933, and by 1938, the hotel was sold. A crew of wreckers was at work when the huge wooden main hotel caught fire and burned. The complex continued to be operated as a resort, using the so-called annex building and dormitory; by the late 1960s, the resort all but ceased to exist. These photographs represent the Kineo area during the first half of the 1900s.

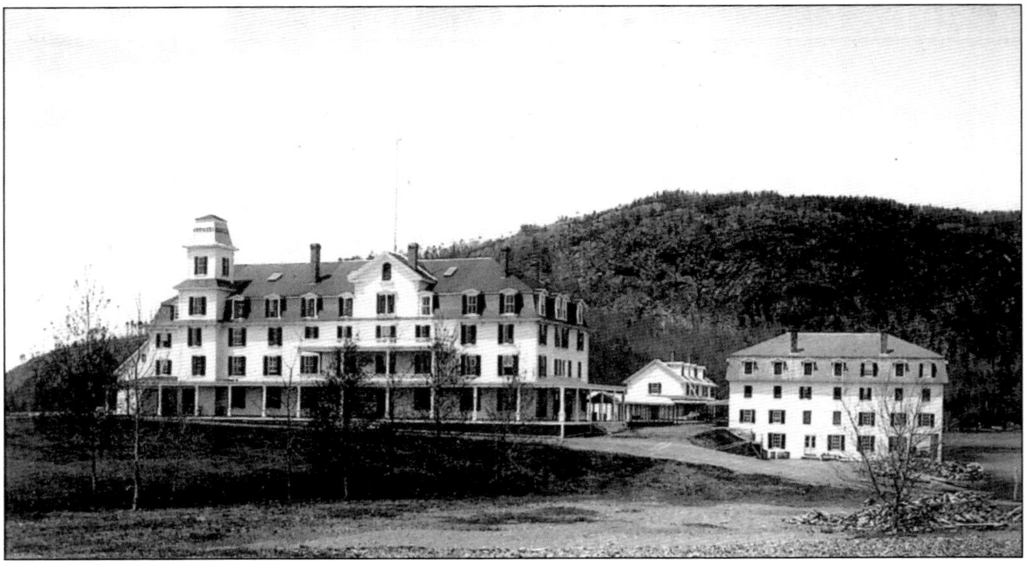

Seen here is an early view of buildings at Mount Kineo. This photograph was taken from the lower peninsula looking north. The building on the left was the main hotel, later replaced by another larger building.

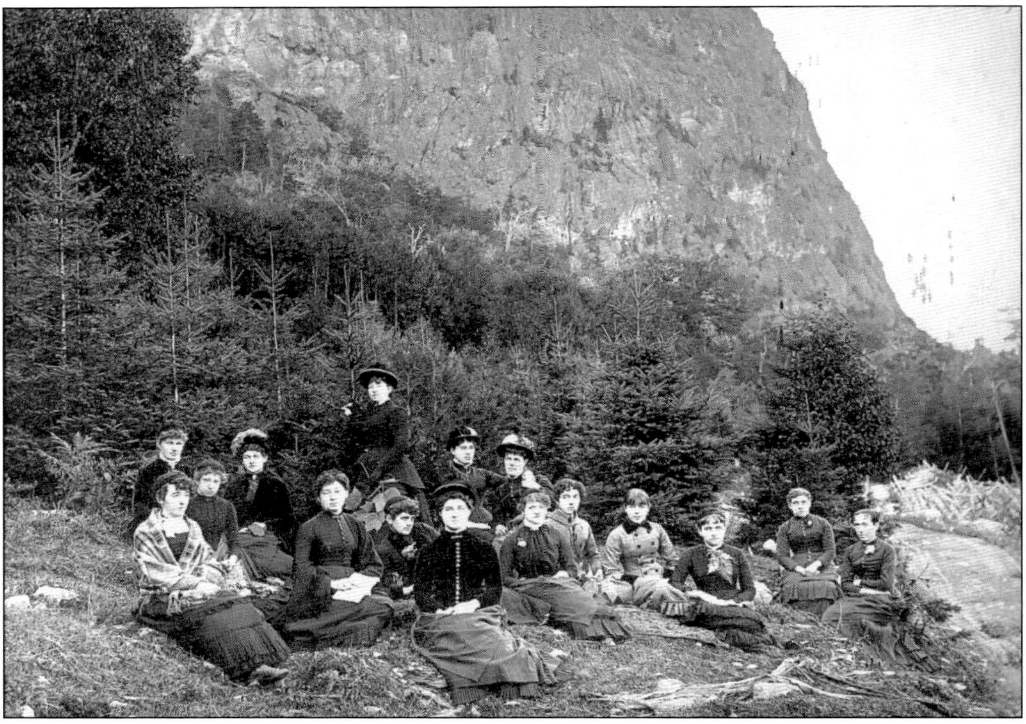

In addition to the hotel at Kineo, the mountain itself brought many visitors in the early days of the 1900s to explore, climb, and enjoy a picnic lunch. This photograph shows a group of 16 young women at the foot of the sheer cliffs. It is not known why there were there.

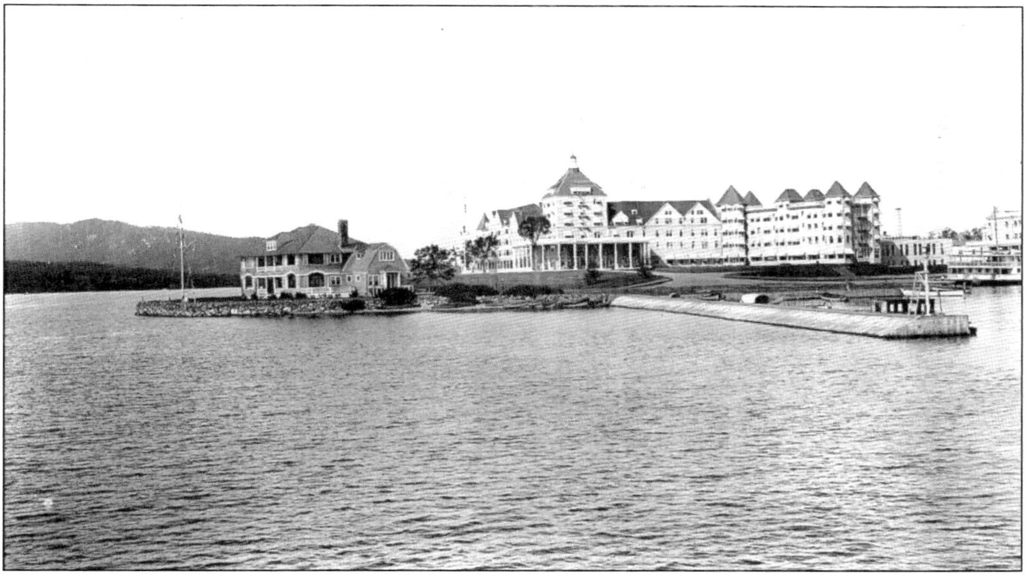

The last Mount Kineo Hotel is shown in this photograph dating from the second decade of the 20th century. The main hotel is at the right center, and on the left at the tip of the peninsula is Breakwater Cottage, so named because of the breakwater at the right in Kineo Cove. This view was taken looking northwest toward Rockwood on the mainland.

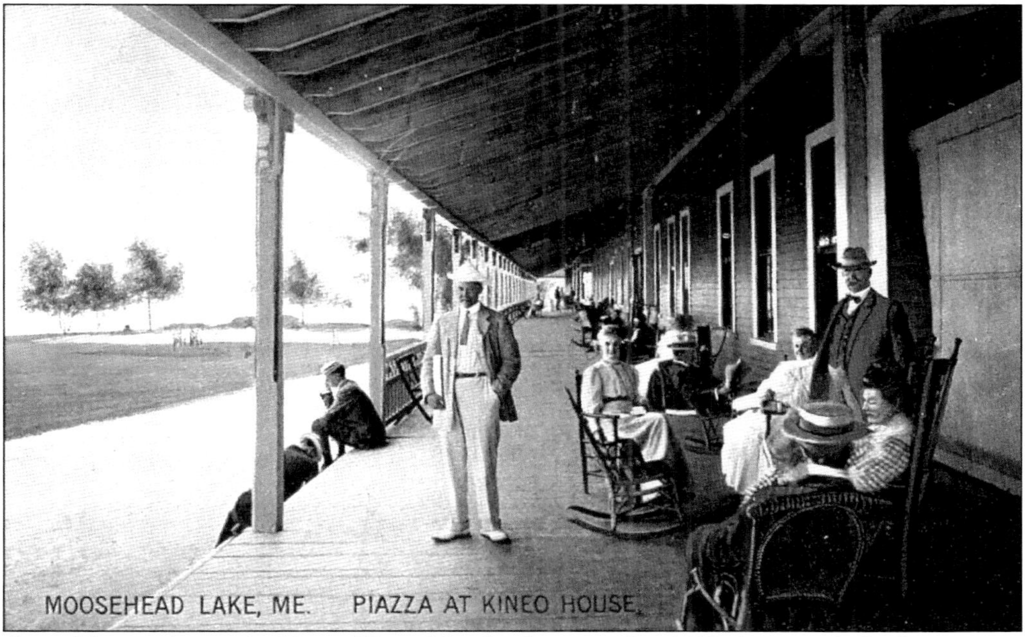

One of the porches at the Mount Kineo Hotel is shown in this 1907 photograph. In the era prior to World War I, hundreds of people came to the Moosehead region to spend several months at the Mount Kineo Hotel. The folks above were likely among those who traveled from big cities to exchange the heat and humidity of summer for cool breezes and brisk temperatures.

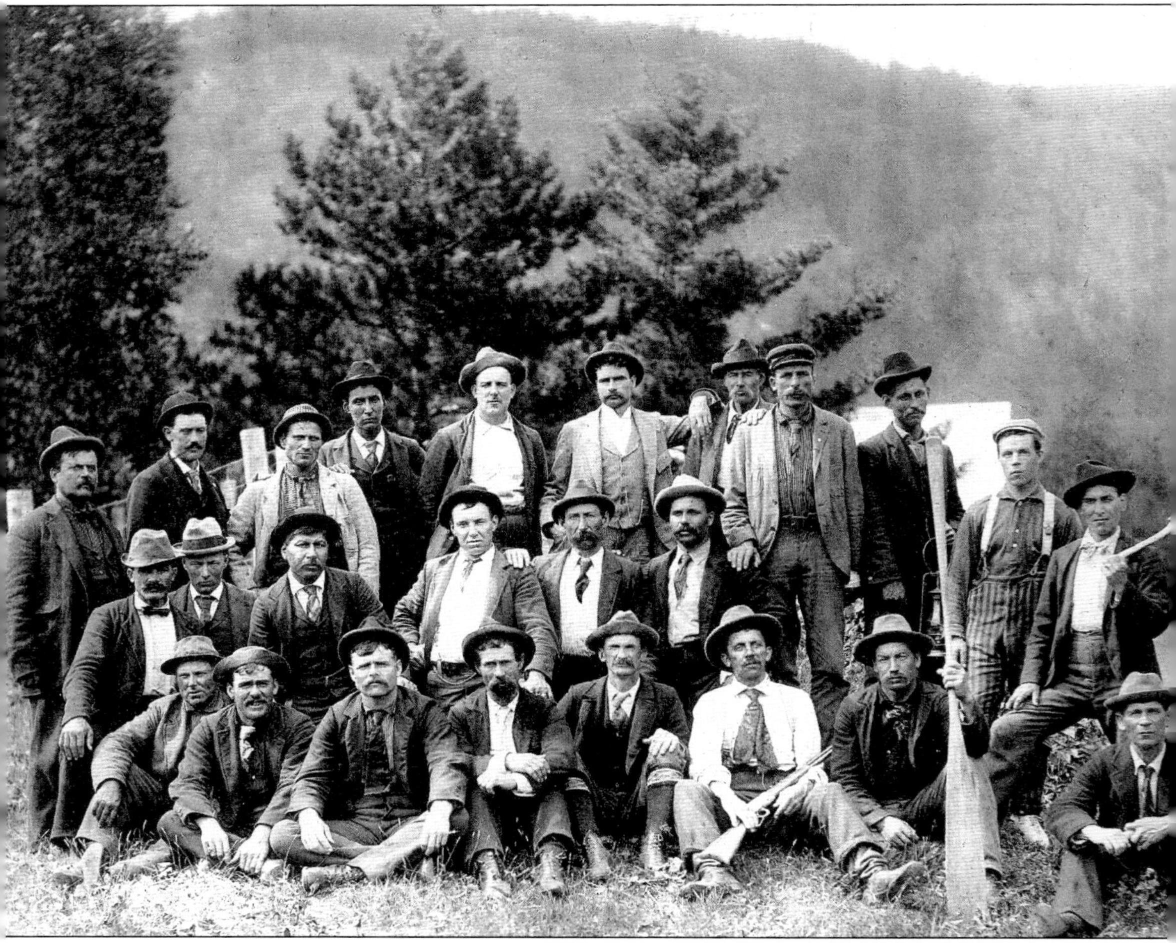

Scores of men from Greenville and Rockwood were employed by the Mount Kineo Hotel to guide visitors on hunting and fishing expeditions. This photograph shows a group of guides in 1912. Among the men pictured here are Bill Meservey, Joe Murray, Amos Thibodeau, Angus Miller, Simon Mayhew, Edgar Harlow, John Mansell, Louis Nicholas, Blackhawk Palmer, Joe Gero, Louis Bernard, Peter Plourde, George Leith, Jim Duff, John Fecto, Roy Nelson, Peter Tomer, Bill Moriarty, Henry Johnson, Oscar Mitchell, Ernest Ham, Frank Tomer, Al Cripps, and Newell Francis.

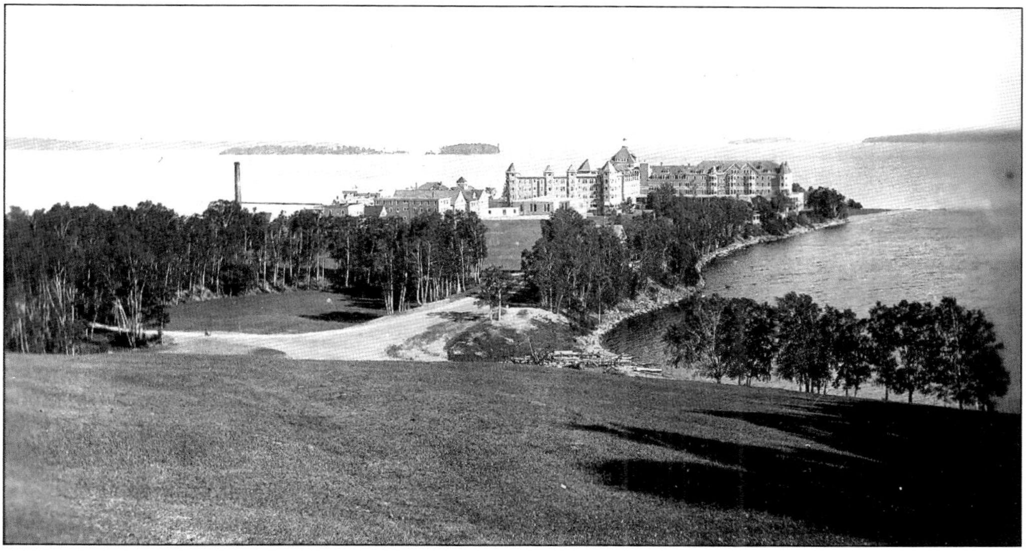

This view looking south from the Kineo golf course in the 1920s shows an expansive view of the Mount Kineo Hotel on the peninsula. The smokestack at the left center is from the heating plant that was located near Kineo Cove. Some photographs show sheep grazing on the steep slope of the golf course.

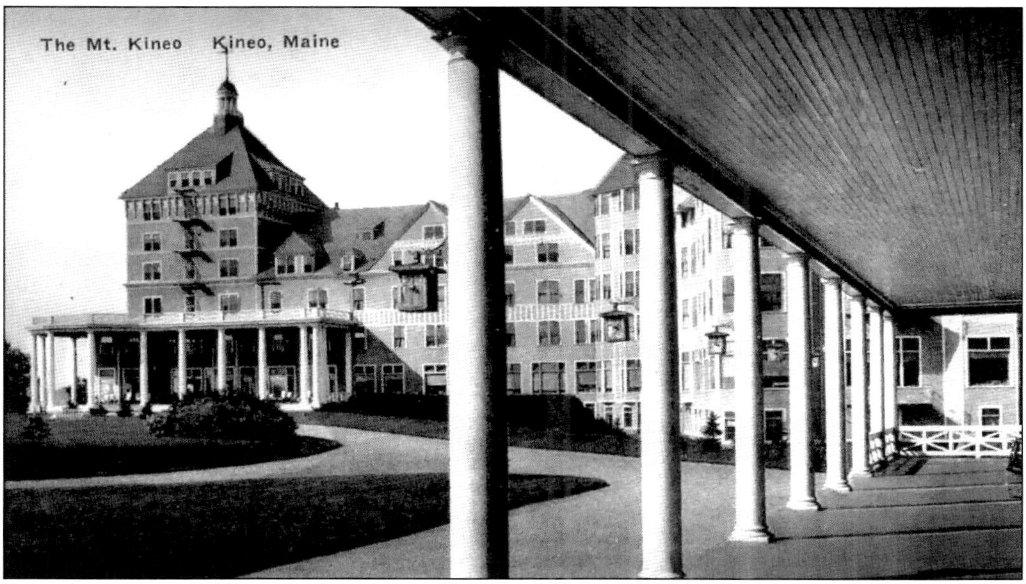

This 1920s photograph offers a sweeping view of the Mount Kineo Hotel. The hotel featured many large porches with white columns. Looking toward the main complex, this view shows one of the wings of the building.

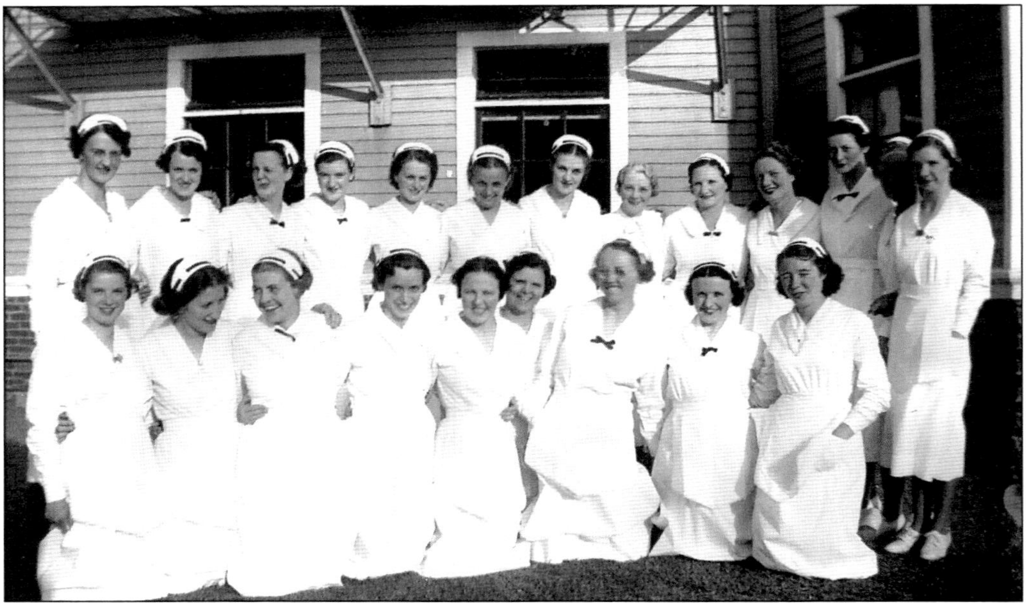

The dining room at the Mount Kineo Hotel was once expected to feed hundreds of people during peak seasons. It required a large kitchen and dining room staff to handle three meals a day. This photograph was taken in the early 1930s and shows 22 ladies who were employed as waitresses. Only one woman is identified. Rhoda Murphy Lamp is at the far left in the second row.

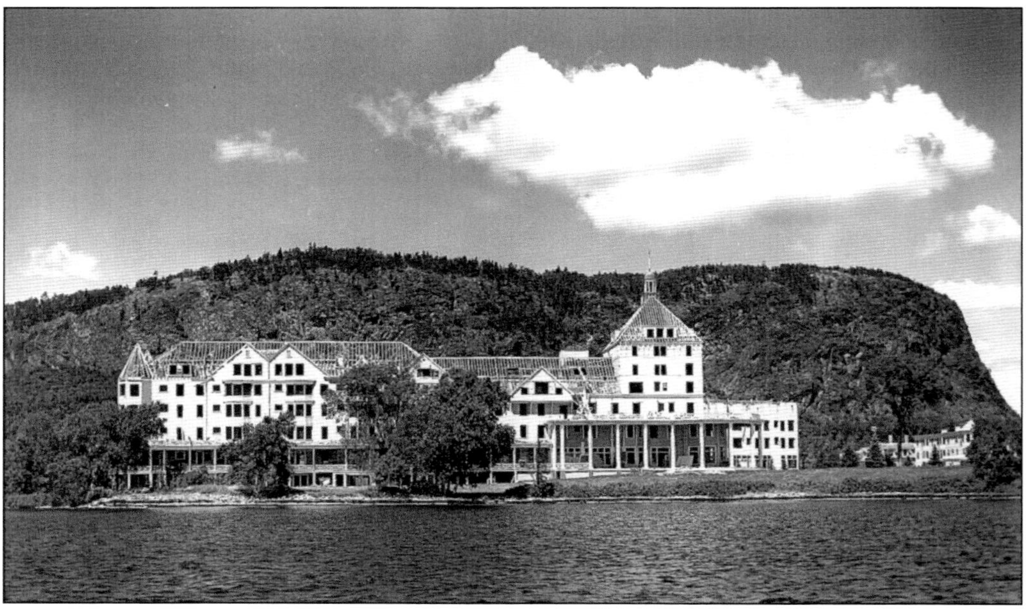

Demolition of the Mount Kineo Hotel took place during 1938. The hotel at one time had accommodations for more than 500, and it was the largest inland water hotel in the United States. But with the automobile increasing in popularity after World War I and more interest in shorter vacations, hotels such as the Mount Kineo went into decline. In the end, the main hotel burned while being demolished. The annex building and dormitory remained.

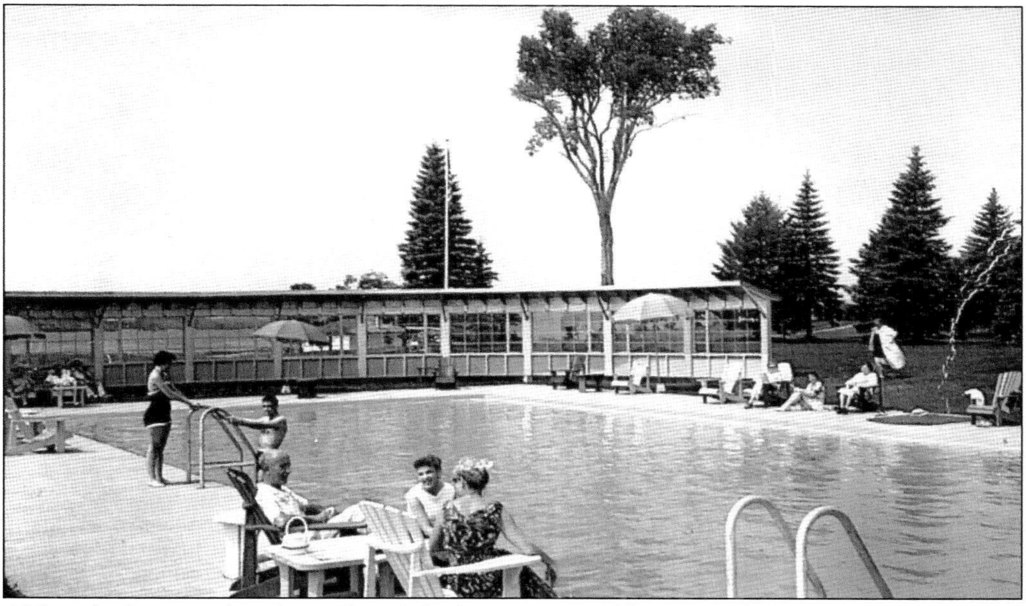

Although the main hotel was demolished prior to World War II, the Kineo name remained with accommodations in other buildings. It underwent several ownerships before being closed for good. This 1950s photograph shows the championship swimming pool with its glassed-in windbreaker. At the time, Kineo resort was a 1,150-acre estate with a private golf course, trapshooting, tennis, and fishing.

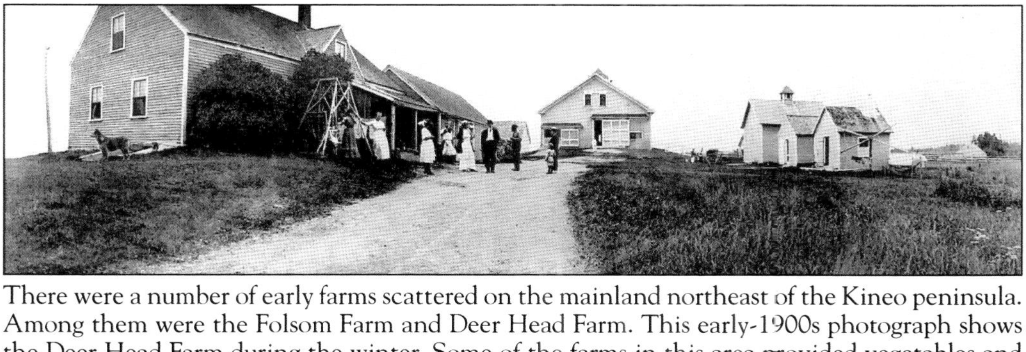

There were a number of early farms scattered on the mainland northeast of the Kineo peninsula. Among them were the Folsom Farm and Deer Head Farm. This early-1900s photograph shows the Deer Head Farm during the winter. Some of the farms in this area provided vegetables and other commodities to the Mount Kineo Hotel.

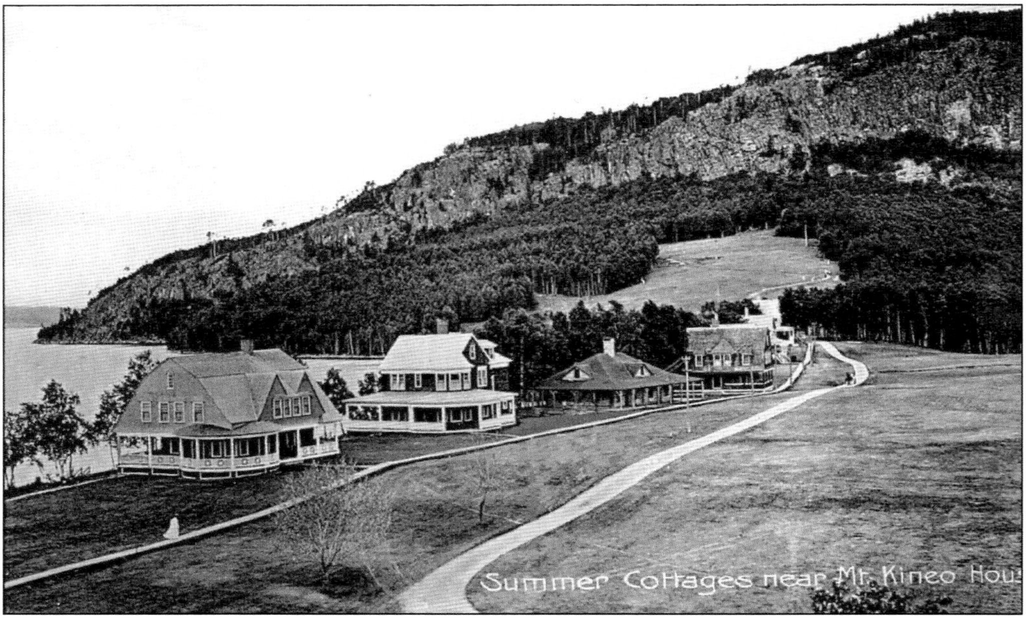

In addition to the Mount Kineo Hotel, a number of privately owned summer cottages were constructed on the west shore of the Kineo peninsula. This photograph was taken c. 1910 and shows several of the cottages; Mount Kineo and the golf course are in the background. Cottages remain today and can be easily seen from the mainland in Rockwood.

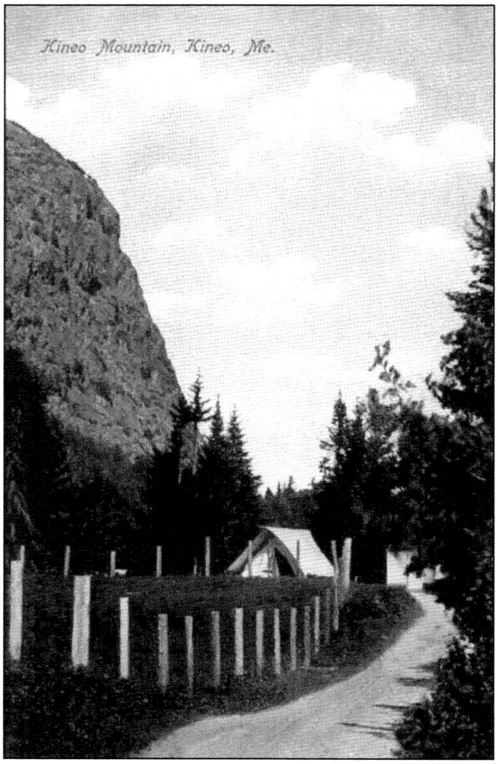

In addition to luxury accommodations in the Mount Kineo Hotel, guests were offered the opportunity to rough it in tents near the base of the cliffs of Mount Kineo. A gravel roadway led from the hotel complex to Pebble Beach and past the location seen in this c. 1920s photograph. This site was also popular with Native Americans in earlier days.

Four

Rockwood

Rockwood has been tied by history, and perhaps at one time in pre-glacial days by geography, to Mount Kineo. Not only was Kineo linked to the Paleo-Indian period but also Rockwood, which has evidence of Native American activity at Birch Point. In the early 1900s, the Maine Central Railroad reached Rockwood, but it was the 1930s before a road was constructed between Greenville and Rockwood. Rockwood is believed to have been settled during the Civil War era. Among the early settlers were families from Nova Scotia and other Maritime Provinces. The first bridge across the Moose River was a floating span built in the late 1800s at the mouth of the river. Another bridge was constructed farther up river around 1914, the same year a road to Pittston Farm was built. The name Rockwood is believed to have come from Hiram Rockwood Page, who decided c. 1909 that the railroad's Kineo station needed a post office. Never a large settlement, Rockwood had two stores and two churches in the early 1900s. The Rockwood Community Church, known affectionately as the Rockwood "Log Chapel," was built in the 1940s and was featured in a *Saturday Evening Post* Christmas issue in the 1950s.

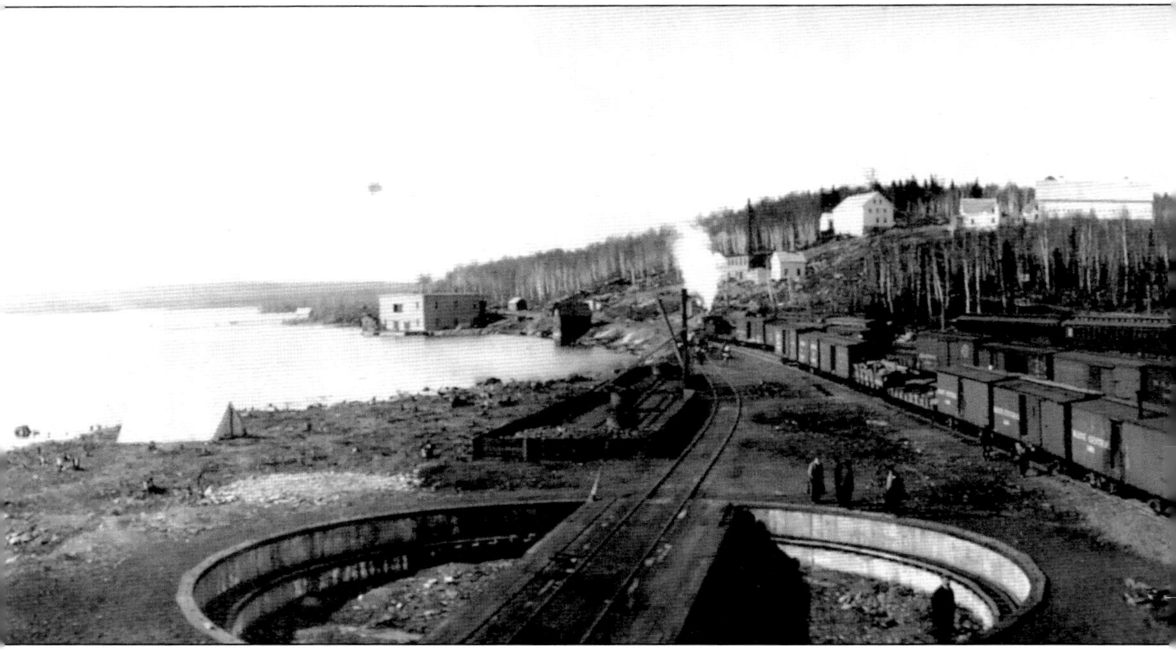

This panoramic view of the Kineo Docks area shows several boxcars of the Maine Central Railroad *c.* 1920. A turntable is shown at the left and buildings of the Great Northern Paper Company are on the hill to the left center. Buildings to the right include the hotel and store.

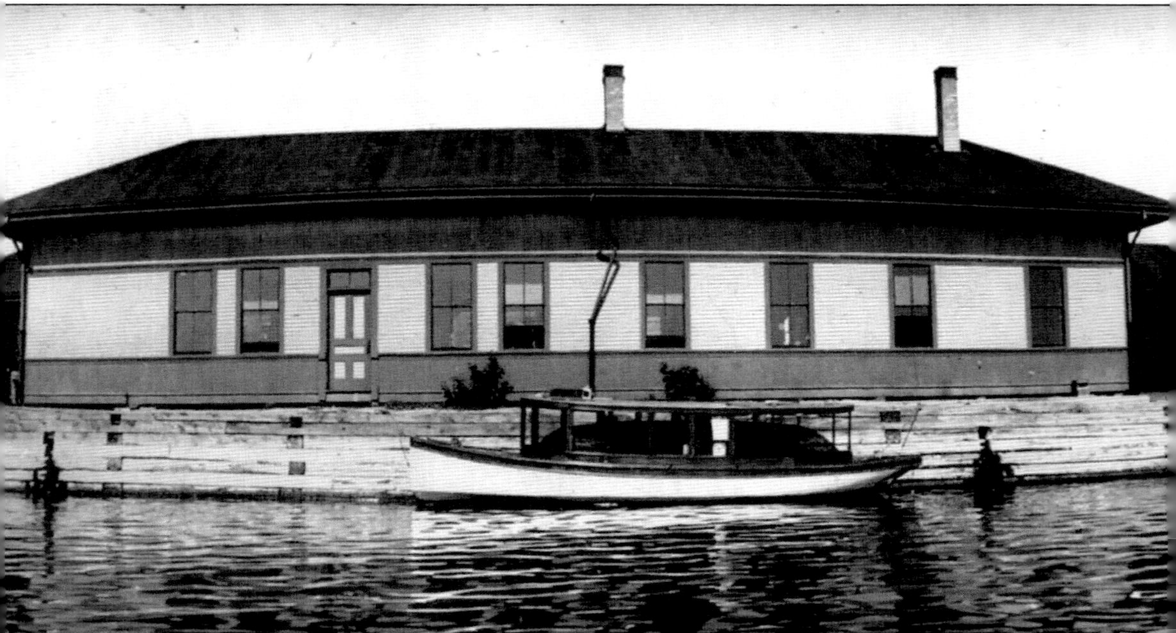

It was a hectic time when a Maine Central Railroad passenger train arrived at the Kineo Station in Rockwood with passengers for the Mount Kineo Hotel. This 1920s photograph shows three steamers lined up at the right to receive passengers; from left to right are the

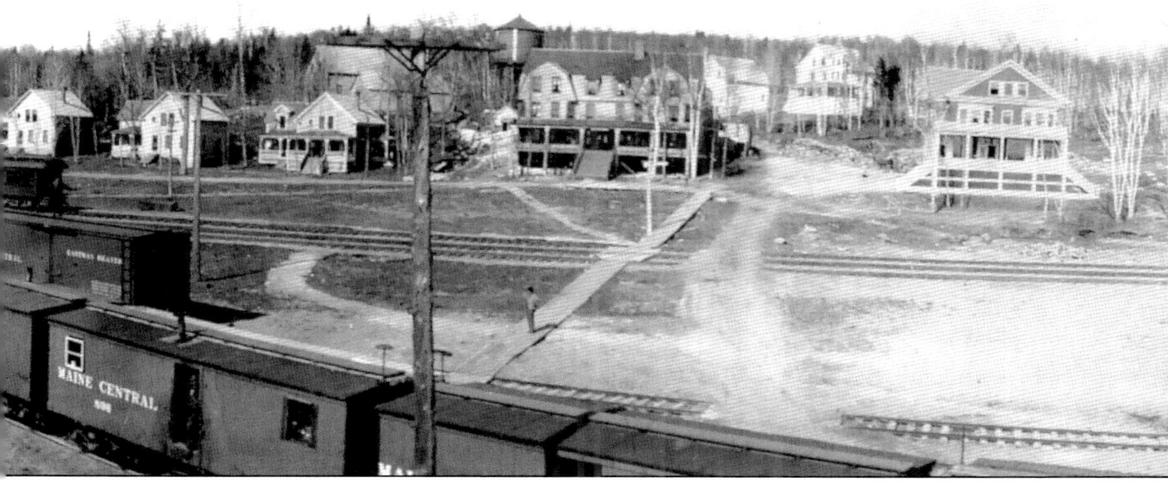

In addition to freight, passengers were also transported on this line (notice the passenger cars at the upper left center). Today, the area in the foreground is a public boat launch.

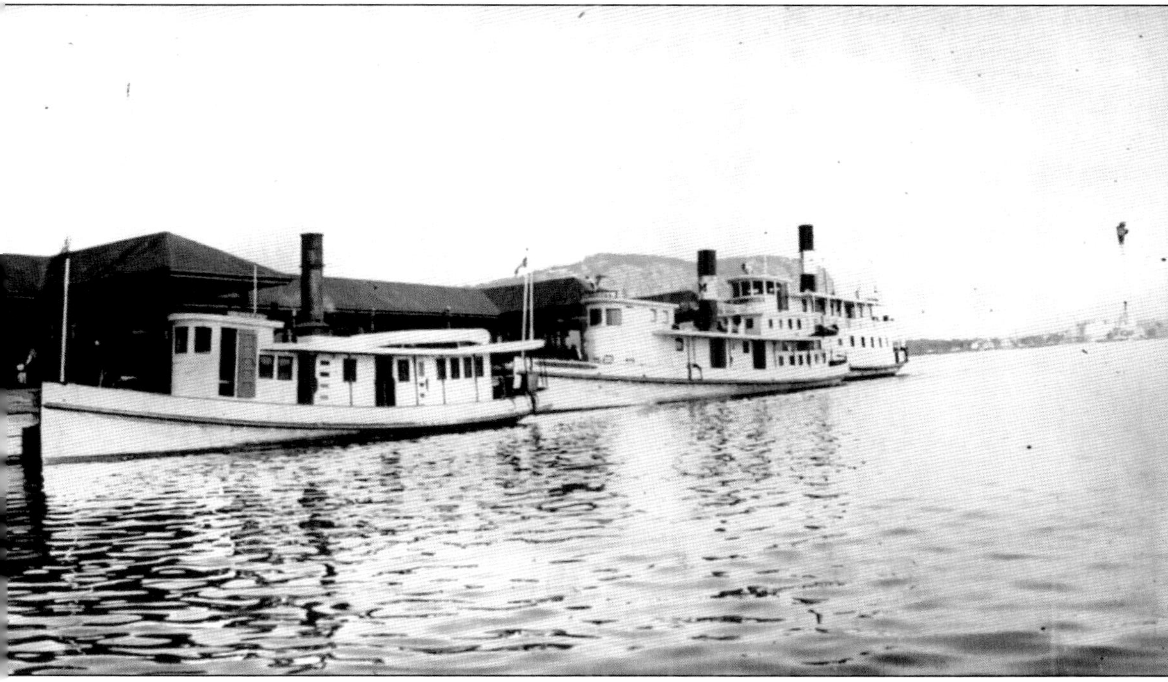

Olivette, *Moosehead*, and *Twilight*. The small craft at the far left is unnamed. The rail line was removed in later years, and the Kineo station was demolished. A set of storage sheds was on the site until it was converted to a public boat launch.

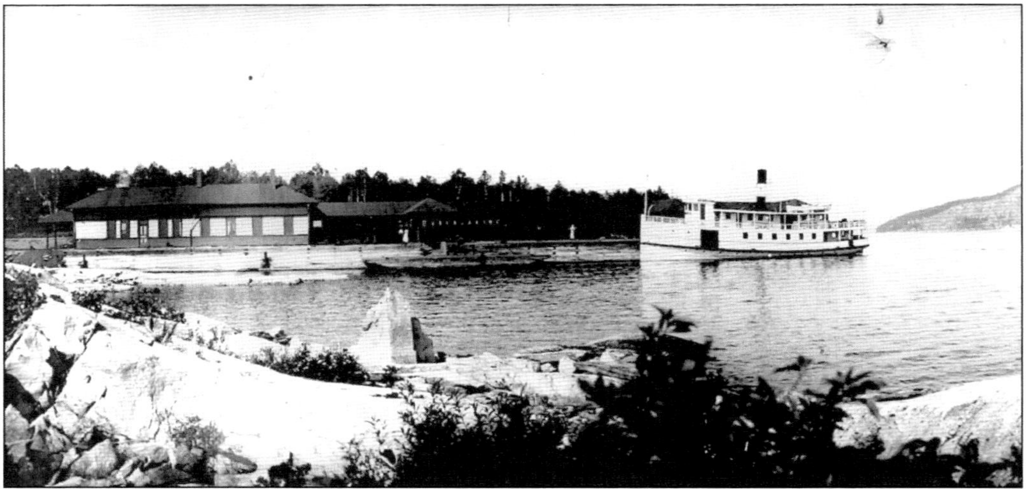

This is another view of the Kineo station of the Maine Central Railroad *c.* 1920. The steamer *Twilight* is docked at the end of the pier. Mount Kineo is in the right background. Thousands of summer visitors were transported from this railroad station to the Mount Kineo Hotel over the decades.

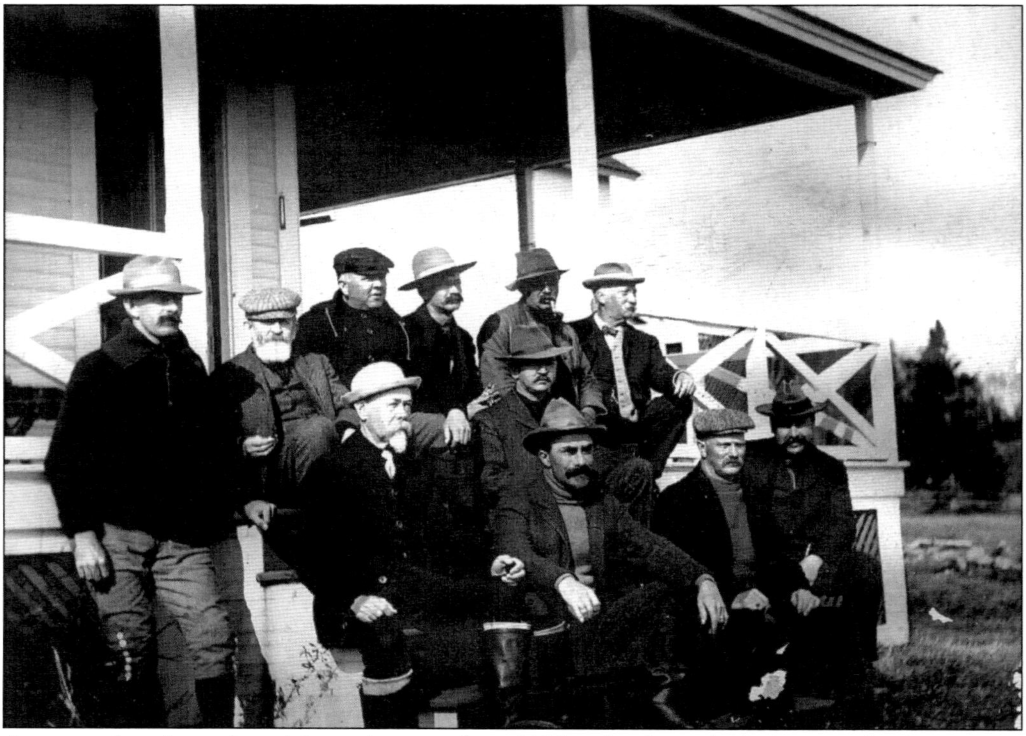

A group of guides gathered for a photograph in 1905 in Rockwood. Unfortunately, their names are not known. Many men in the Rockwood and Greenville area were employed during the early 1900s at the Mount Kineo Hotel as guides during the summer and fall months. They also worked at a number of other sporting camps in the area such as Maynard's-in-Maine on the Moose River.

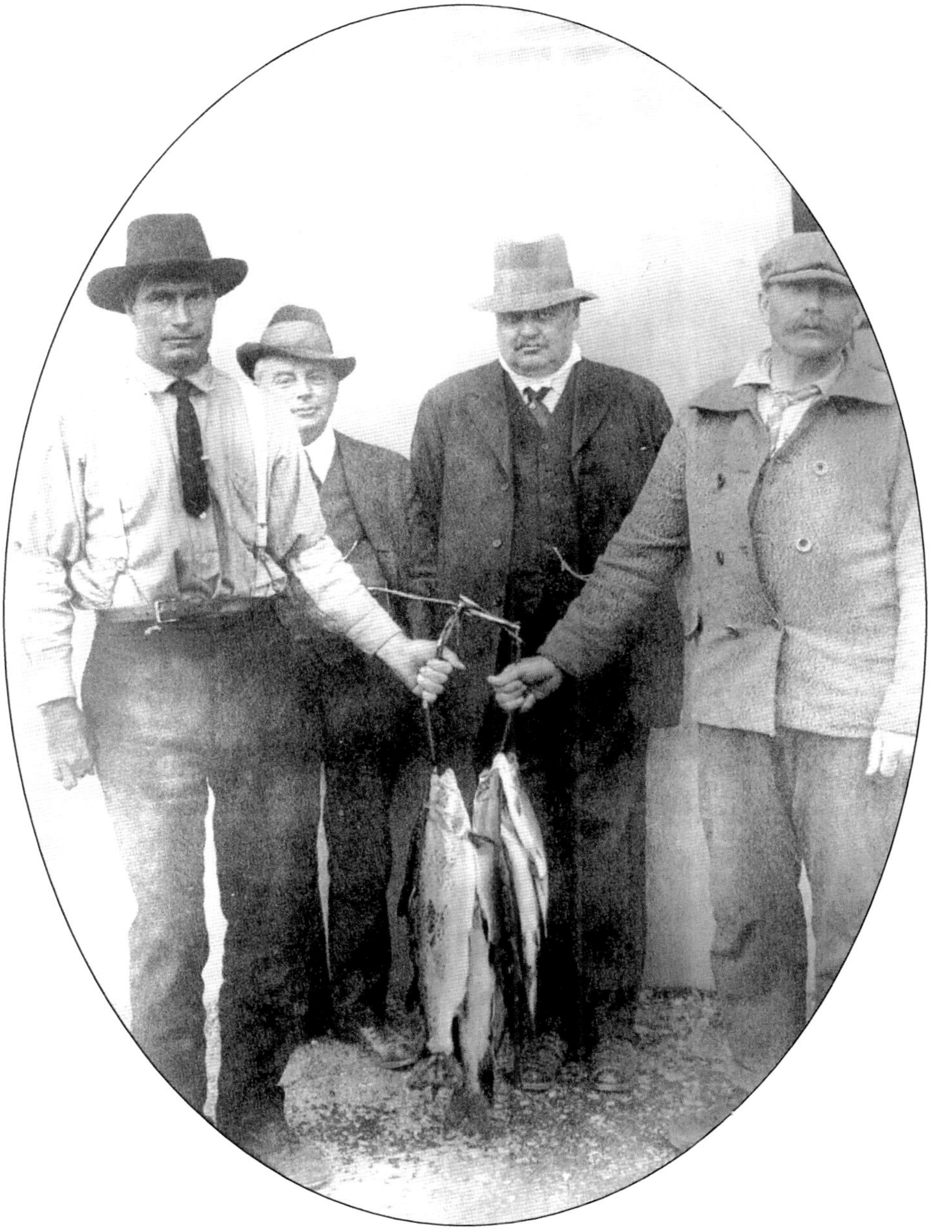

Two well-known guides who worked at the Mount Kineo Hotel during the early 1900s were Duncan Matheson (left) and Crawford Johnson (right). They are shown with two sports and a string of fish at the Mount Kineo Hotel c. 1905. Matheson was born in Charlottetown, Prince Edward Island, and moved to Greenville in 1884. He died in Greenville in 1944. Johnson was born at Seven Islands and lived in Rockwood for 74 years. He died in 1959.

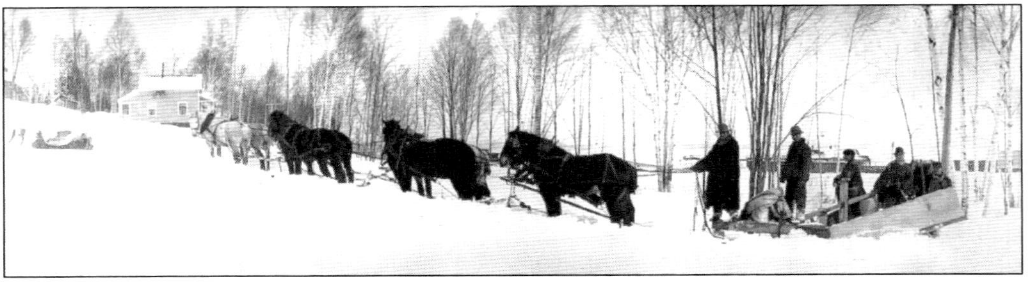

This panoramic view shows a Great Northern Paper Company snowplow at work in Rockwood in 1910. The plow was pulled by a team of eight horses and opened a one-lane roadway. The photograph was taken on Northern Hill. The Maine Central Railroad Kineo station is located in the right background. The extra weight in the rear of the plow helped to cut through the snow.

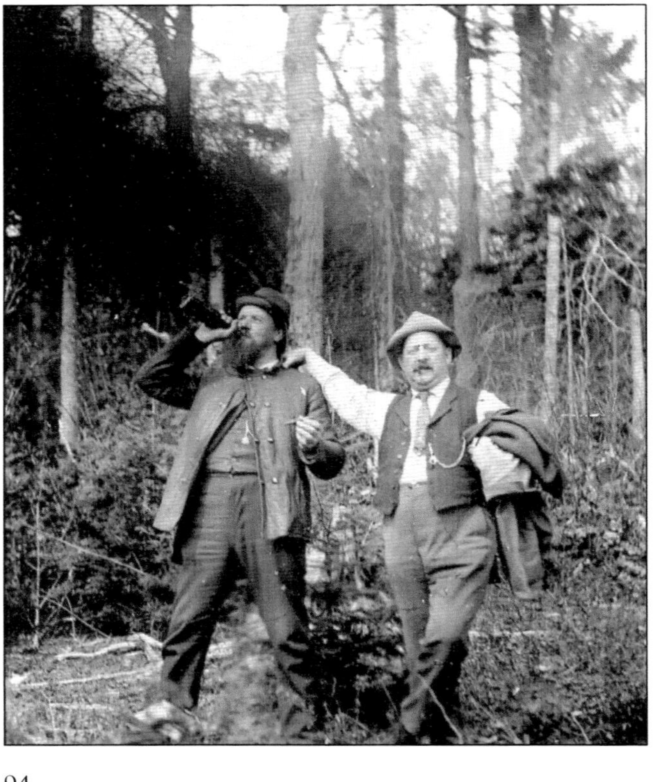

Hunting and fishing were and still are major activities in the Moosehead region. In this c. 1910 photograph, David Fales (left) is apparently imitating a moose call while his friend Billie McKenie listens. Hamming it up for the camera was a feature of many early photographs. The men were residents of Rockwood.

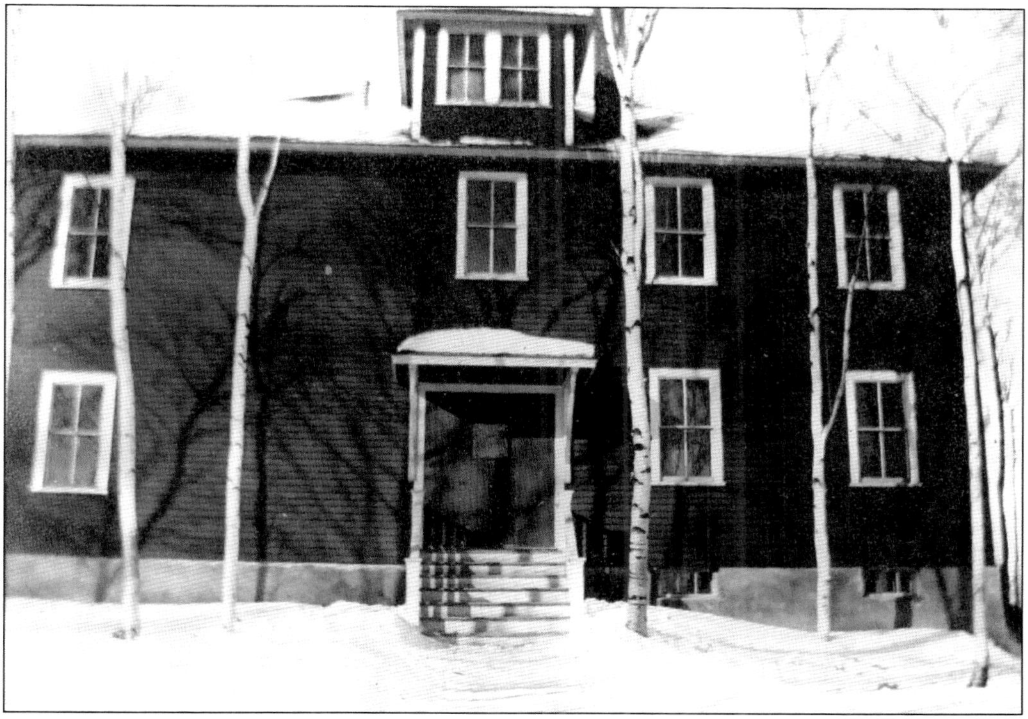

For many years, this building was known as the Rockwood Hall and school building. There have been several different schools in the Rockwood area, along both the Moose River and in the village.

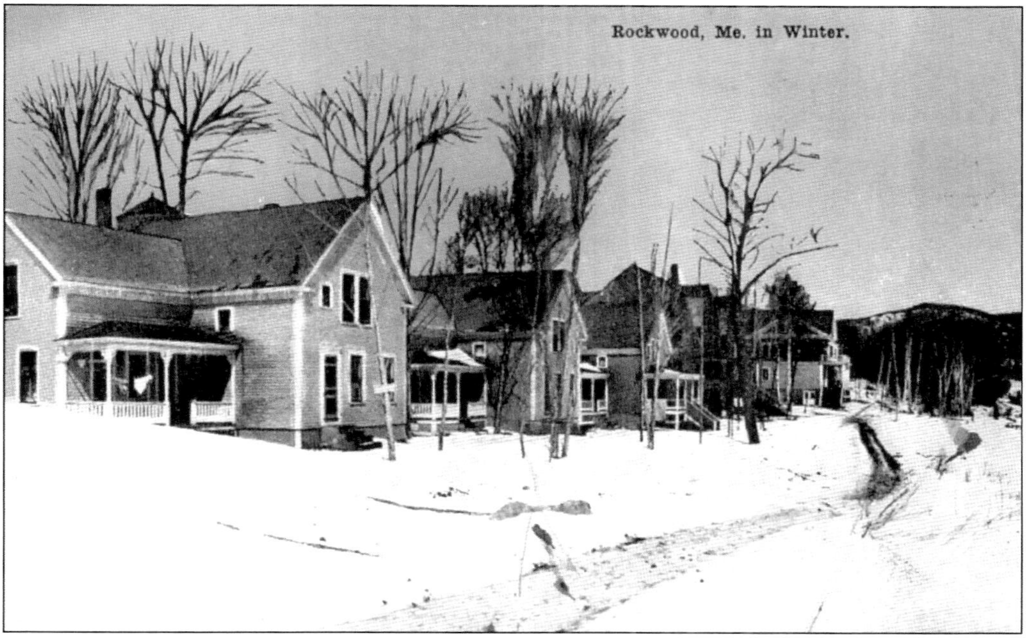

This view of Rockwood along the Moosehead Lake waterfront was likely taken in the 1920s. Several of the buildings shown are no longer standing.

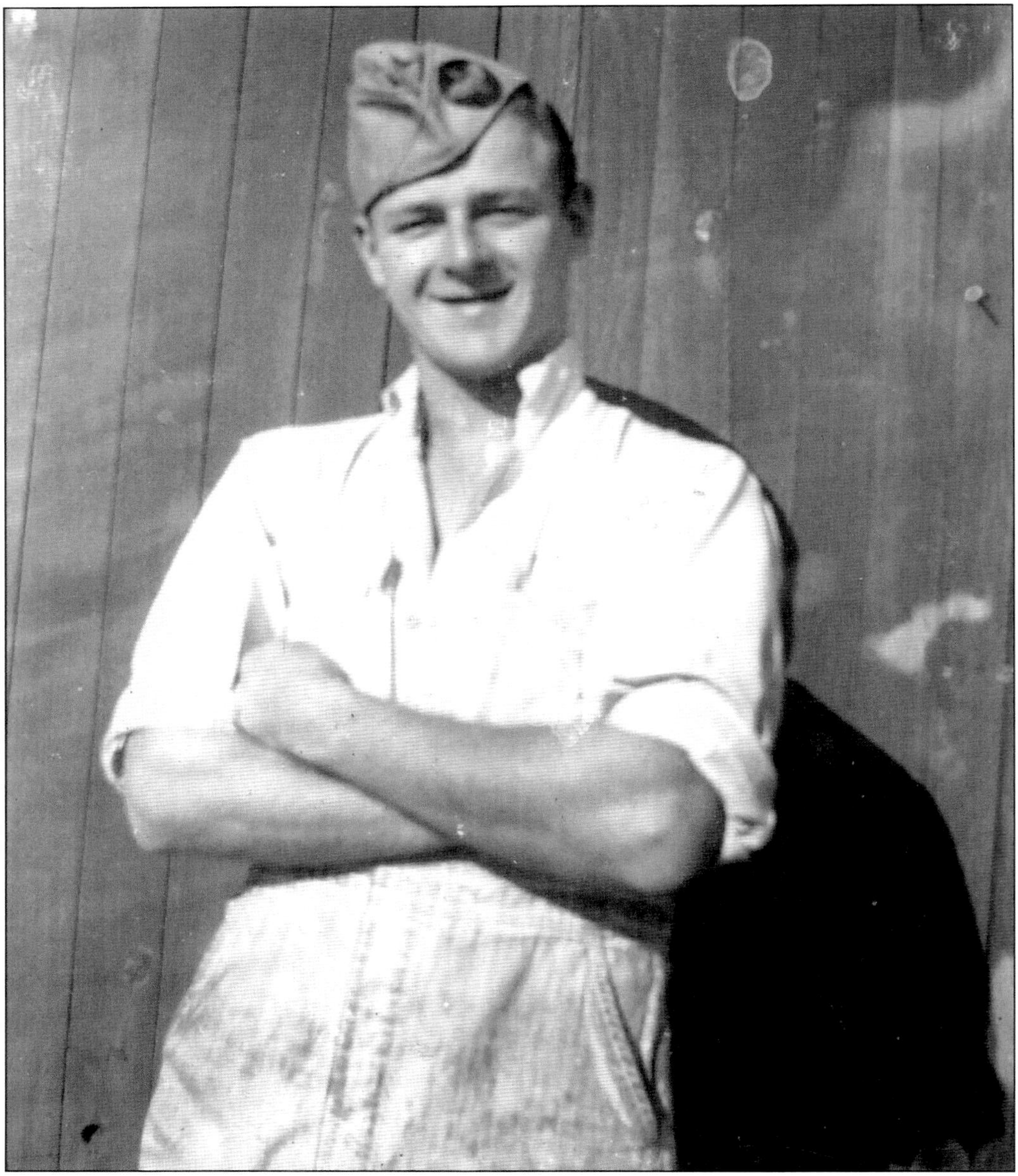

Frederick York was the only Rockwood man killed in action during World War II. He was born on August 12, 1918, in Rockwood, son of Ralph and Nora Smart York. He attended the one-room Rockwood school and graduated from Higgins Classical Institute in Charleston. He had a passion for flying and went to flying school in Englewood, California. After graduating, he became a member of the U.S. Army Air Corps. He signed up after being told that if he volunteered for the Flying Tigers American Group or the Royal Air Force American Eagle Squadron in the United Kingdom he would be given the rank of captain in the U.S. Army Air Corps upon return to the United States. In the early morning hours of September 18, 1942, he was killed when his Spitfire crashed during aerial combat with a German pilot. At the time of his death, he was a sergeant pilot in the Royal Air Force, a rank equivalent to second lieutenant in the U.S. Army Air Corps.

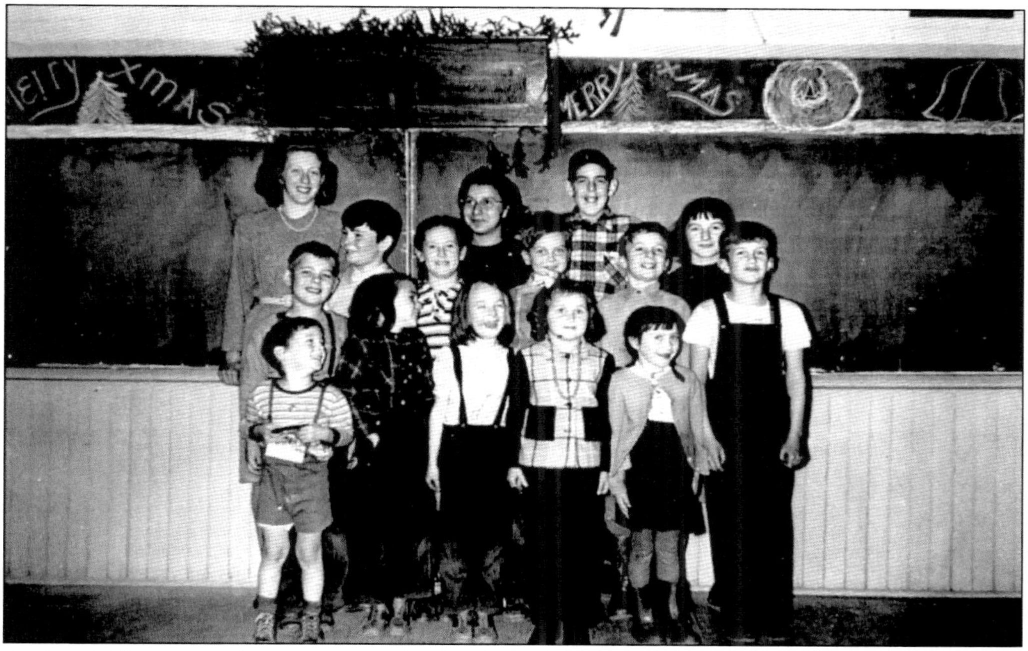

Louise Sullivan was the teacher at the Rockwood Village School when this photograph was taken in November 1948. From left to right are the following: (first row) Maurice Richards, Jack Rancourt, Gail Rancourt, Deanne Rancourt, Jo-ann Whitten, Lorraine Tupper, and Guy Whitten; (second row) Scott Fraser, Sharon Fraser, Donald Ayer, Ron Rancourt, and Marie Tupper; (third row) Louise Sullivan, Virginia Gardiner, and George Fogg.

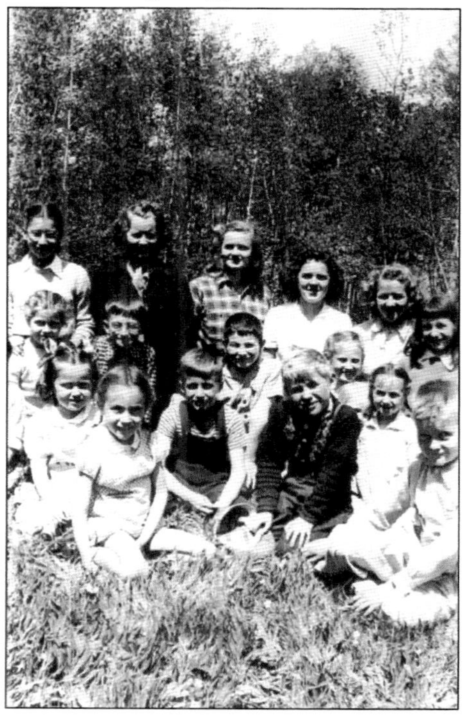

Pupils of the Rockwood Village School settled down for a photograph during an outing in the 1940s. Students are, from left to right, as follows: (first row) Jo-ann (Whitten) Somers, Gail (Rancourt) Turmel, Guy Whitten, Maurice Richards, Deanne Rancourt, and Donald Ayer; (second row) Sandra (Whitten) Ryder, Jerry Hyson, Scott Fraser, and Sharon (Fraser) Breton; (third row) Virginia (Gardiner) Pelletier, Annie Macomber (teacher), Betty (Ames) Moreau, Donna (Hamilton) Ryder, and Fern (Richards) Moulton.

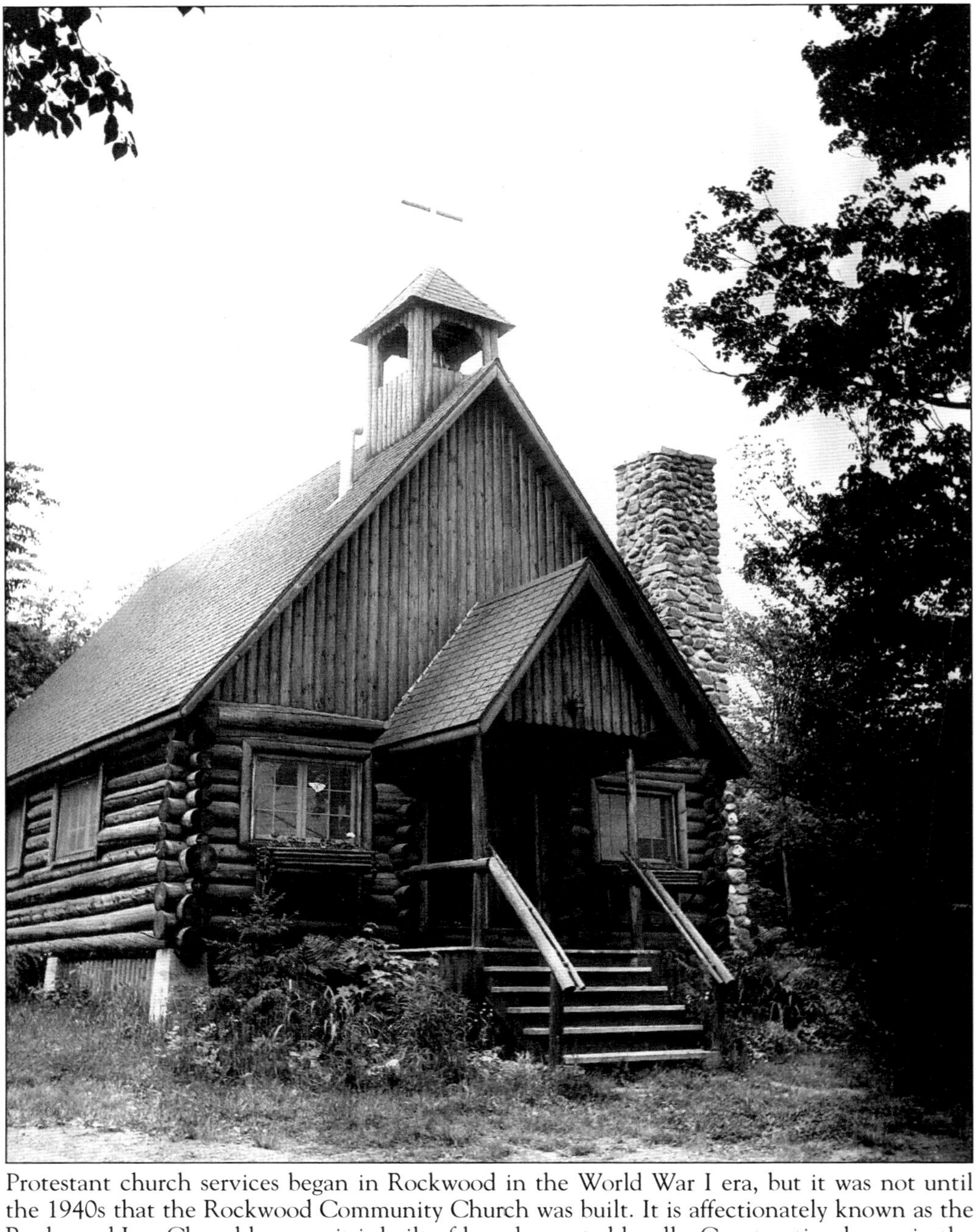

Protestant church services began in Rockwood in the World War I era, but it was not until the 1940s that the Rockwood Community Church was built. It is affectionately known as the Rockwood Log Chapel because it is built of logs, harvested locally. Construction began in the summer of 1948. Construction did not take long and the building was dedicated on October 17, 1948, with three services. The first wedding took place in the chapel on November 21, 1948, when Frances Grace Cyr of Rockwood exchanged vows with Frederick H. Bigney, son of Mr. and Mrs. Fred D. Bigney of Greenville.

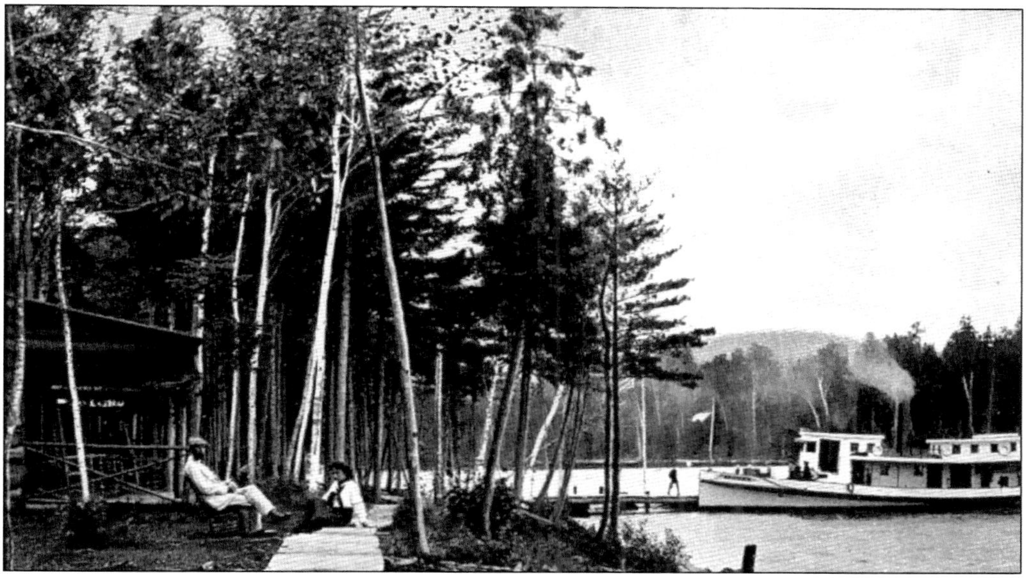

This *c*. 1900 photograph shows a steamer that has pulled up at the Gilbert & Coombs Camps at West Outlet (south of Rockwood). The sporting camp operation was located midway between Rockwood and the East Outlet (Kennebec River) of Moosehead Lake.

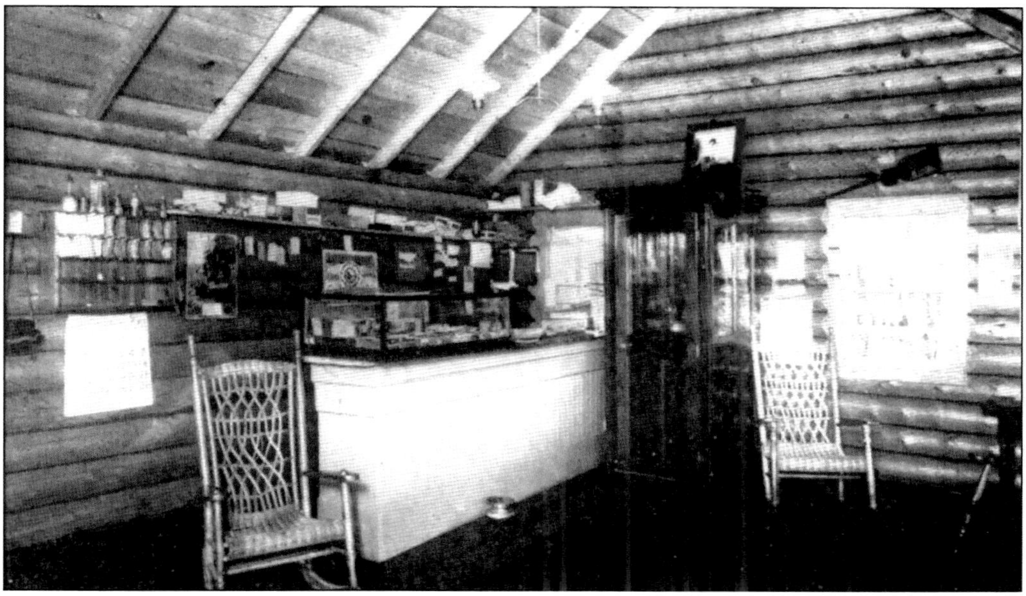

This interior view of West Outlet Camps (then known as MacKenzie's West Outlet Camps on Moosehead Lake) shows the office, located in one of the log cabins. At the time, the sporting camps featured continuously available hot and cold water, electric lights, and heat.

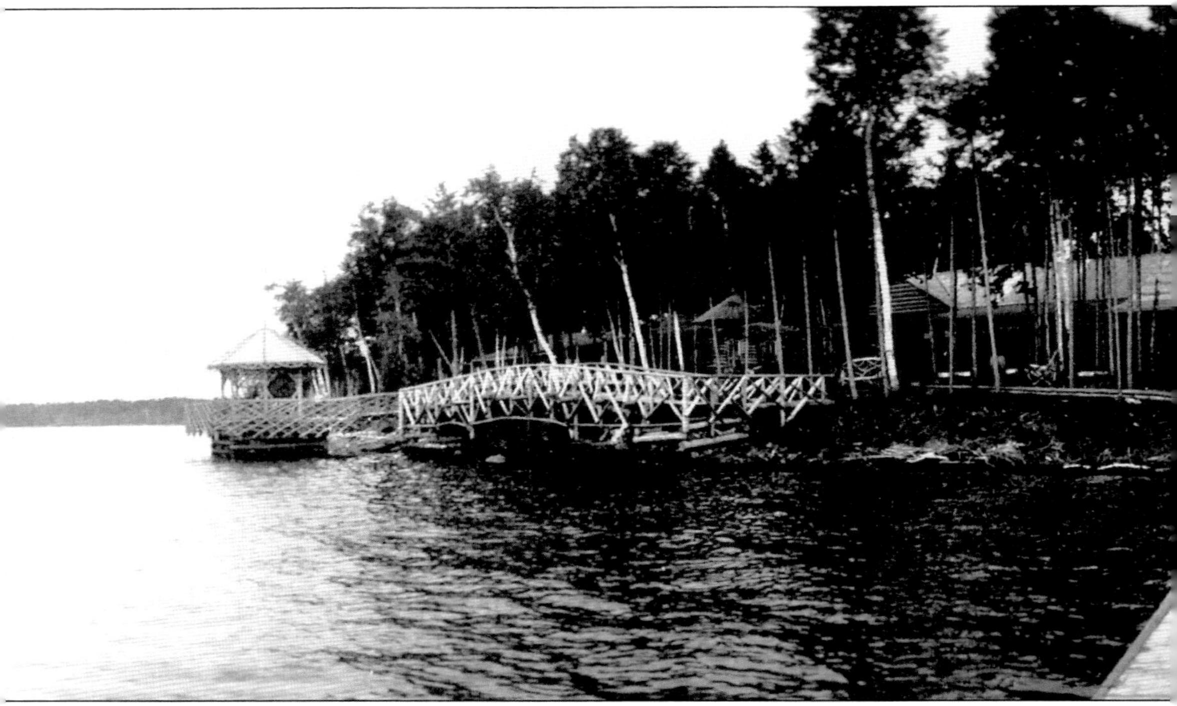

These panoramic photographs of West Outlet Camps from Moosehead Lake provide views of summer and winter scenes. The top photograph was taken from the end of the long pier that extended into the lake and offers a nice view of the vessel *West Outlet* before it had been put

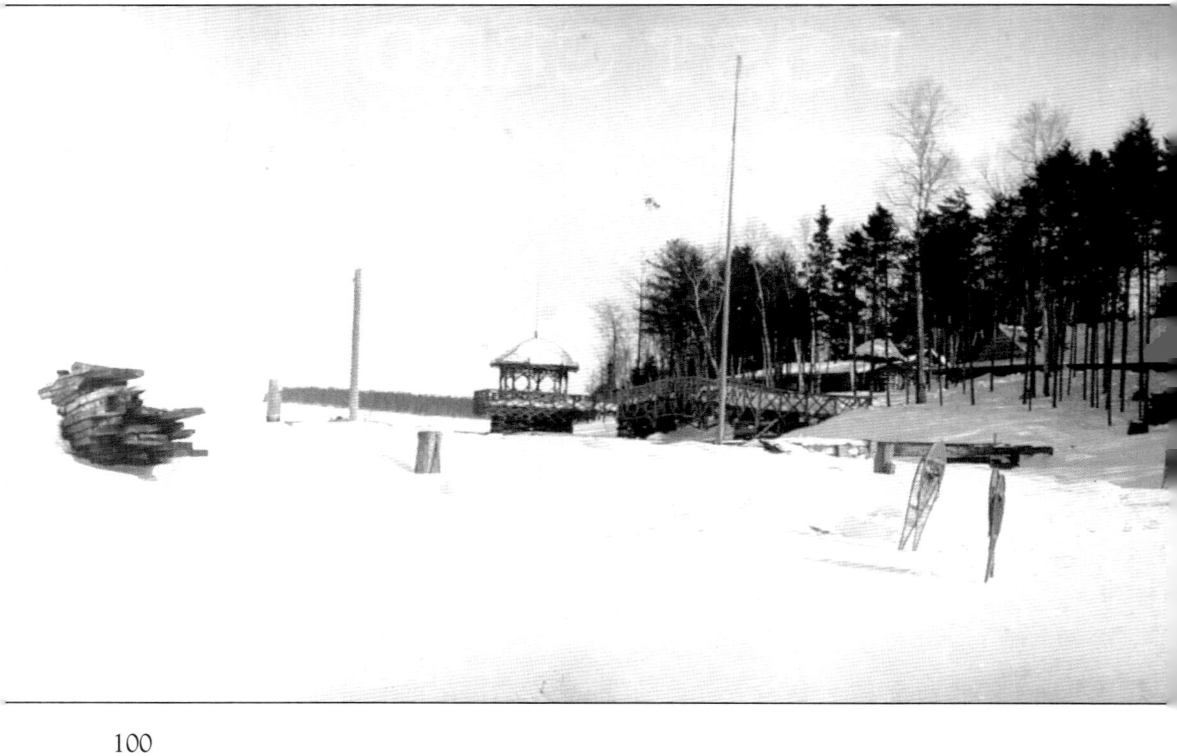

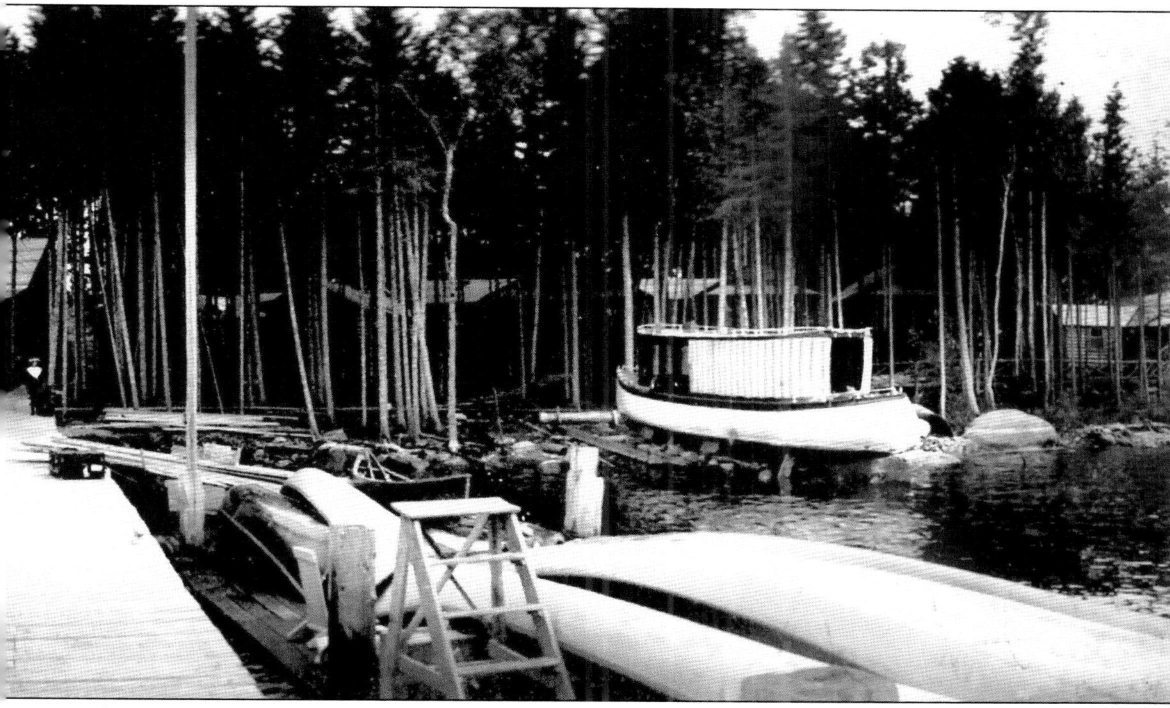

into the water for summer transportation. The bottom photograph is essentially the same scene in winter, with the *West Outlet* in wraps. There is a nice view in each photograph of the gazebo at the far left, which juts out into Moosehead Lake.

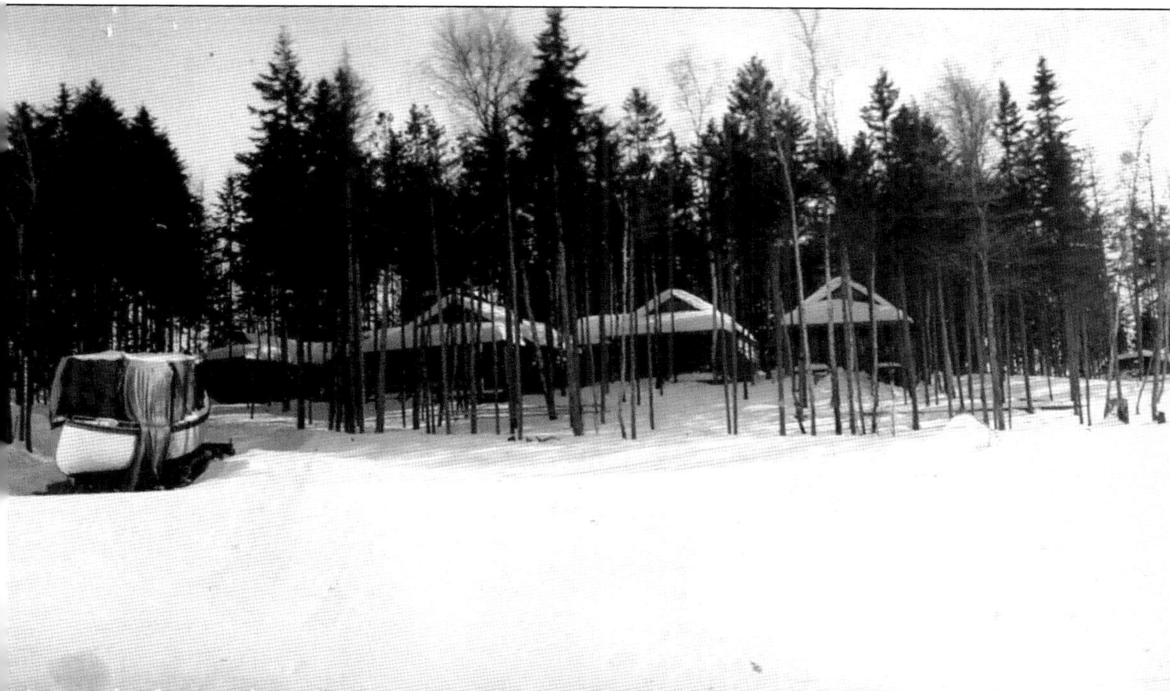

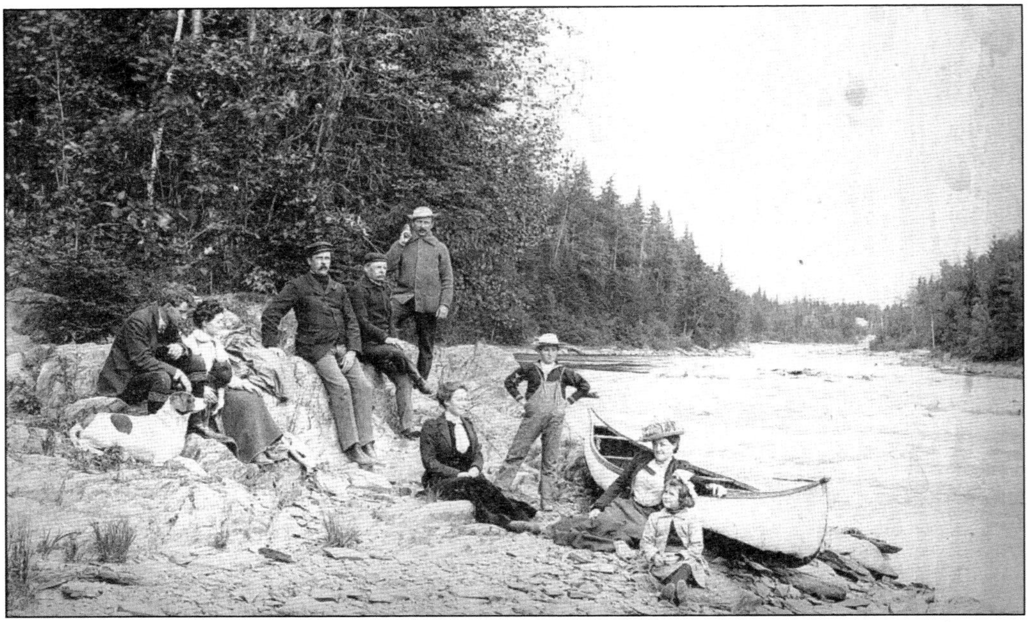

The Kennebec River has been a favorite waterway for canoeing for generations. In the very early 1900s, these people posed for a photograph below the East Outlet dam at Moosehead Lake, apparently while on a canoeing expedition. The Kennebec River is also popular for fishing and whitewater rafting.

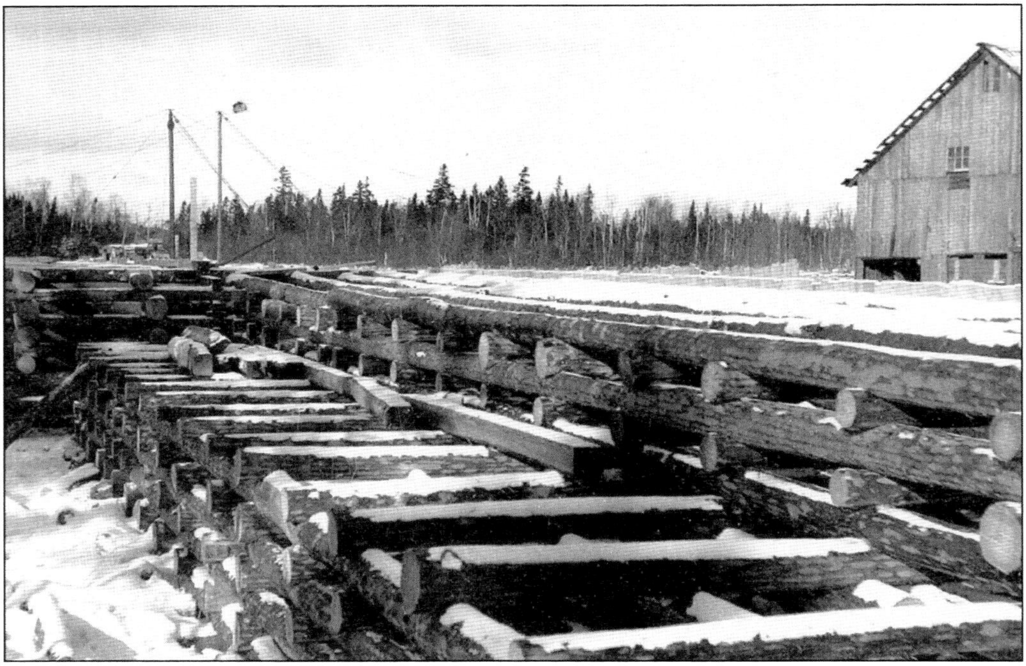

The first dam at East Outlet was a wooden structure, shown here *c.* 1900. This photograph was taken in the winter and shows the sluiceway between the two poles at the left center. This dam was later replaced with a more modern structure.

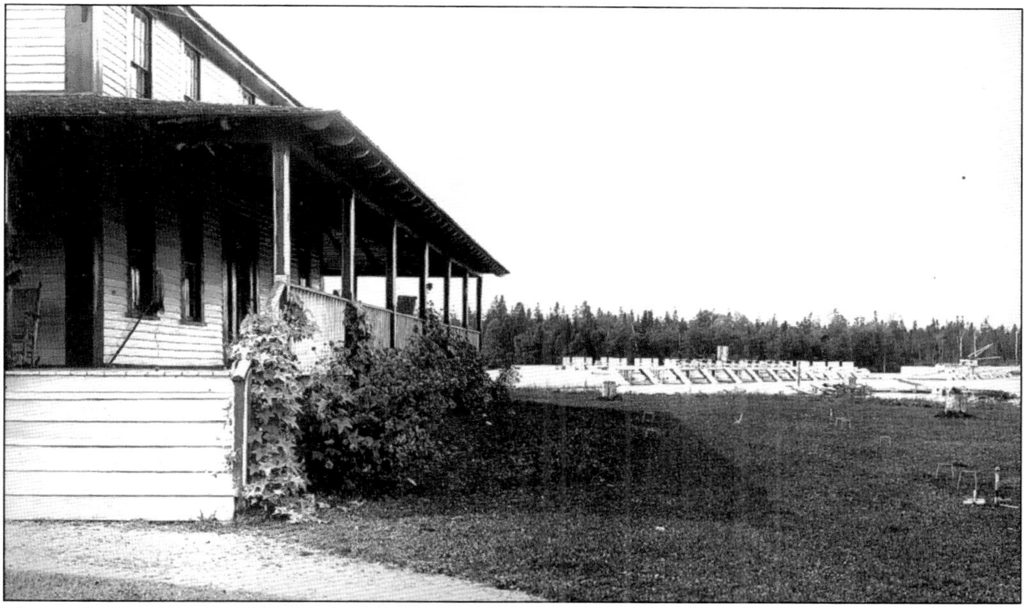

This early 1900s view of the East Outlet Dam also shows the porch of the Outlet House, which later became Wilson's Camps. Notice the croquet game set up on the front lawn at the right center.

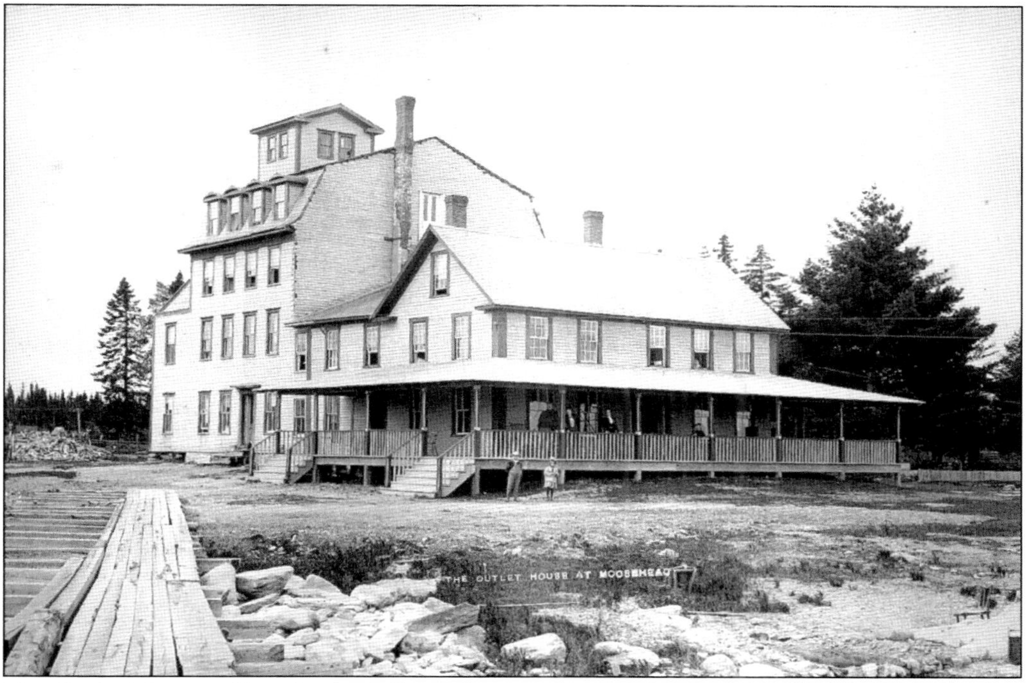

The Outlet House at East Outlet is shown here in the early 1900s. This photograph was taken from the East Outlet Dam on the Kennebec River and was one of many published by E. R. Starbird of Brunswick, Maine, in this era under the title *The Woods of Maine*.

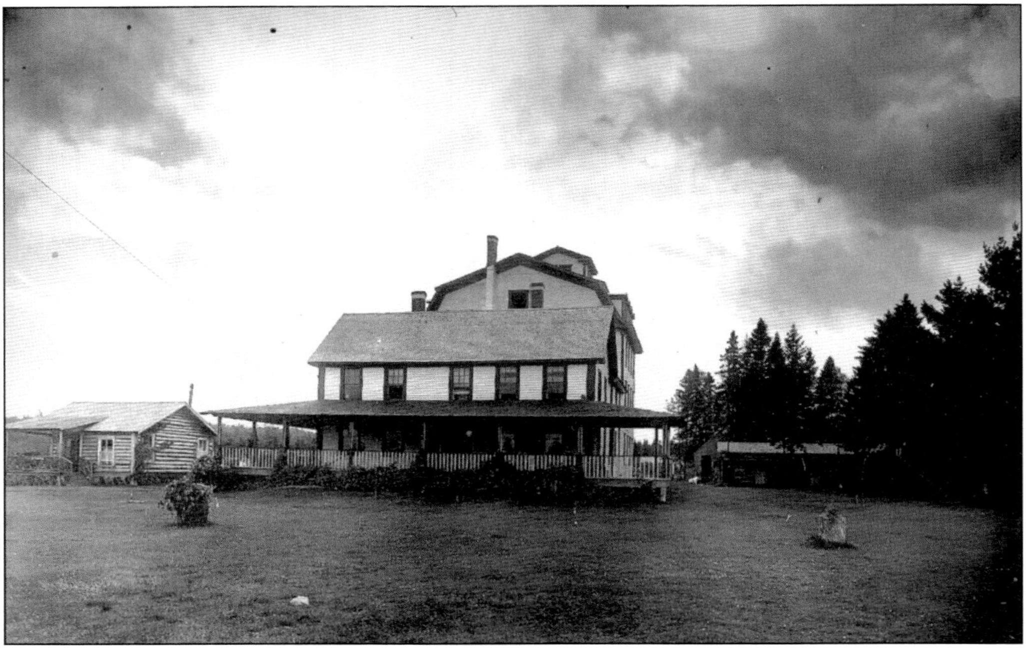

Here is another view of the Outlet House; this one is taken from the south. The house featured large wraparound porches on the first floor. This site is now known as Wilson's on Moosehead Lake.

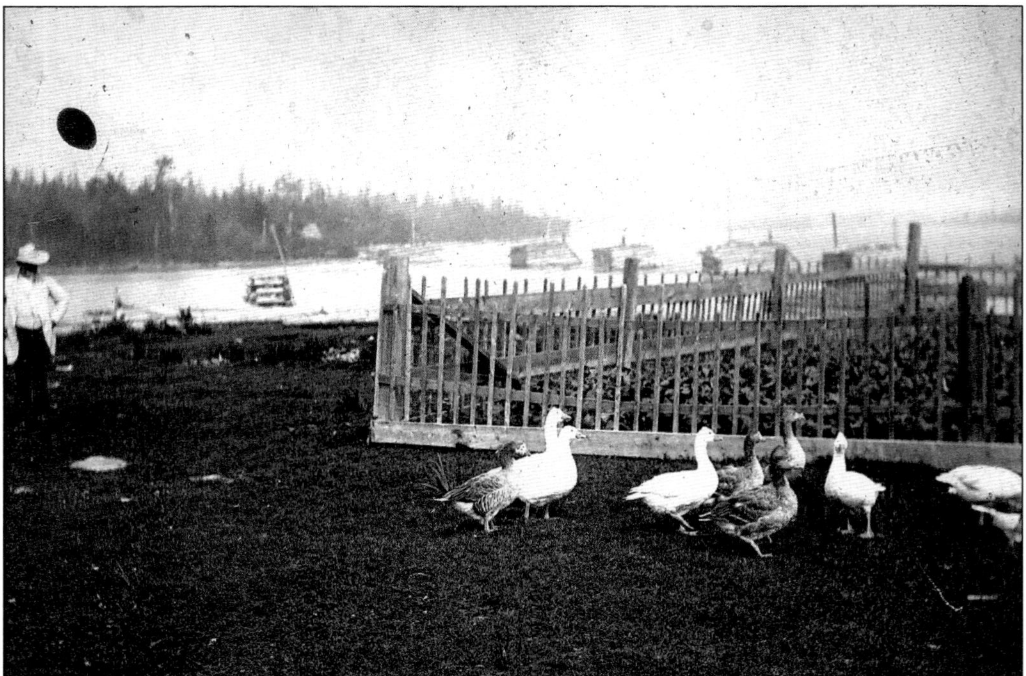

A gaggle of geese eye the vegetable garden at the Outlet House in very early 1900s. Notice the breakwater for the East Outlet Dam at the rear center.

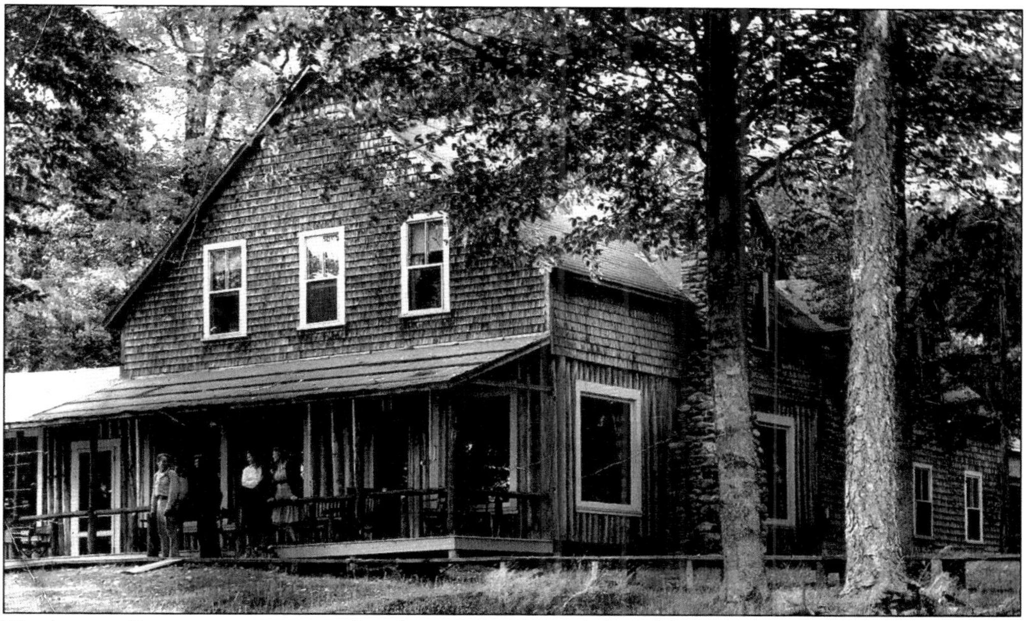

Tomhegan Camps, as it was earlier known, is one of the oldest sporting camp operations in northern Maine. Featuring several individual camps and a main lodge, it was a very popular destination in the 1940s, when this photograph was taken. Shown under the porch, from left to right, are Bob Folsom, Margie Spinney, and Blanche Spinney.

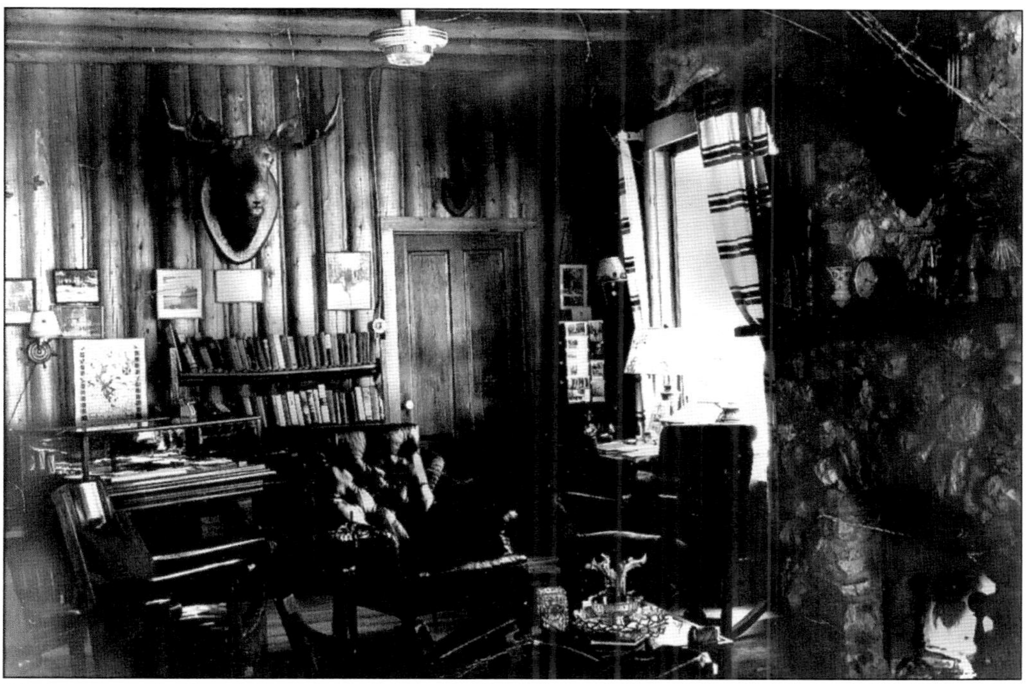

This view of the Tomhegan Camps main lodge shows the library c. the 1940s.

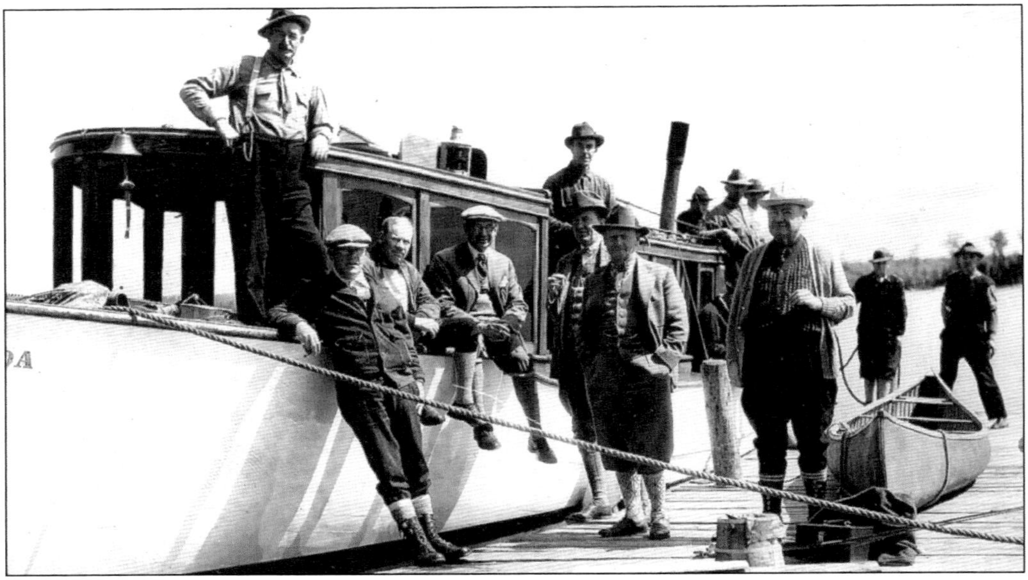

These sports were ready for an outing on Moosehead Lake when this photograph was taken at the Tomhegan Camps dock. Jim Finley (top left) was the owner of the boat and a guide at Tomhegan Camps. The photograph was likely taken c. the 1920s.

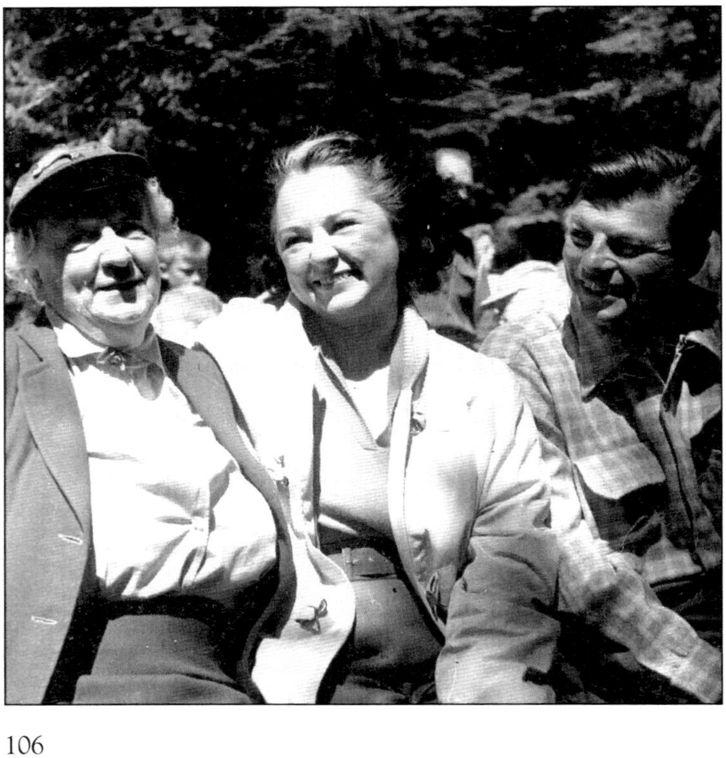

These folks posed for a quick photograph at Tomhegan Camps in the late 1940s. Shown, from left to right, are Alice Statler, Marjorie Spinney McBurnie, and Keith McBurnie. Marjorie McBurnie was born at Tomhegan and is the daughter of R. P. and Blanche Spinney. The Spinneys built the camps on the shore of Moosehead Lake prior to World War I. Keith McBurnie died in 1984, and Marjorie McBurnie still lives at Tomhegan.

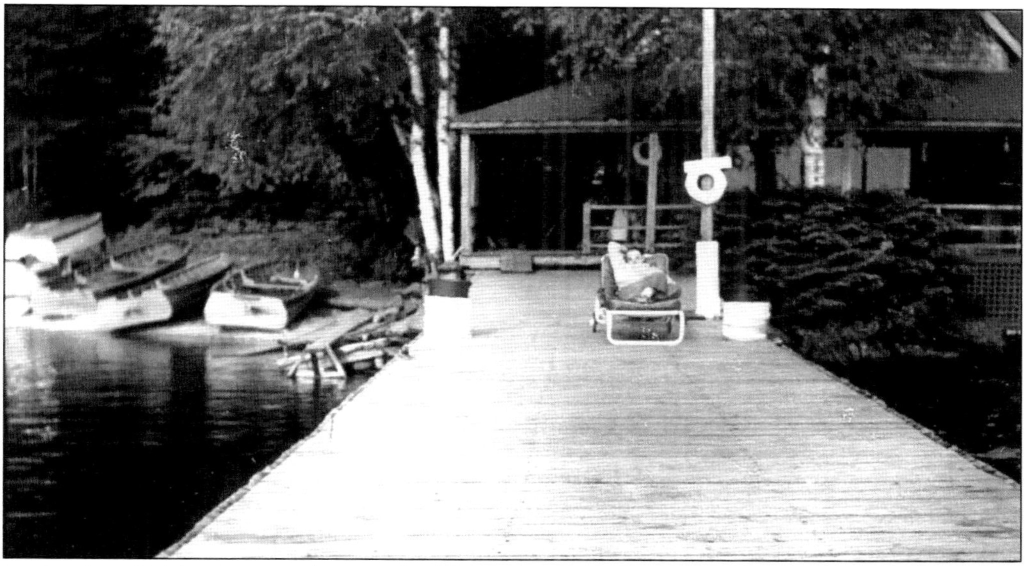

In this late 1940s photograph, inscribed "a paying guest," a guest takes it easy on the dock at Camp Caribou in Ogontz, above Rockwood. It was likely used as a publicity photograph for a brochure. At the time, Camp Caribou was owned by Charles Umsted and his wife. Charles Umsted was also postmaster in Ogontz, a small settlement on the shore of Moosehead Lake that never had more than a few scattered summer camps in addition to the sporting camp operation. Camp Caribou is now a private camp.

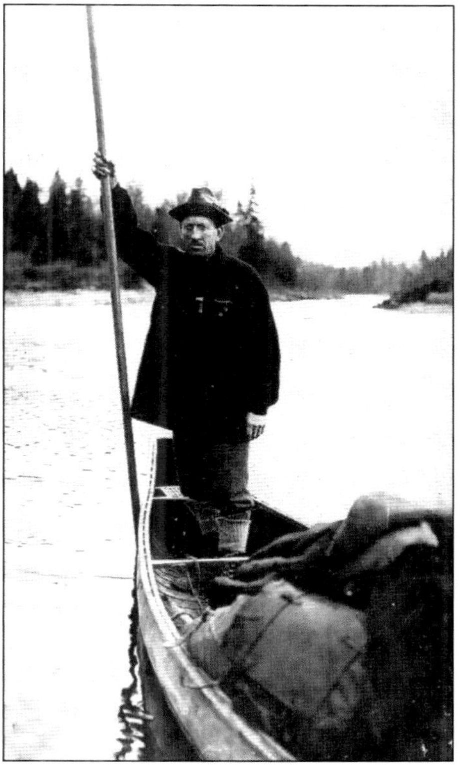

J. Asa Larrabee and his wife, Caroline, were early owners of Camp Caribou at Ogontz. Here J. Asa Larrabee is shown poling a canoe in 1922, apparently toting supplies to a campsite.

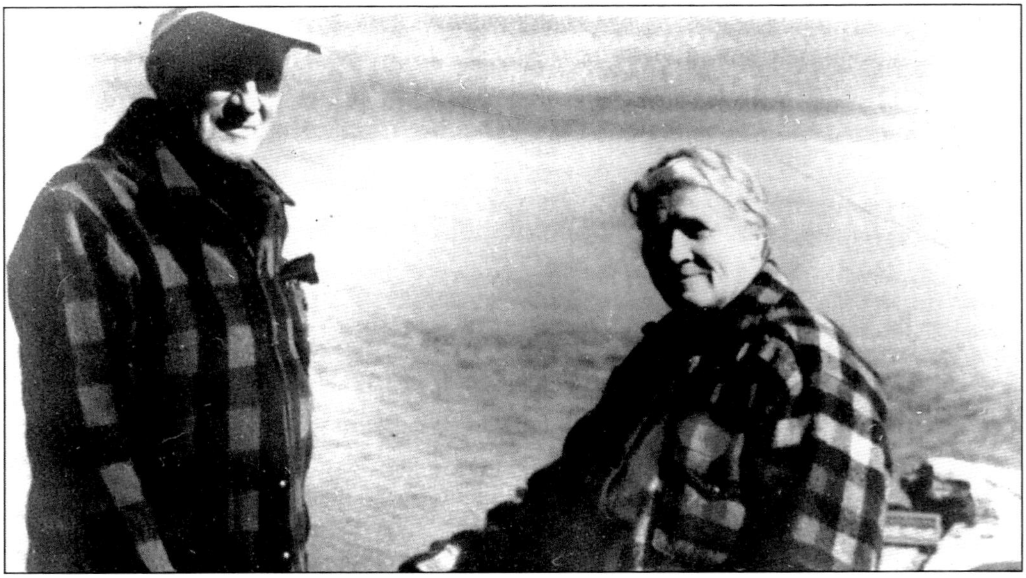

J. Asa and Caroline Larrabee spent many years catering to guests at Camp Caribou in Ogontz. In addition, J. Asa Larrabee was postmaster at the post office located in the main lodge at the camp. This photograph, taken in June 1950, shows the Larrabees as they prepare to leave Camp Caribou for the last time after selling the sporting camp operation to Charles Umsted and his wife.

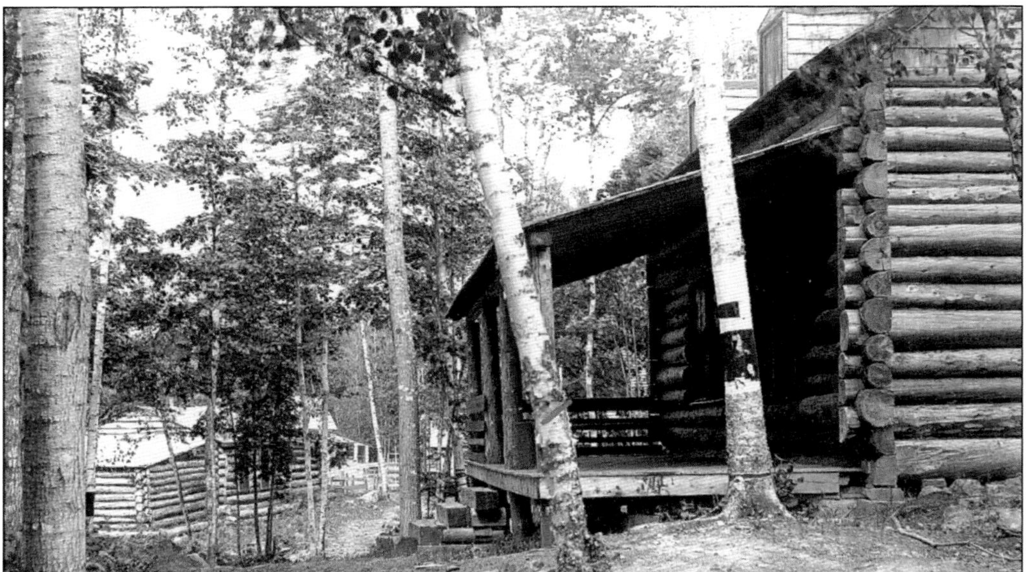

Marr's Sporting Camps at Indian Pond was another popular sporting camp operation in the early 1900s at the spot where the East and West outlets of the Kennebec River converge. The sporting camp operation was started by Mike Marr, who emigrated to Maine from Canada in 1892. There were at least two devastating fires at the camps, one c. 1898 and again in 1941. In 1952, Marr's Sporting Camps were sold to Central Maine Power Company, and the site was flooded with the creation of the Harris Dam.

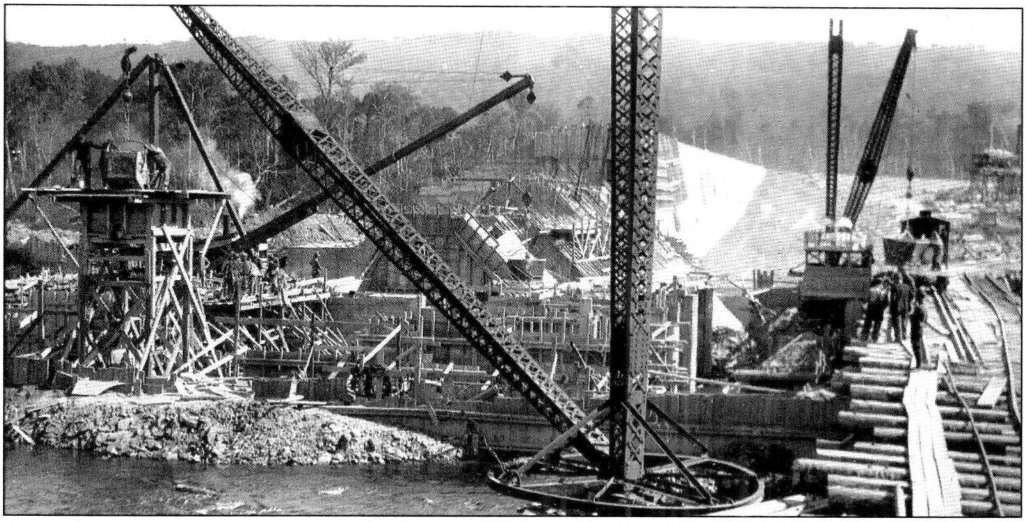

This photograph, taken on October 1, 1926, shows construction of the Brassua Dam. This dam is located at the outlet of Brassua Lake at the Moose River and helps control flow into Moosehead Lake near Rockwood.

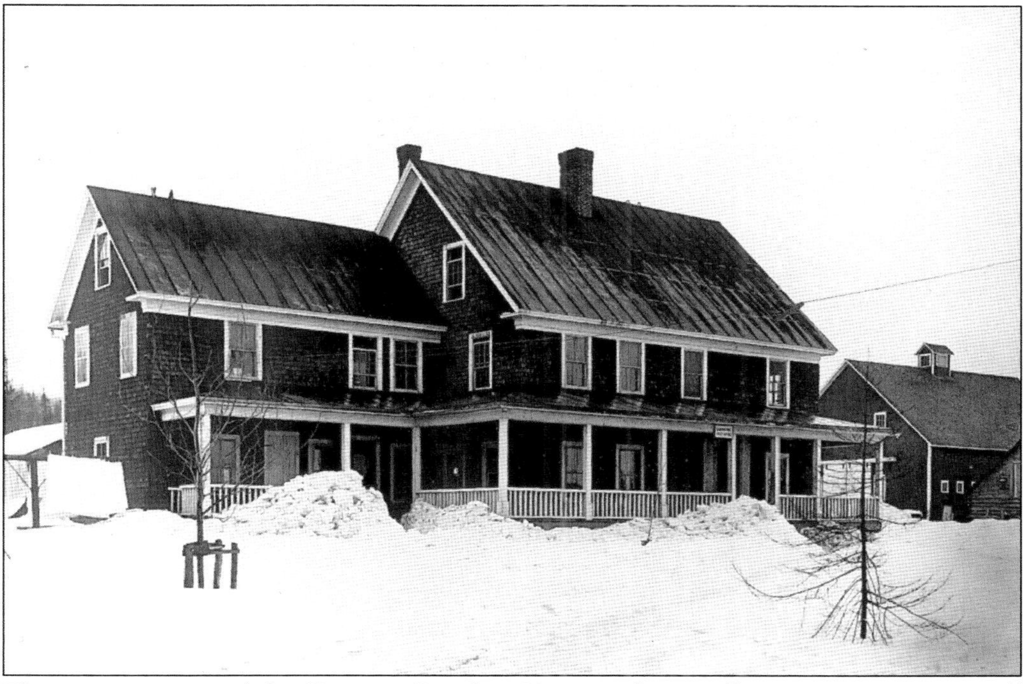

This is a rare view of the Tarratine Boarding House and post office. Tarratine was a small settlement along the Canadian Pacific Railroad west of Rockwood. The post office operated for only a few years. This photograph was taken on March 17, 1914; notice the Tarratine post office sign over the porch at the center of the main house. The approximate site today is known as Tarratine Crossing, where the railroad tracks cross Route 15 on the Rockwood-Jackman Road.

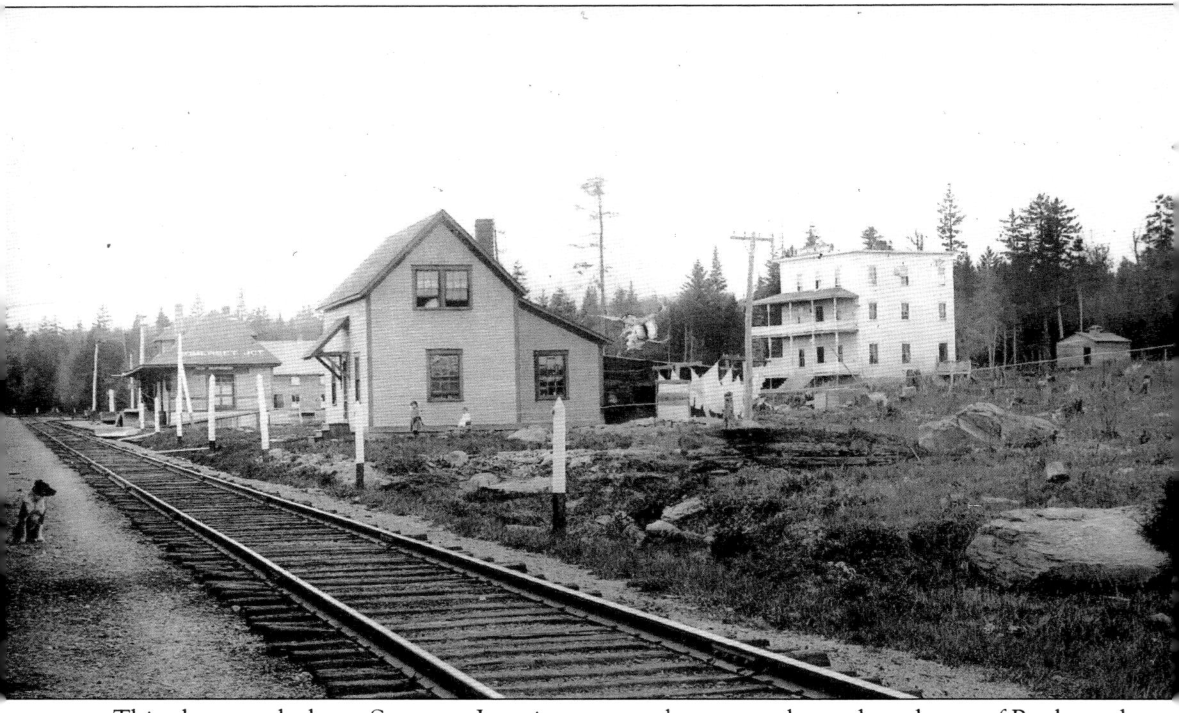

This photograph shows Somerset Junction, now a ghost town, located southwest of Rockwood. At one time, this settlement, located in Misery Gore Township, had several buildings, including the railroad depot at the far left. Located at the left center is the Pomerleau House, and at the far right is the Munster House. The settlement was situated where the Canadian Pacific Railroad and Maine Central Railroad's Kineo branch crossed. Today there are only a few foundations and summer camps in the area, which can be reached by a gravel road that is the old Maine Central Railroad track bed that runs from near West Outlet at Rockwood to Route 201 south of Jackman.

Five

KOKADJO

As woods operations expanded north of Greenville, it was inevitable that a road would be constructed along the east side of Moosehead Lake. The road was constructed in pieces during the very early 1900s. The need for a road to the new Ripogenus Dam became apparent when construction materials needed to be transported during the mid-1910s. The settlement of Kokadjo (shortened from the Native American name *Kokadjoweemgwasebemis*, or "Kettle Mountain," which rises to the north) predates by decades the coming of the road. The earliest known reference to Kokadjo (also spelled Kokad-jo) was in 1844, when a Deacon Ford built a camp at the mouth of the Roach River. Thomas W. Smith operated a small farm and had a woods operation beginning in 1853. It was in the 1880s that an inn was started. Until 1914, Kokadjo was reached either by steamer on Moosehead Lake to the Roach River or by a woods trail used by oxen and horses from Lily Bay. Before the road was built, a small general store was opened at Kokadjo, and the building remains today, although it is no longer used. A post office was opened with the name Roach River in 1890 and was changed to Kokadjo in 1910 (it closed mid-century). In 1931, the Hollingsworth & Whitney Company, which had owned the Roach River House, sold it to Jack and Jean Richards of Greenville, and although it was closed during World War II, it reopened following the war. There is little at Kokadjo today to link it with the past. Perhaps the most poignant reminder is a large barn behind the Kokadjo Trading Post that was a part of the Roach River House of earlier days.

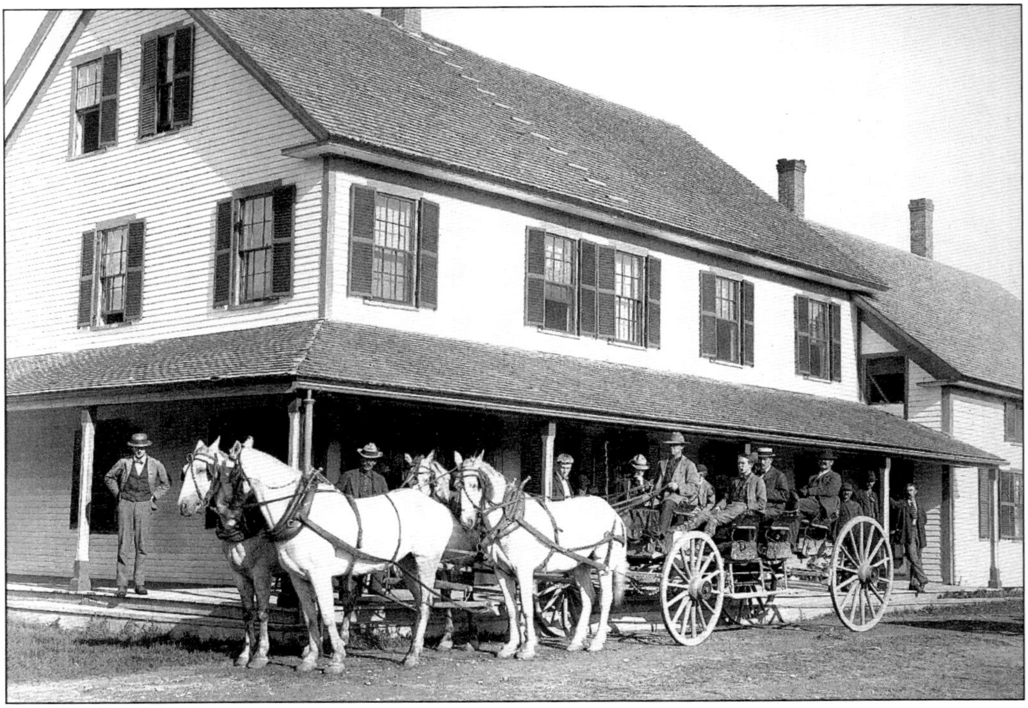

The Roach River House was for many years located on the shore of the Roach River at the outlet of First Roach Pond in Kokadjo. This photograph dates from the very early 1900s and shows a group of people perhaps ready to make the long journey to Greenville.

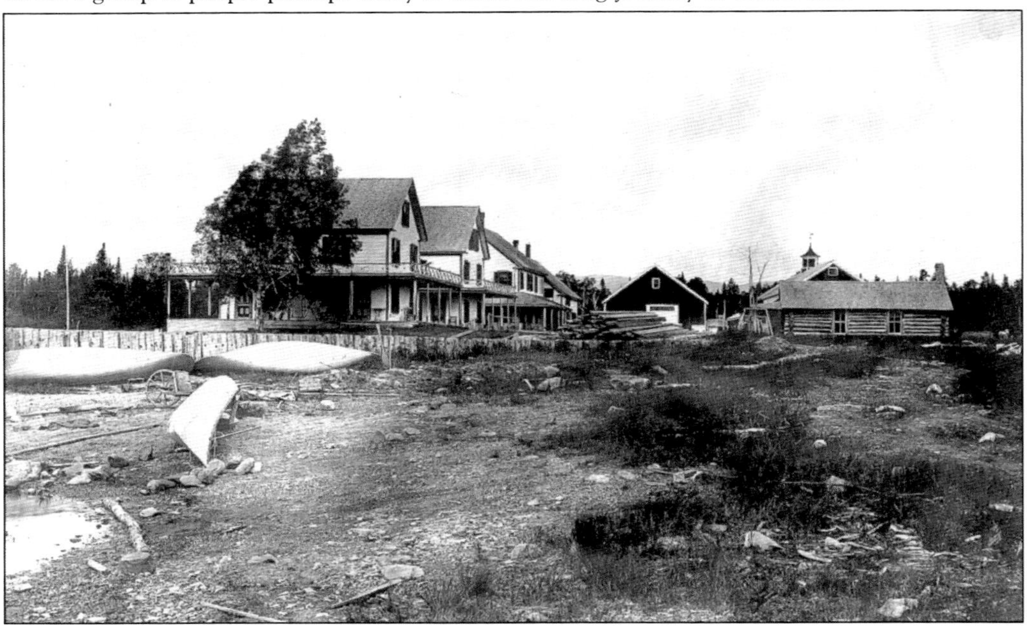

This c. 1910 view of the Roach River House was taken from the shore of First Roach Pond. The barn at the far right behind the log cabin is still standing, but all of the rest of the buildings are now gone.

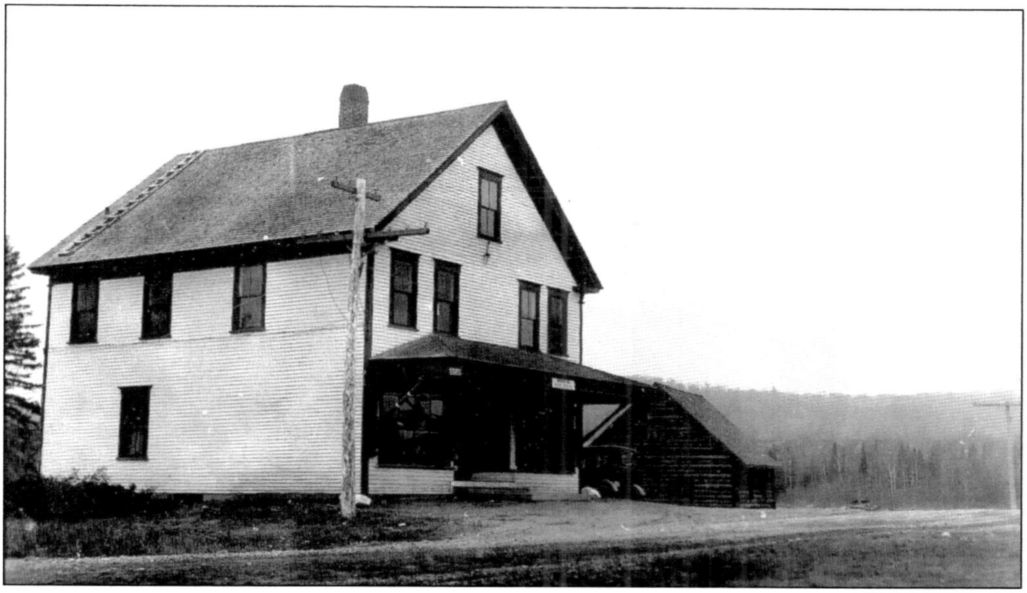

The building shown here on the left housed the Kokadjo General Store and the post office and was moved when the road from Lily Bay to Ripogenus Dam was constructed in the early 1900s. Originally on the north side of the road, it was moved across the road to a point near the shore of First Roach Pond. This photograph was taken in the 1920s. The sign on the porch shows it is the Kokadjo (spelled here as Kokad-jo)post office.

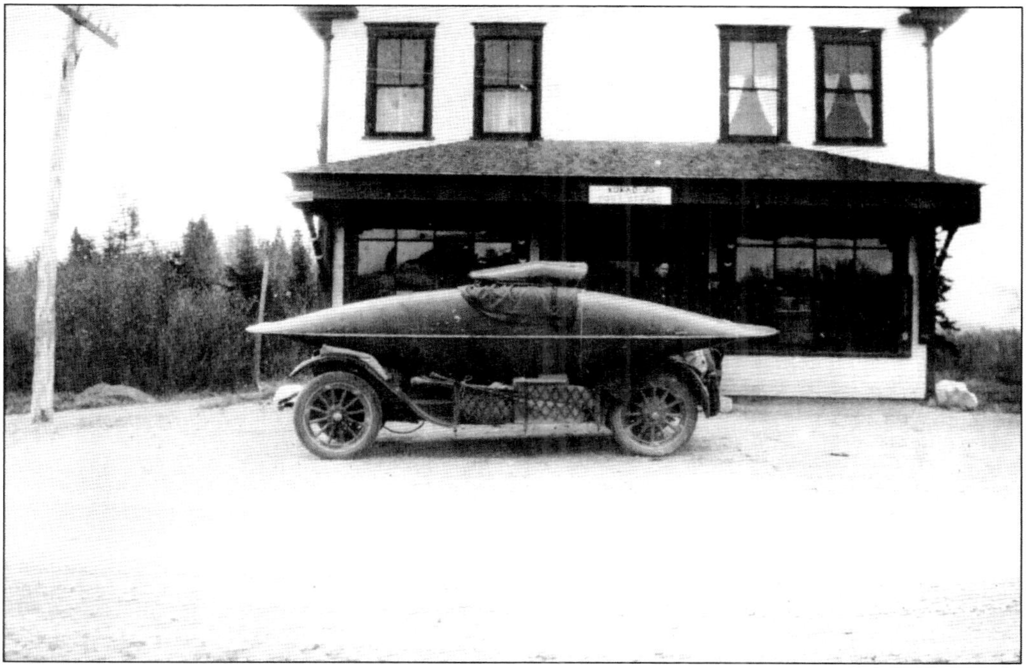

Here is another view of the front of the Kokadjo General Store and post office, also from the 1920s. The car in front has a canoe strapped to its side, thus creating a rather odd-looking vehicle.

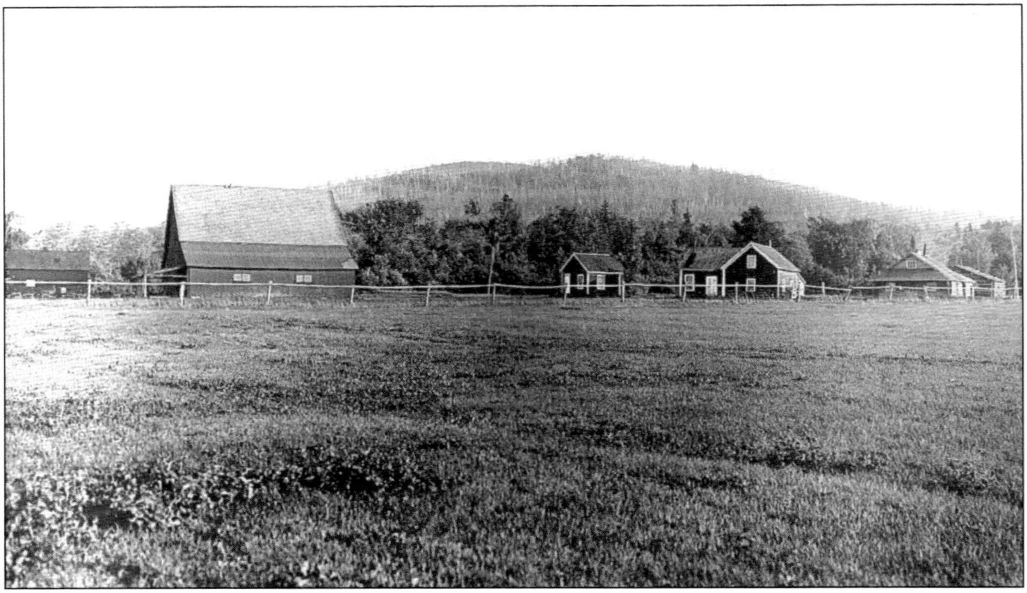

A roadway was constructed from a point south of Kokadjo along the west shore of First Roach Pond during the early 1900s. This roadway went to West Branch Pond Camps and other locations when lumbering was active in this region. A particularly level piece of land along First Roach Pond was known as Frenchtown Field, shown with a set of farm buildings in this photograph taken on September 18, 1914.

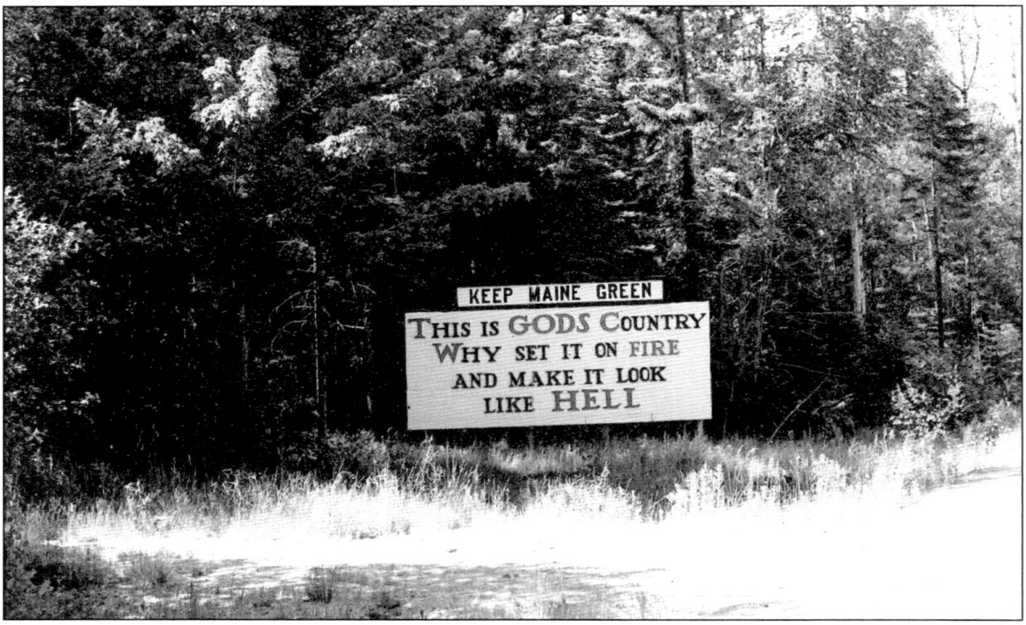

This sign warning motorists of the dangers of fire was erected by Great Northern Paper Company and has remained in the same spot for decades. It is the only official billboard in Maine, a state that abolished billboards many years ago.

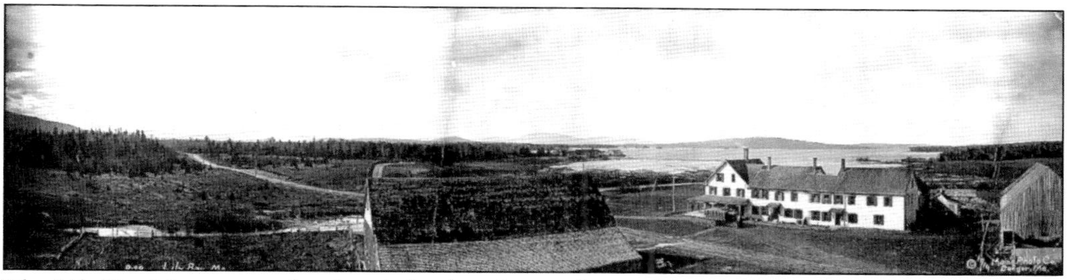

The Lily Bay House was a landmark for decades on the road from Greenville to Ripogenus Dam. The farm was a destination for woodsmen who traveled into the North Woods aboard a steamer from Greenville. The steamer landed at the distant point of land between the barn building at the left and the main house. The men stayed overnight at the Lily Bay House before walking into the woods. The farm also produced garden goods for lumber camps and lodged horses from woods operations in the summer. These buildings are no longer standing. This photograph was taken in 1919 by a Bangor photographer.

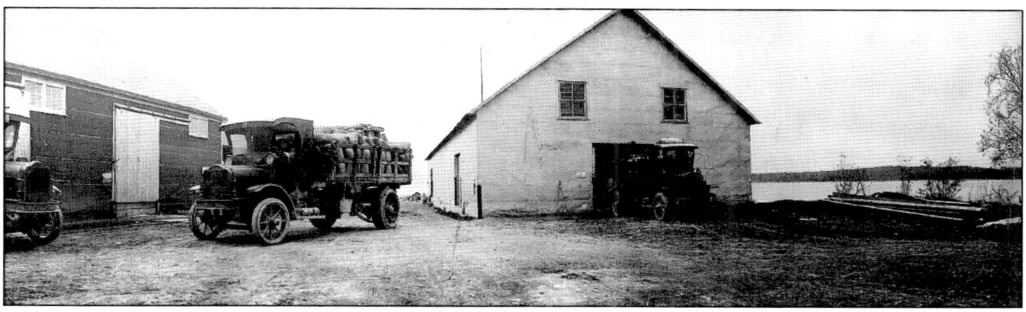

The Lily Bay Storehouse was located at the point where steamers docked on trips up Moosehead Lake from Greenville. It was a popular landing for goods, as well as lumbermen, being transported into woods operations. This 1919 photograph shows trucks being loaded with goods destined for woods camps. The building at the left is no longer standing, but the building at the right remains to this day.

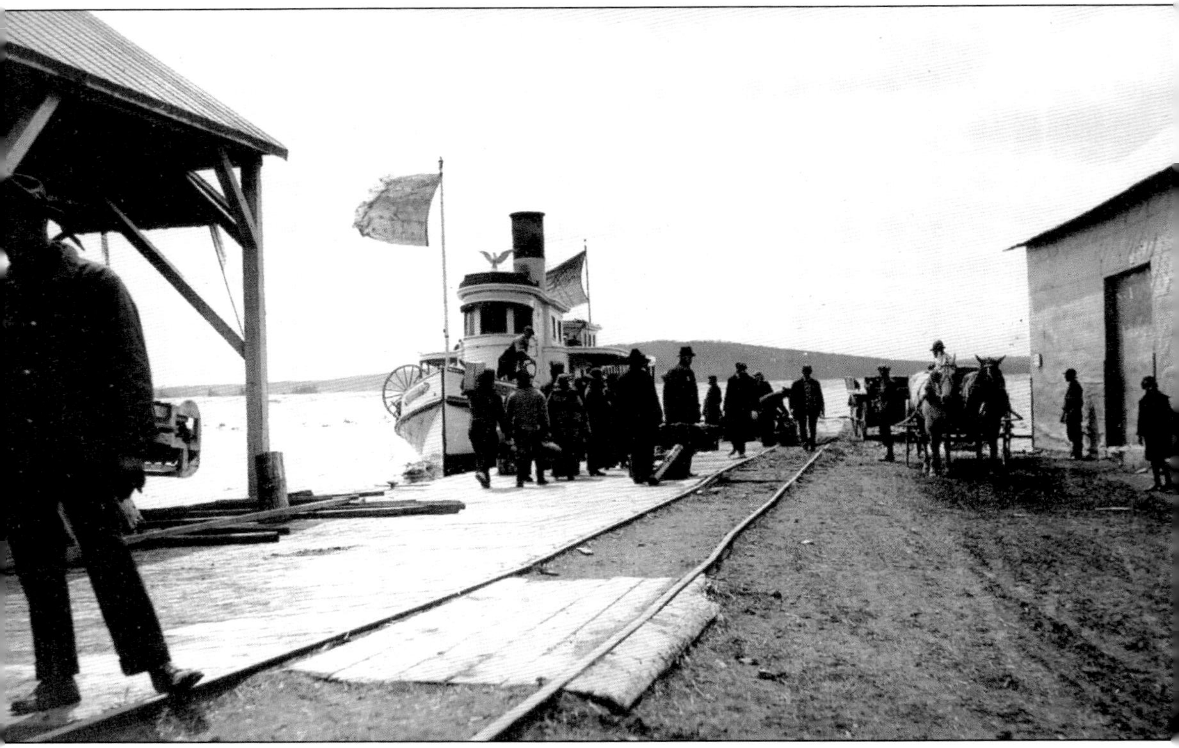

The steamer *Louisa* is shown at the Lily Bay dock, with the storehouse at the far right. This c. 1920s photograph was taken shortly after the steamer had arrived with the passengers it was transporting.

Six

The North Woods

The term North Woods when used here applies to the large geographical area lying north of a line from roughly Greenville to Rockwood and stretching to the Aroostook County line. There are several settlements that are not included in the scope of this book, notably Chesuncook Village, but the pages that follow will give readers a sense of man's hand in the region during the first half of the 1900s. Northeast Carry, Seboomook, the Lily Bay House, Grant Farm—these are all areas that are steeped in history. Northeast Carry has been used by travelers for centuries, for it is here that Native Americans made the carry from the West Branch of the Penobscot River to Moosehead Lake, and in their footsteps came early explorers and sportsmen. The same can be said of Seboomook, which is also known as the Northwest Carry, for it was here that an overland carry was made between Moosehead Lake and Carry Brook or Seboomook Lake and eventually into what is now Canada. It was also here at Seboomook that a small settlement existed, thanks to the woods industry and later tourism (the Seboomook House was a popular destination). It is not widely known that one of five World War II prisoner-of-war camps in Maine was located at Seboomook in the mid-1940s. All that remains today of the camp, which housed scores of German soldiers, is a mess-hall chimney standing as a silent sentinel in the woods.

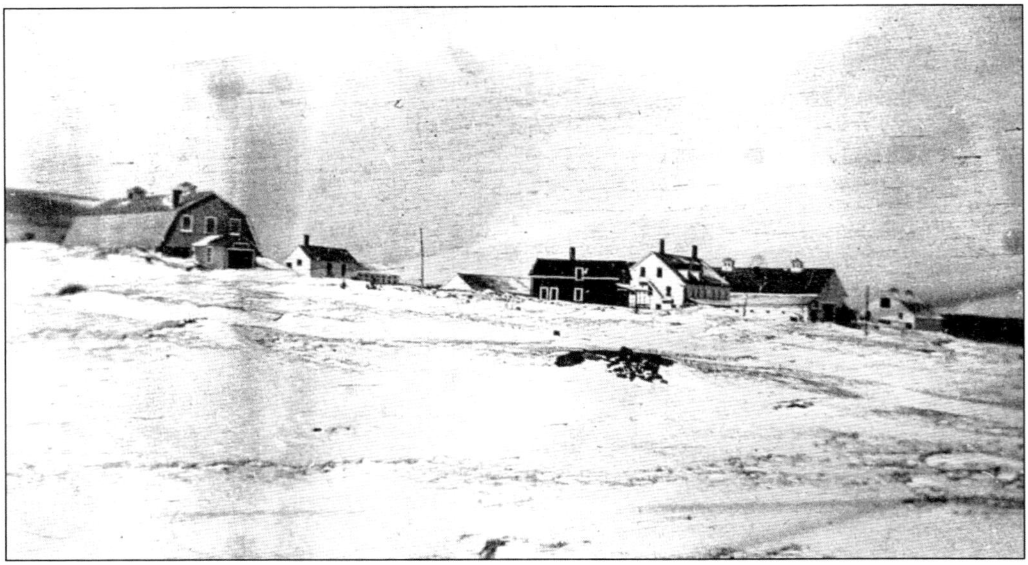

Grant Farm was located high on a hill several miles beyond Kokadjo in Township 2, Range 13, in the area designated as West of the Easterly Line of the State. Thomas Grant built a log house on this spot in 1840, and before the end of the 1800s, several farm buildings had been constructed. The farm was sold to Great Northern Paper Company in 1901 and was used to grow vegetables and hay for woods camps and to lodge working horses during the summer. None of these buildings remain today, although there is a commanding view of Mount Katahdin from the location.

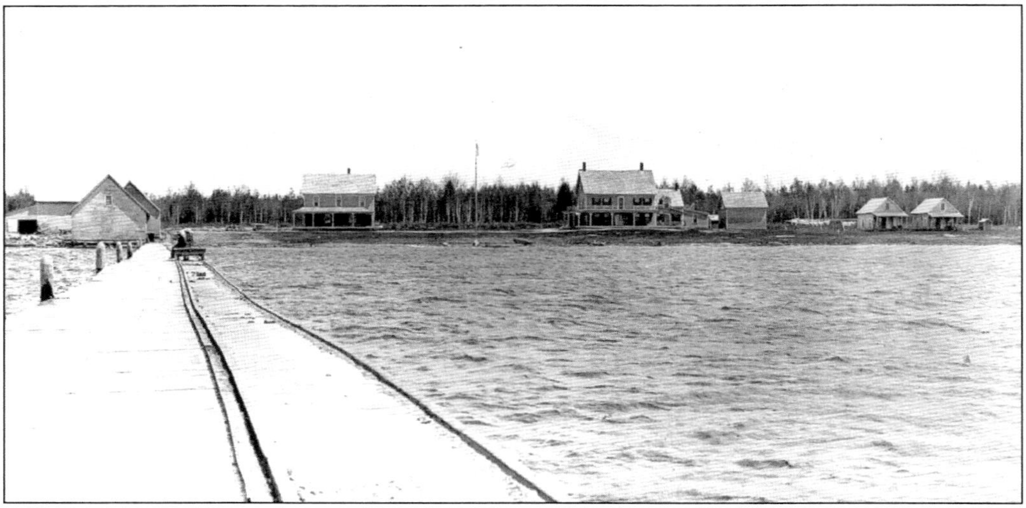

Northeast Carry has been a popular crossing from Moosehead Lake to the West Branch of the Penobscot River for centuries. Early Native Americans used this route, and later explorers and woodsmen used the carry. This c. 1910 view shows the long pier that once extended far into Moosehead Lake. The water was shallow at this point and steamers had to dock a long way from land. The rails on the right side of the dock were used by a horse-drawn rail cart (shown in the center of the background at the far left) to transport goods to the storehouses shown at the far left center. In the center is a store, and the Winnegarnock House, an overnight hotel, is located to the right center.

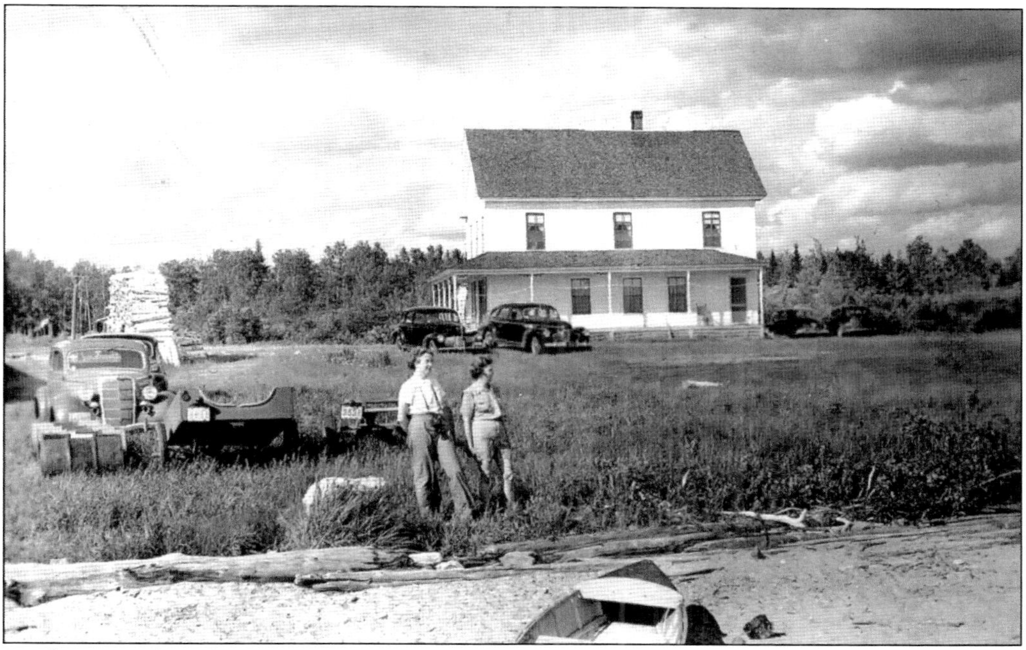

By the time this photograph was taken at Northeast Carry c. 1950, the store, shown here, was being used as a summer camp. The Winnegarnock House is no longer standing, but this building remains.

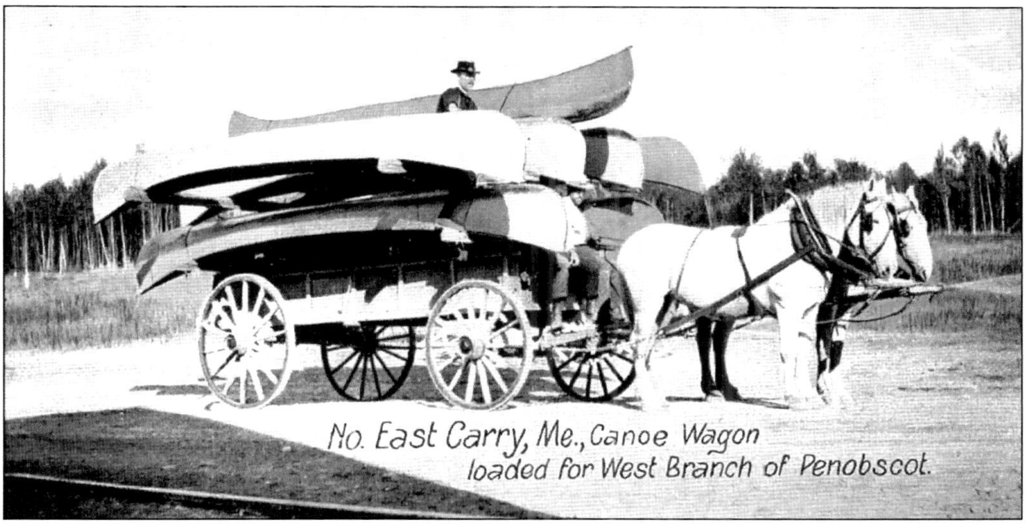

In the early 1900s, a horse-drawn wagon was used to transport canoes and other goods, as well as people, across the carry from Northeast Carry to the West Branch of the Penobscot River. From here, people could travel the West Branch to Chesuncook Lake and other points north. In the 1800s, an ox team pulled a wagon on rails (partially visible at lower left center) across the carry, a distance of less than two miles.

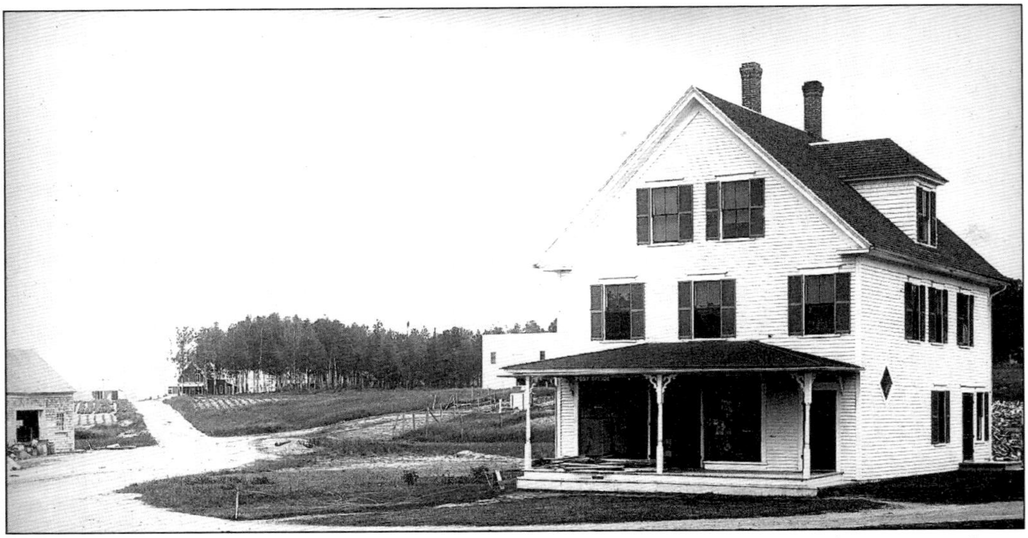

The store at Seboomook was located a short distance from the Seboomook House and was part of a large complex of buildings at the Northwest Carry of Moosehead Lake. There was a German prisoner-of-war camp at this spot during World War II; following the war, all of the buildings were demolished.

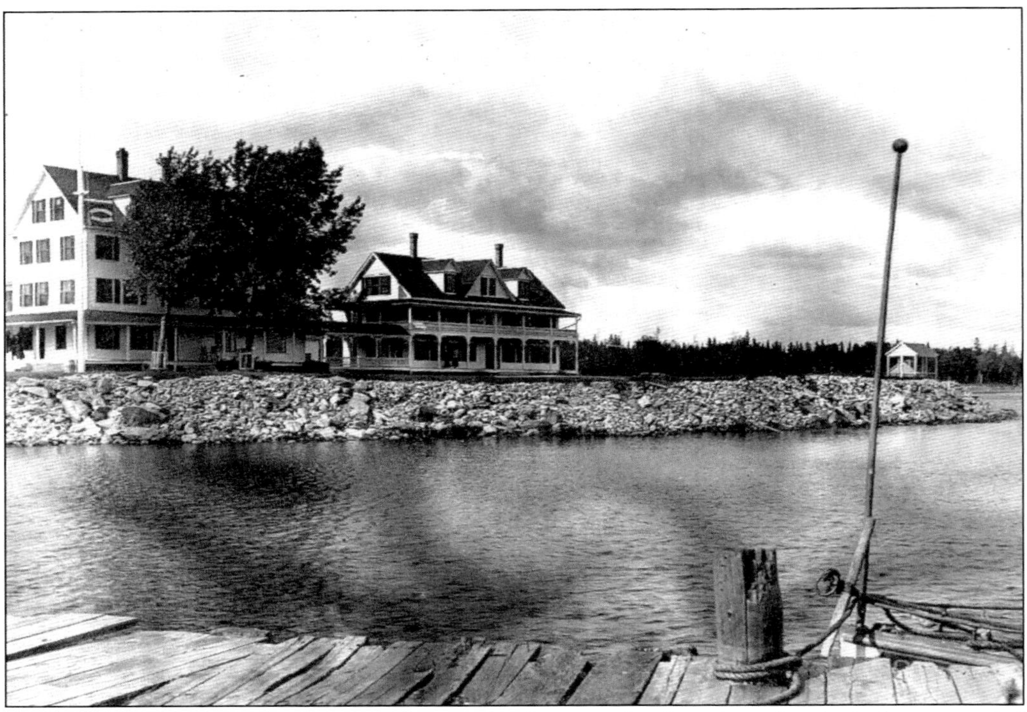

The Seboomook House is shown in this 1930s photograph taken from the dock that extended into Moosehead Lake. Steamers from Greenville and Kineo brought passengers to this dock for decades. This location is now the site of the Seboomook Wilderness Campground; none of these buildings remain.

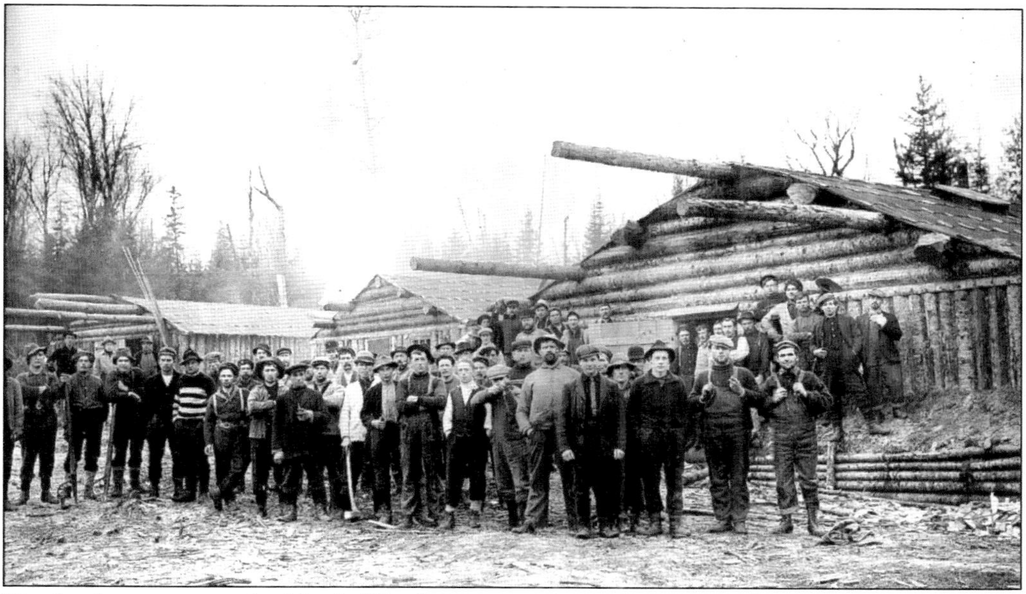

The lumbering era in the North Woods began in the early 1800s and continued well into the 1900s. Countless woods operations have harvested timber from thousands of acres, first with horse and oxen and the brute strength of woodsmen and later with chain saws and skidders. This 1911 photograph shows a Great Northern Paper Company woods crew posing for a photograph. The site was located between Rockwood and Canada Falls.

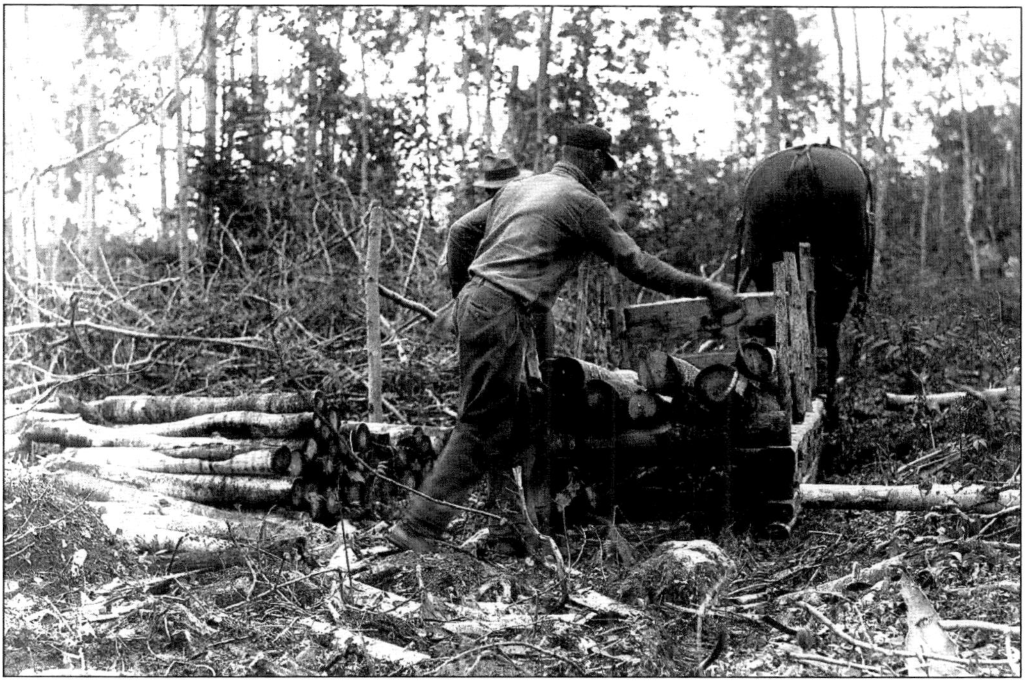

This photograph shows two men at work cutting pulp or firewood and loading it onto a horse-drawn sled. Its location unknown, this photograph was taken in the 1940s. Woodsmen's work was very difficult in those days and remains as difficult today.

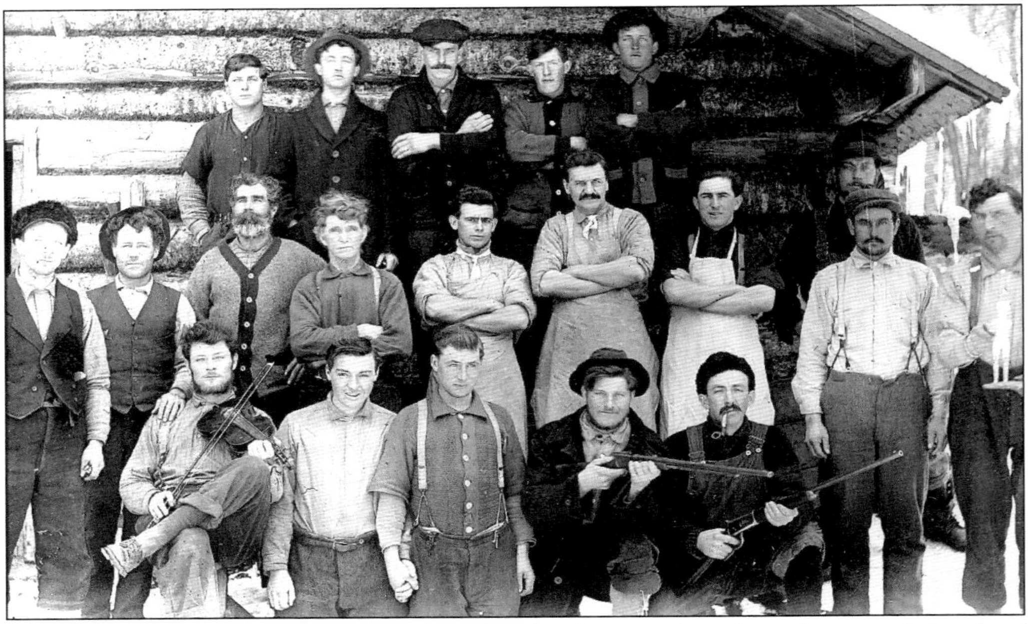

This photograph of a woods crew in the Moosehead region dates from the second decade of the 20th century and shows a man with his fiddle (likely the only kind of live entertainment the men had during the long winter nights), two others with rifles, and the head cook and his workers.

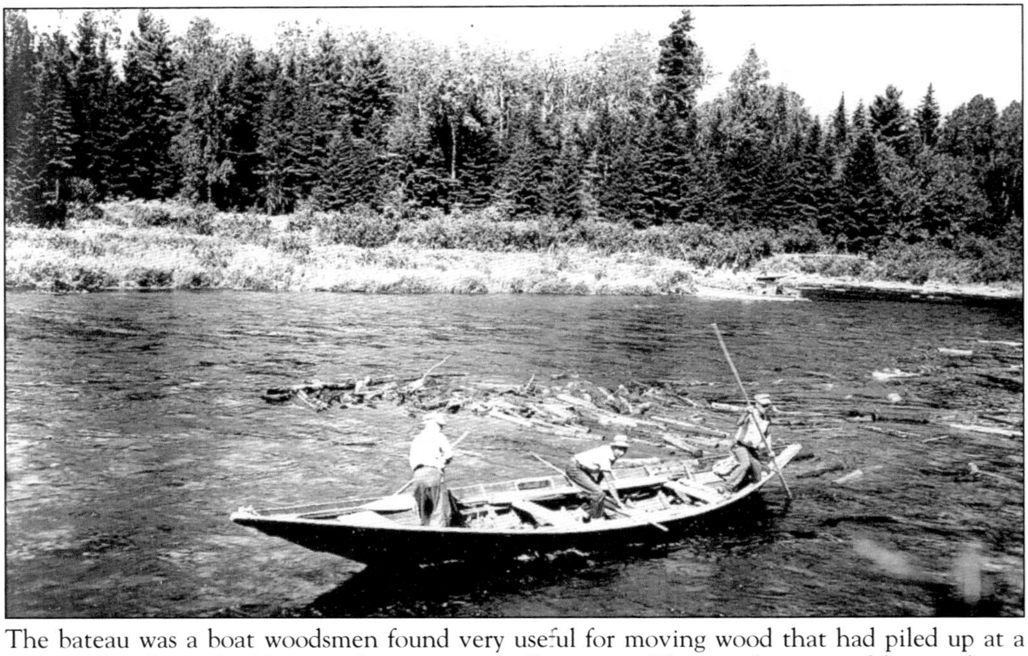

The bateau was a boat woodsmen found very useful for moving wood that had piled up at a waterway's edge or had become hung up in shallow areas. The woodsmen used long poles to move the wood and also to steer the bateaux. This 1940s photograph shows three men on the West Branch of the Penobscot River working behind a log drive and removing logs that had become tangled. The man seen at the far right is steering the bateau using his pole.

Seven

RAILROADS OF THE NORTH WOODS

There have been three railroads that have served the majority of Moosehead area residents and visitors, and today only one line still exists for freight only. Several other lines have also existed over the decades. In years past, it was not unusual to hear the lonesome whistle of a train in the more remote areas to the north. Following the Civil War, and with a period of prosperity felt throughout Maine, the Bangor & Piscataquis Railroad began inching toward the Moosehead region by 1869. It reached Dover and Foxcroft (at the time two separate towns) and then Guilford by 1871. In 1875, it reached Abbot and was in Blanchard by 1877. Only a few miles from Greenville, it was delayed there for seven years. But by July 1884, the problems had been solved and the rails reached Greenville Junction. In 1888, the Canadian Pacific Railroad reached Greenville Junction from the northwest. Both the Bangor & Aroostook Railroad (the name had been changed from Bangor & Piscataquis) and the Canadian Pacific Railroad served the Greenville area for decades. The Maine Central Railroad built a line to Rockwood to provide transportation for the hundreds of people traveling each summer to the Mount Kineo House resort. The Kineo station lasted until the 1930s. Farther to the north, the Seboomook Lake & St. John Railroad was constructed in the 1920s to help with the removal of logs from the woods. It was reported that great obstacles had to be overcome to build the short line of only 18 miles. There was a narrow-gauge railroad at Carry Brook near Seboomook, constructed in 1914 to haul railroad ties cut on the Penobscot watershed to Moosehead Lake. The Chesuncook-Chamberlain Railroad, the Tramway, and the Eagle Lake & West Branch Railroad were other North Woods rail lines used for transporting timber. All of these lumbering lines are now gone; although traces of rails or other artifacts are occasionally found if a person knows exactly where to look. Unfortunately, few original photographs of these railroads exist today.

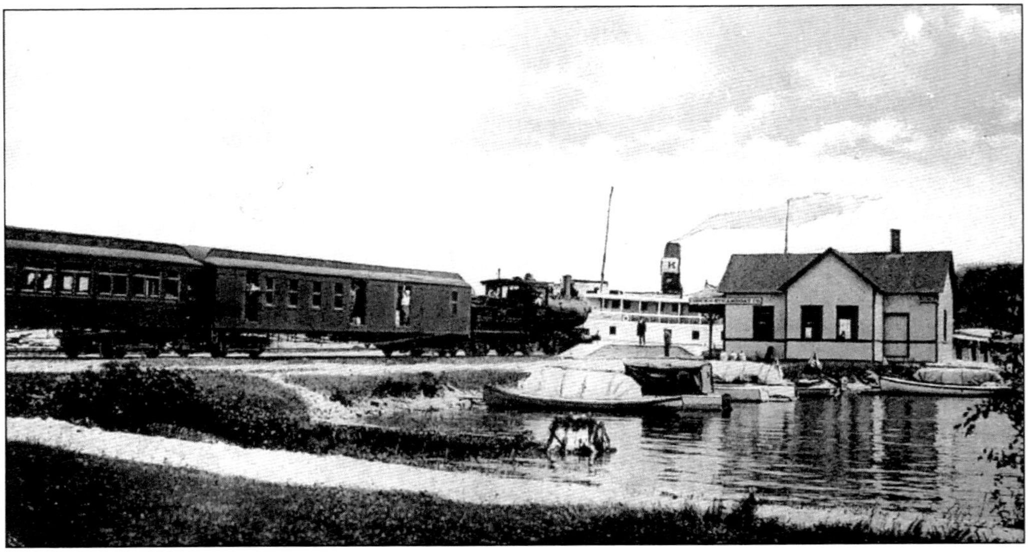

The Coburn Steamboat Company maintained a small office at the end of the Junction Wharf where passengers arriving on a Bangor & Aroostook train could purchase tickets for transportation up Moosehead Lake on steamers such as the *Katahdin*, which is shown in the right center background. Railroad tracks ran down to the end of the wharf, as seen in this *c.* 1910 photograph, for the convenience of passengers.

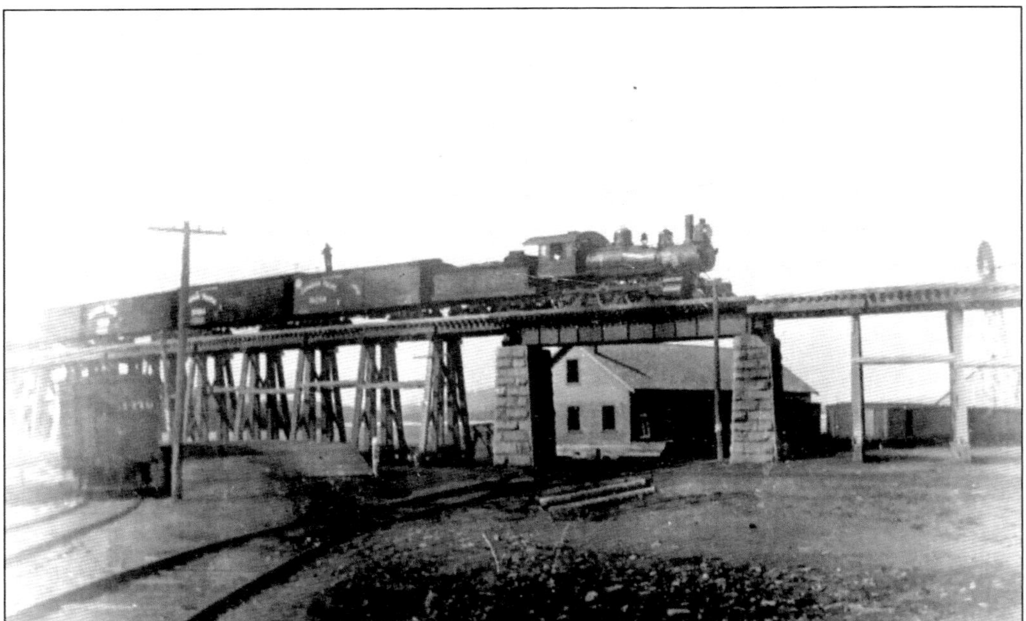

This is a rare, *c.* 1900 view of a Canadian Pacific Railroad train on the long trestle at the Junction Wharf. The view looks east-northeast toward Moosehead Lake and shows the rails of the Bangor & Aroostook Railroad under the trestle. The Canadian Pacific Railroad arrived at Greenville Junction in 1888, four years after the Bangor & Piscataquis Railroad, which was later renamed the Bangor & Aroostook Railroad.

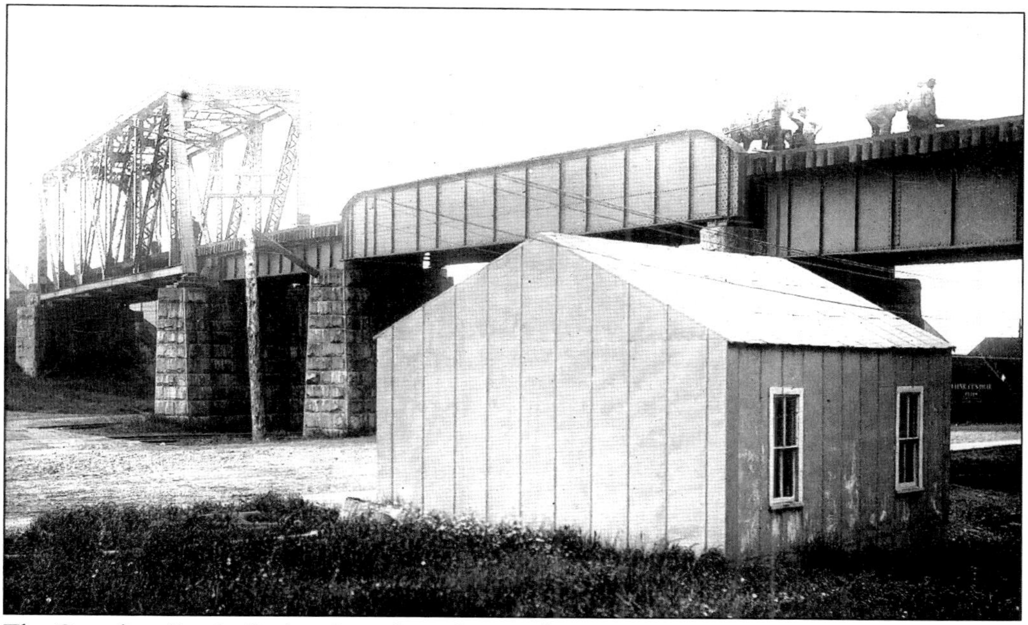

The Canadian Pacific Railroad trestle at Greenville Junction is shown here *c.* 1910. Men and horses are at work on the track in the upper right corner, and rails of the Bangor & Aroostook Railroad can be seen in the lower center, underneath the trestle. Notice that many of the wood pilings holding up the trestle in the previous view have now been replaced with stone.

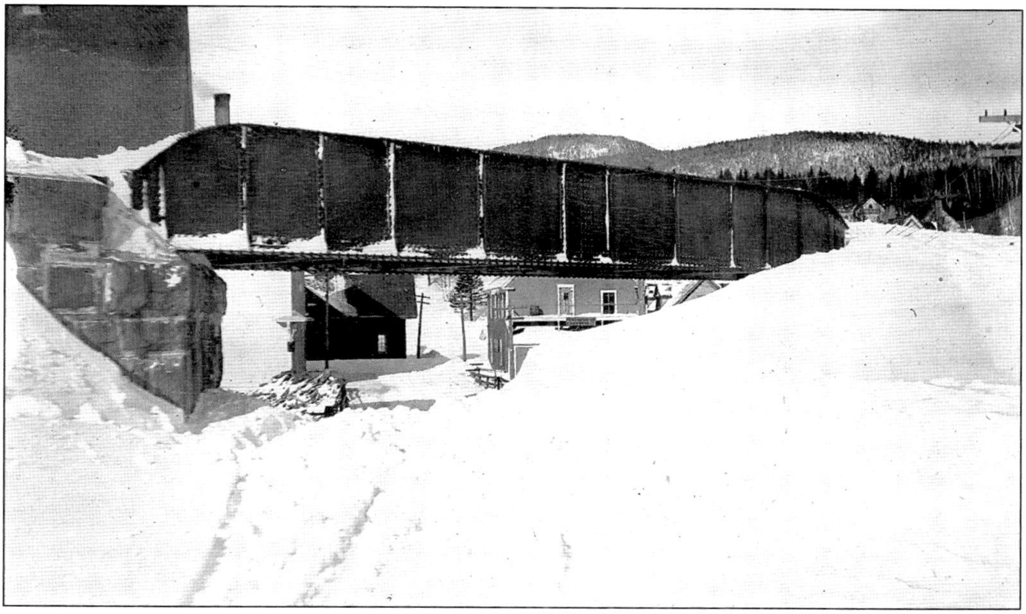

This is a winter scene showing West Street (now Pritham Avenue) where the Canadian Pacific Railroad trestle crosses the road. This *c.* 1920s view was taken from the front of the A. A. Crafts residence and looks to the west. The roof of the A. A. Crafts Store can be seen in the upper left corner. Notice how the snow has drifted to approximately 10 feet high on the right side of the trestle. The same trestle remains today at this location.

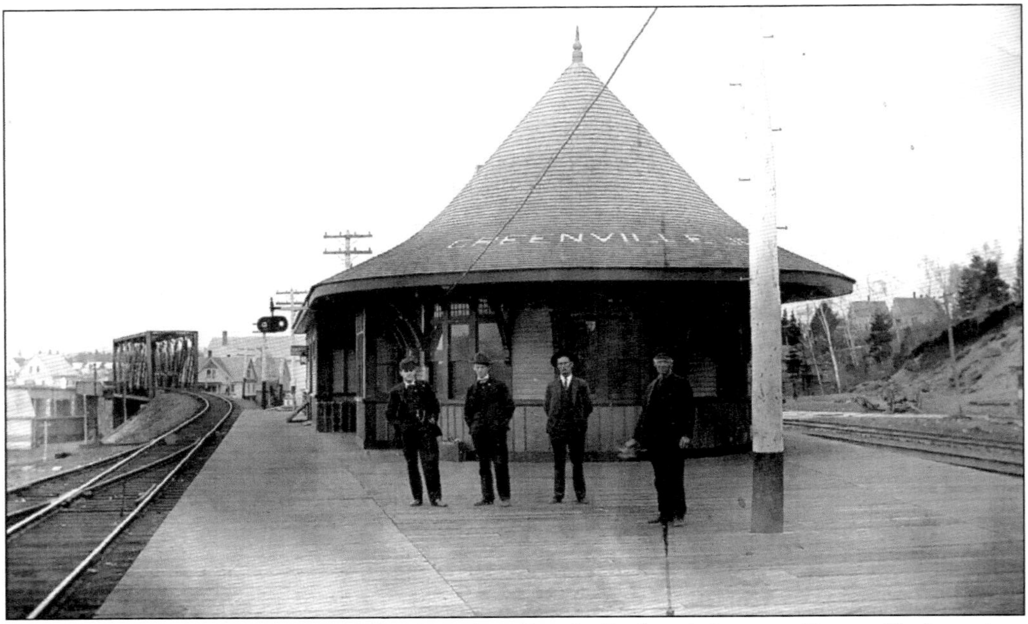

Shown here is a c. 1900 view of the Canadian Pacific Railroad depot in Greenville Junction. The building was constructed in the 1880s and featured a sweeping roofline. The building remains at the site today, although it is severely deteriorated. The men shown here are believed to be local employees of the Canadian Pacific Railroad.

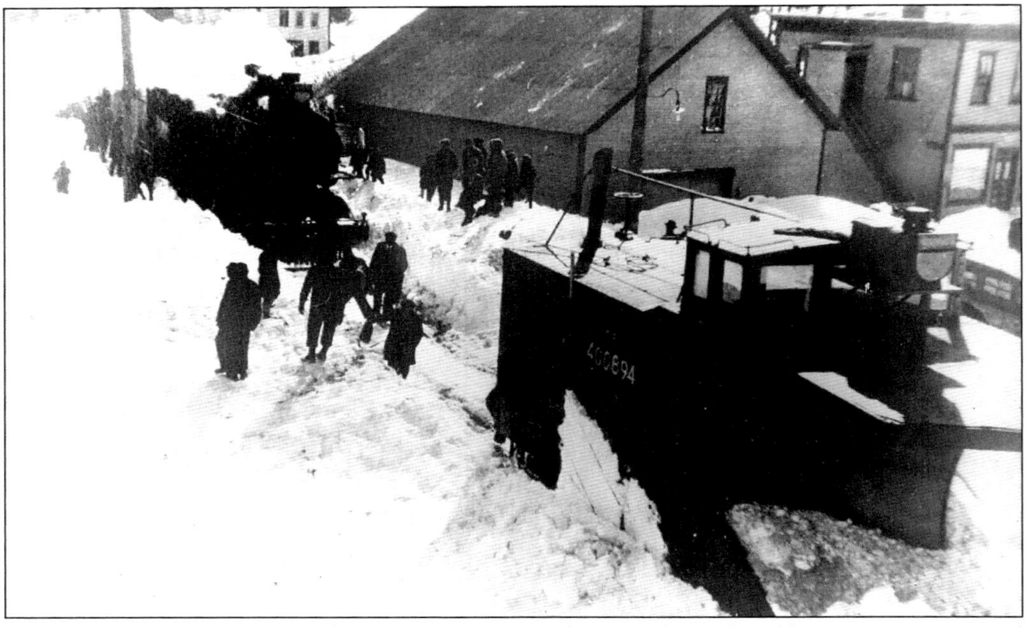

Even trains can fall victim to deep snow. This Canadian Pacific Railroad locomotive was mired in deep snow after a storm in the 1930s on the Atlas Plywood spur line in Greenville village. It required the railroad snowplow, seen on the right, to extricate the locomotive. The spur line crossed West Street (Pritham Avenue)behind the Shaw Block and to the west of Harris Drug Store. The rails were removed decades ago.

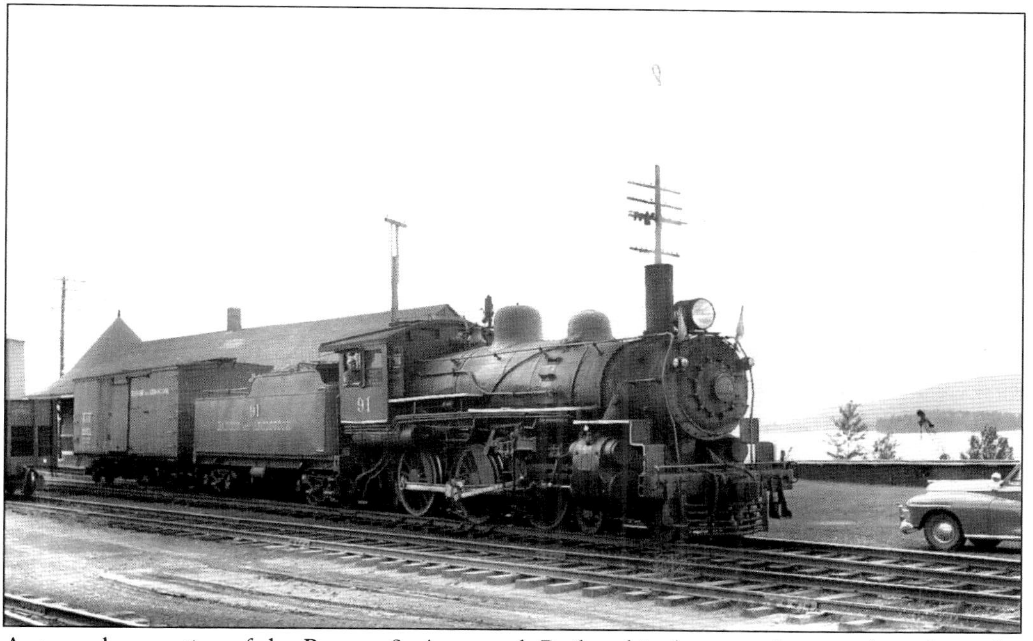

A steam locomotive of the Bangor & Aroostook Railroad is shown with its coal tender and a boxcar in Greenville Junction during 1948. The Canadian Pacific Railroad depot is shown in the background on the left. The steam era was coming to an end during this period, and steam locomotives of the Bangor & Aroostook were replaced with diesels.

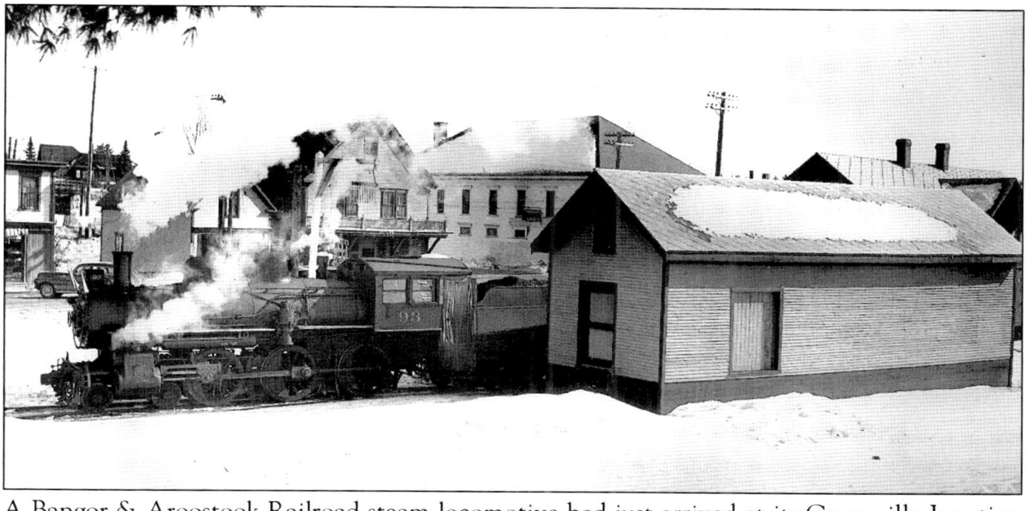

A Bangor & Aroostook Railroad steam locomotive had just arrived at its Greenville Junction depot when this photograph was taken on February 24, 1948. The building on the right is a storage shed, and the main depot building is the structure with two chimneys located on the far right. In the center background, the large building is the former A. A. Crafts Store, now known as the Depot. It is the only one of the buildings shown that still remains. The area where the locomotive and storage building are located is now the approximate site of Breton's Store.

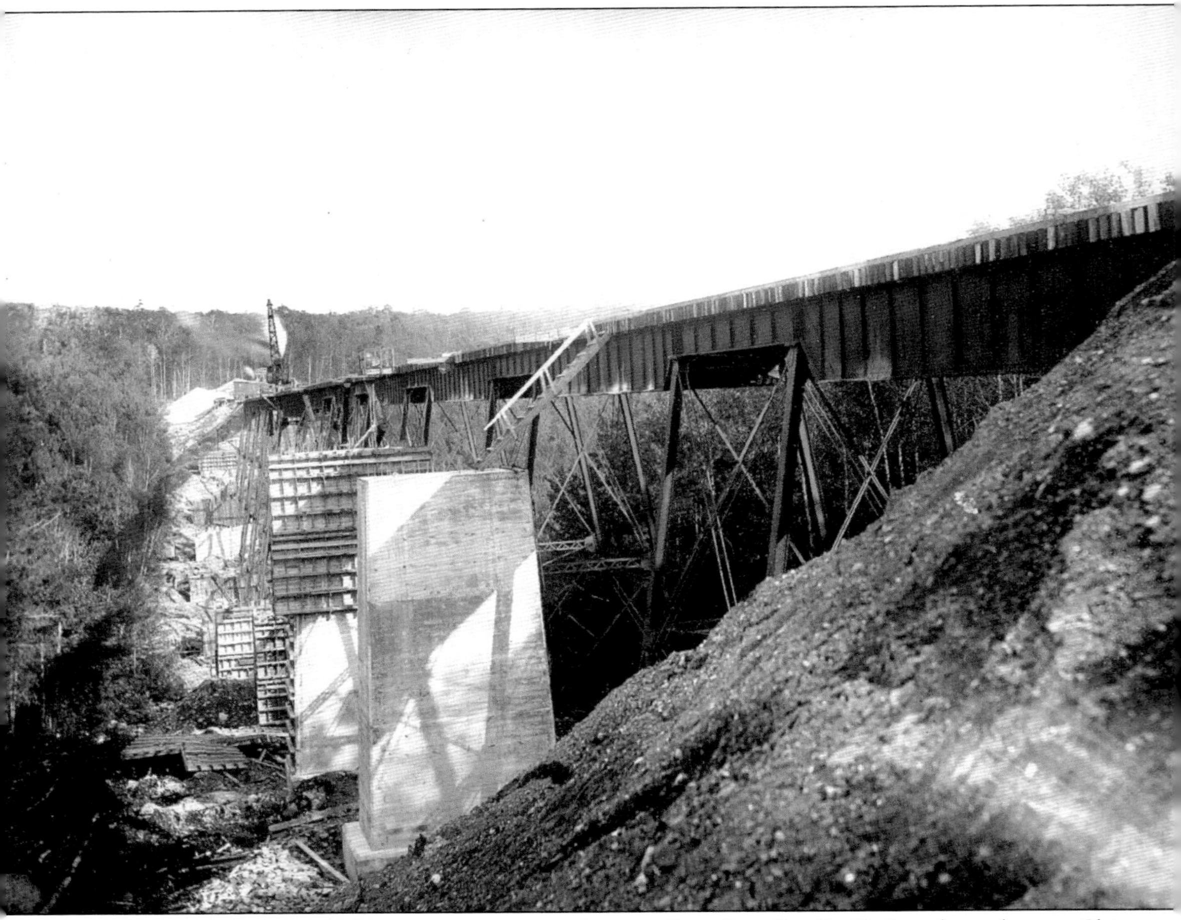

This rare photograph shows construction of a new Canadian Pacific Railroad trestle over Ship Pond Stream near Onawa in Willimantic Township. The dramatic drop where trains cross the stream is a much photographed location. The trestle was reconstructed during 1927–1928, and this photograph, taken by Onawa photographer H. F. Pierce, shows a steam crane at work in the distance.

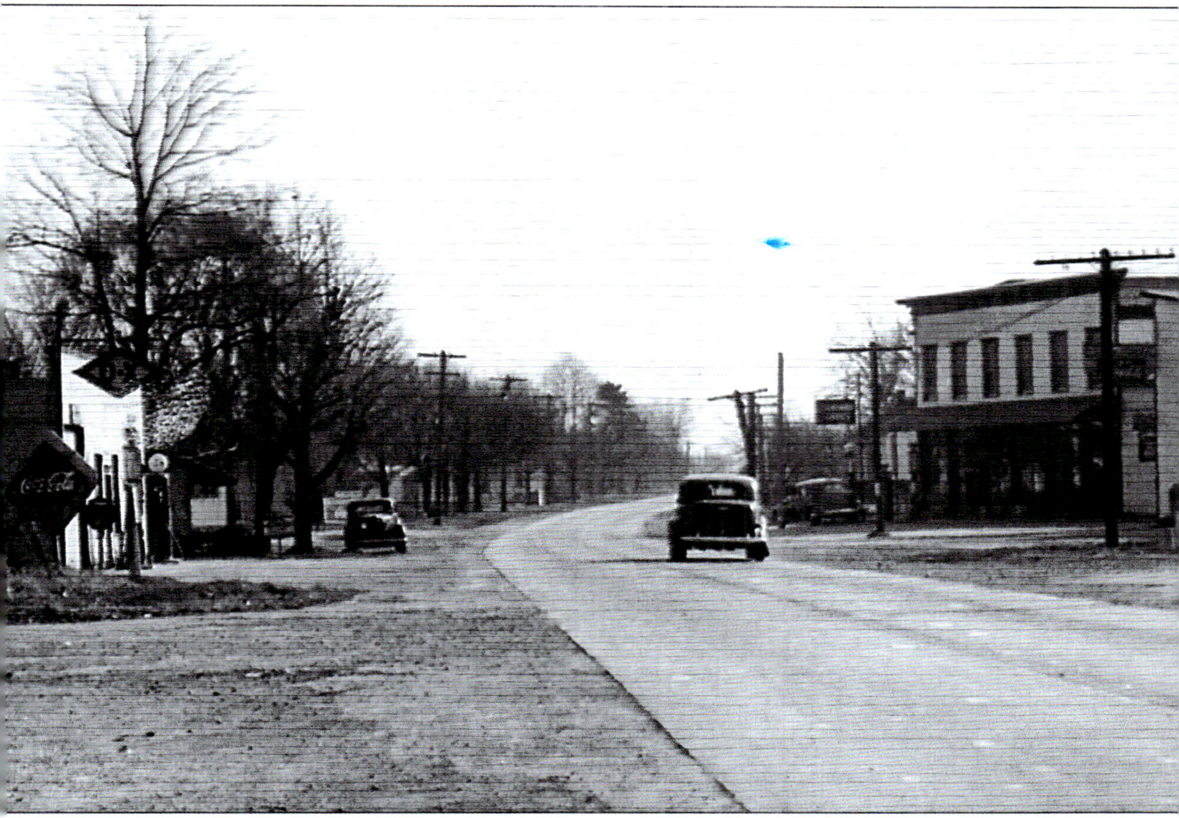

HIGHWAY 56 LOOKING EAST, IRELAND. Alf's D-X service station is on the left. Across the street, on the right, is Steinhart, Weidenbenner, and Bartley's Store. Settled mainly by descendants of Irish immigrants, Ireland strives to maintain its Irish heritage, despite the many German-named families now living in town. (Photograph courtesy of Anthony Wigand.)

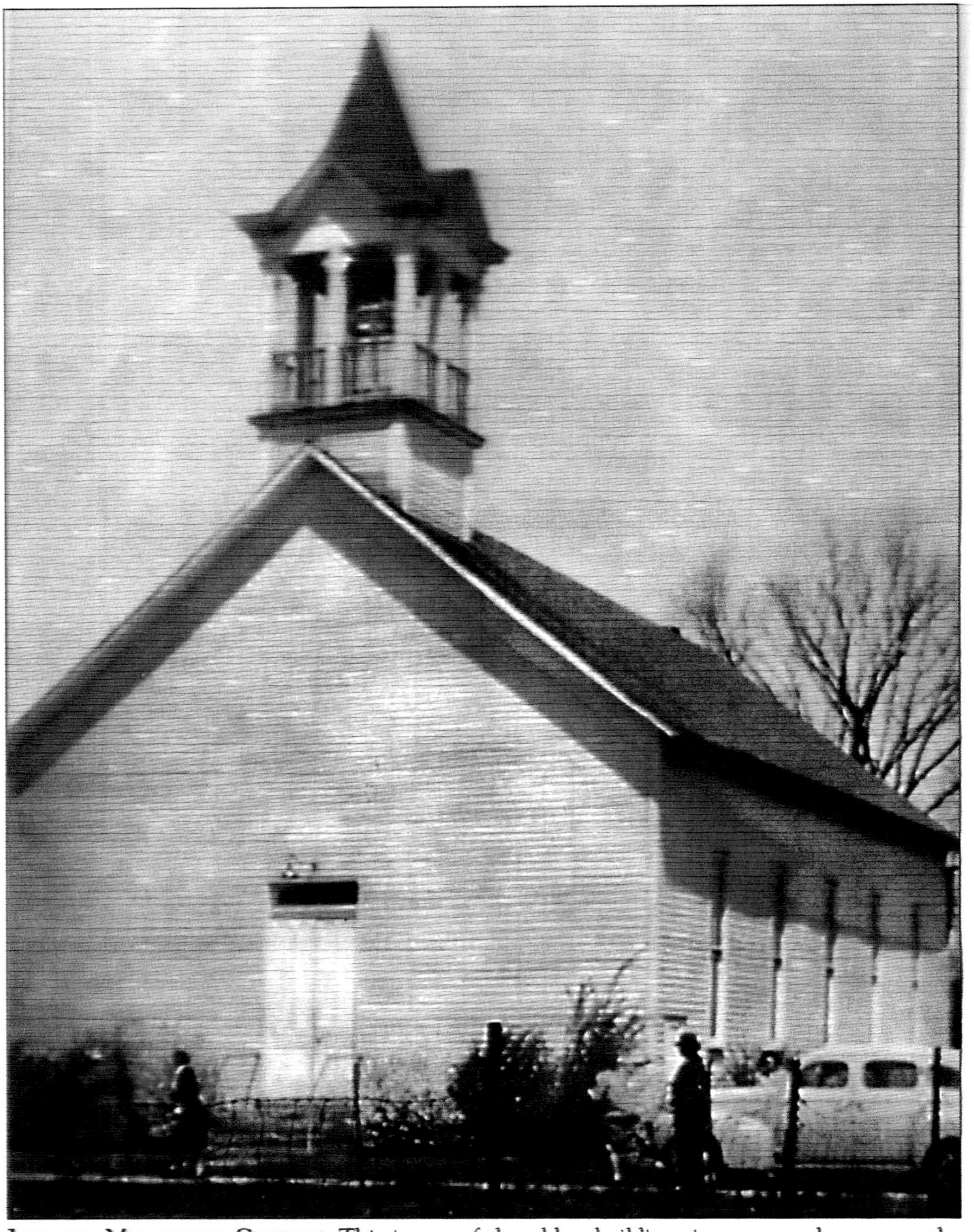

IRELAND METHODIST CHURCH. This is one of the oldest buildings in town, and was once the Ireland Methodist Church; currently, it is the Ireland Historical Society. Built in 1878, the church was dedicated in 1880 and was remodeled in 1952. Two outstanding church members were Dr. Lilly Dexter Greene, a missionary in Indiana for 48 years from 1894 until her death in 1942, and Senator Samuel H. Stewart, who served his country during the Civil War. Stewart fought in many battles and was a prisoner of war at Andersonville, Georgia. Returning to Ireland after the war, he was elected to the Indiana Senate. (Photograph courtesy of Delbert Himsel Jr.)